Value Creation of Corporate Restructuring

Corporate Finance and Governance

Edited by Dirk Schiereck

Volume 17

Zur Qualitätssicherung und Peer Review der vorliegenden Publikation

Die Qualität der in dieser Reihe erscheinenden Arbeiten wird vor der Publikation durch den Herausgeber der Reihe geprüft.

Notes on the quality assurance and peer review of this publication

Prior to publication, the quality of the work published in this series is reviewed by the editor of the series.

Ulrich Erxleben

Value Creation of Corporate Restructuring

A Market Cycle and Industry View

PL ACADEMIC RESEARCH

III. List of Figures

IV. List of Abbreviations

AROA	Abnormal Return On Assets
$R^2_{adjusted}$	Adjusted Coefficient of Determination
ADR	American Depository Receipts
approx.	Approximately
AV	Average
bn	Billion
BMP	Boehmer, Musumeci, Poulsen's Standardized Cross-Sectional Test
B/M	Book-to-Market
BHAR	Buy-and-Hold Abnormal Return
CAPEX	Capital Expenditure
CAPM	Capital Asset Pricing Model
CAR	Cumulative Abnormal Return
EBITDA	Earnings Before Interest, Taxes, Depreciation, and Amortization
ECB	European Central Bank
EMH	Efficient Market Hypothesis
EUR	Euro
FF	Fama and French Industry Classification
FF3F	Fama-French-3-Factor
FF4F	Fama-French-4-Factor
FTSE	Financial Times Stock Exchange
e.g.	For example
GST	Generalized Sign Test
HML	High Minus Low
ICB	Industry Classification Benchmark
M/B	Market-to-Book
MD	Median
M&A	Mergers and Acquisitions
mn	Million
OLS	Ordinary Least Squares
P/E	Price-to-Earnings
R&D	Research and Development
ROA	Return on Assets
SEO	Seasoned Equity Offering
SDC	Securities Data Corporation

Section B adds an industry perspective to the discussion of determinants of M&A and divestment value creation. Previous research mainly focuses on individual firm characteristics, omitting overall industry effects. While the effects of industry structure and dynamic on corporate restructuring activity are well documented (e.g., Mitchell and Mulherin 1996, Harford 2005, Komlenovic et al. 2011), little empirical evidence exists with regard to the implications on value creation potential. The analyses, therefore, contribute to the debate on determinants of M&A and divestment success by providing an explanation for variations based on industry characteristics.

Besides its contribution to current research, this thesis also aspires to be relevant for practitioners. The study addresses financial investors by providing guidance with regard to expected stock market returns related to corporate restructuring events based on prevailing market environment and industry context. Firm management can use the results as guidance regarding a promising time to look for external growth and to assess the value drivers of corporate restructuring in their industry context.

The structure of this document is illustrated in Figure 1.1. Succeeding this introduction, Chapter 2 contains a descriptive analysis of European M&A over the last 20 years. The objective of Chapter 2 is to establish the starting point and research motivation by conducting an initial analysis of European M&A from an industry and market perspective to test the intuition that significant differences in corporate restructuring success exist over time and across industries. The findings constitute the motivation for the in-depth examination in Section A and B. Chapter 3 briefly discusses the research foundation of the presented analysis including definitions of corporate restructuring as used throughout this study and a discussion of the applied research approach. The main body of this document is divided in Sections A (Chapters 4 and 5) and Section B (Chapters 6 and 7) that include the main results of the examination. Section A presents the discussion and analysis of corporate restructuring in the context of different market cycles. The discussion is split in a M&A (Chapter 4) and a divestiture piece (Chapter 5). Section B focuses on corporate restructuring from an industry view. Analogous to Section A, the discussion is separated in an analysis of takeovers and divestments in Chapters 6 and 7 respectively. Some parts of the different sections may appear repetitive as descriptions of the empirical approach reappear. This is owed to the cumulative nature of my dissertation. Chapters 4 to 7 are designed as standalone studies that refer individually to common core literature and econometric approaches. The methodology applied, however, also differs between sections in some core aspects. Chapter 8 summarizes the individual results and draws a final conclusion combining M&A and divestment results in a joint discussion. It also proposes areas for further research based on the presented findings.

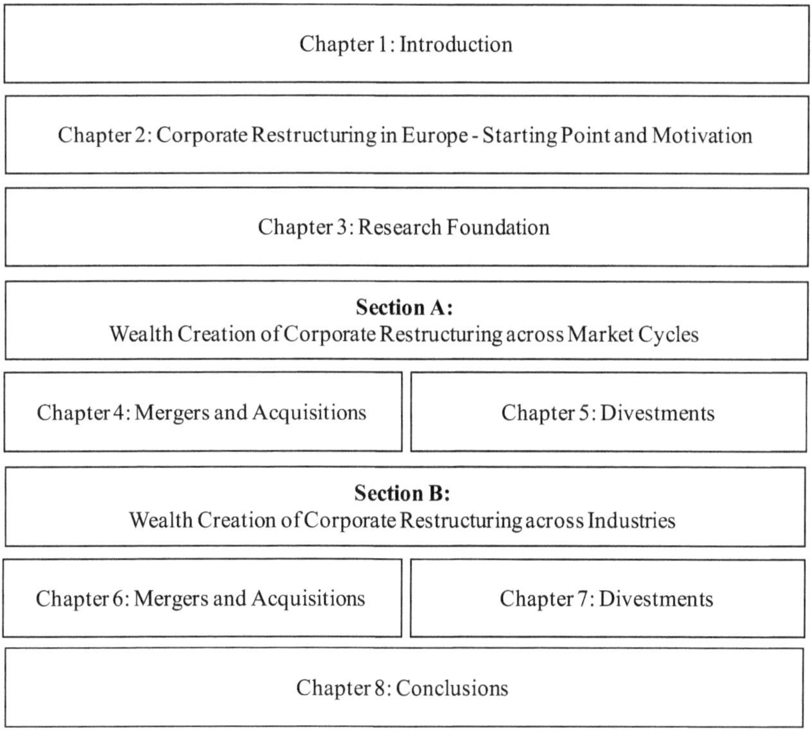

Figure 1.1: Structure of book

and EUR 52 bn) as well as in 2006 (EUR 20 bn). The finding shows that despite positive announcement effects, on average some large failures in boom markets led to significant value destruction for acquirers' shareholders. These results are also consistent with findings from Moeller et al. (2004) for the two decades from 1980 to 2001.

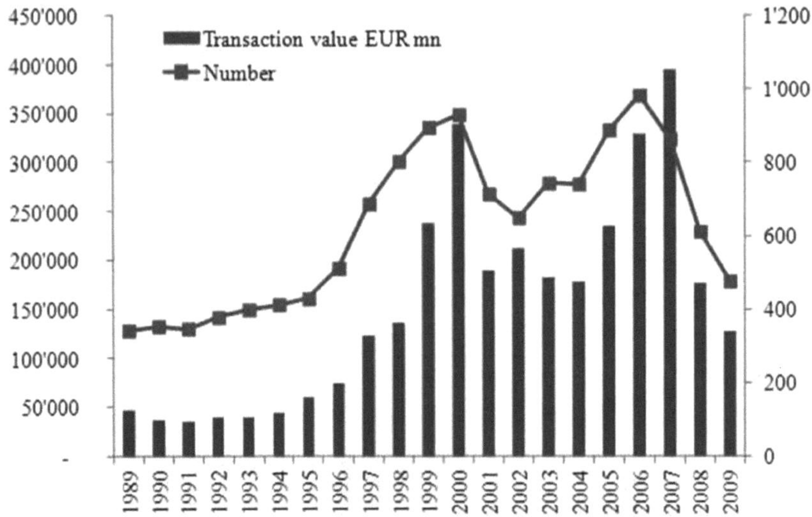

Figure 2.2: Divestment activity of European sellers 1989 - 2009[2]

The value creation over time for divestments shows a different pattern (see Figure 2.4). The average annual CAR for divestments is higher than for acquisitions with a CAR of 0.98%. It ranges from 3.77% in 1993 to 0.23% in 2002. Value creation in absolute terms shows an aggregated value creation of EUR 72 bn between 1989 and 2009. In contrast to acquisitions, the highest absolute value creation is observed in years of booming stock markets with the highest corporate restructuring activity. In each of the two years 2000 and 2007 EUR 15 bn of shareholder value was generated from the divestment of firm assets.

These findings provide an indication that M&A success is influenced by the market phase during which corporate control transactions are executed. Section A (Chapters 4 and 5) of my thesis therefore conducts a detailed analysis of value creation in different market phases. The main underlying hypothesis hereby is that acquisitions in weak market environments outperform transactions in booming markets. From a divestment perspective the hypothesis is reversely that asset sales in strong markets create more value than divestments in weak markets. These predictions are supplemented by the analysis of specific transaction characteristics that determine the success of transactions in different market environments.

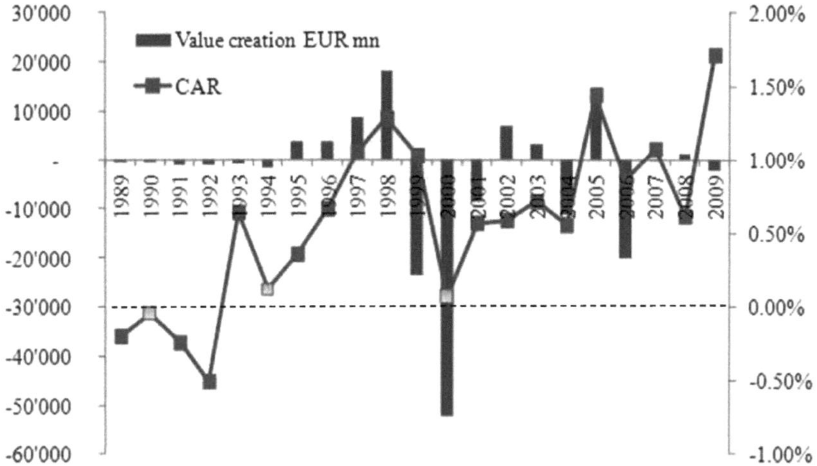

Figure 2.3: Wealth creation of M&A for shareholders of European acquirers 1989 - 2009[3]

3 The short-term abnormal announcement returns (CAR) per year are the average of individual European acquirer's/seller's abnormal returns of the specific year between 1989 and 2009. CAR are calculated for three days around the announcement [-1/+1] using the Market Model as proposed by Brown and Warner (1980 and 1985). The Market Model factors are estimated based on an OLS regression of an observation period of 180 trading days prior to a 41-day event period around announcement [-20/+20]. The statistical significance of the results are tested with a t-statistic. All results with a confidence level below 10% are marked as filled data points in the chart while insignificant data points show gradient fillings. The absolute EUR values are calculated as abnormal change in individual firm's market values in the three days around announcement. The value effect is computed as 3-day CAR times the market capitalization two trading days before the announcement. The individual results are then aggregated by year. Transactions are included in the analysis when (i) the acquirer's/seller's headquarter was in an European country; (ii) the transaction value was reported and larger than EUR 10 mn exceeding 1% of the acquirer's/seller's market capitalization; (iii) more than 50% of the targets ownership rights were transferred to the acquirer. Transaction data was received from Thomson Reuters' SDC database. Capital market data was downloaded from Datastream.

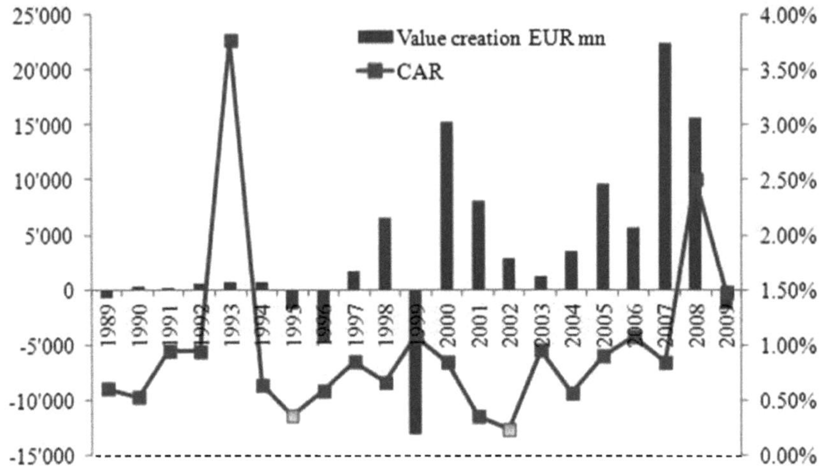

Figure 2.4: Wealth creation of divestments for shareholders of European sellers 1989 - 2009[3]

2.2 Corporate restructuring across European industries

In addition to a time series perspective on corporate restructuring, an industry view is taken to complete the discussion of corporate restructuring activity in Europe. Figures 2.5 and 2.6 summarize M&A activity and announcement returns within 52 ICB sub-sectors for acquisitions and 42 ICB sub-sectors for divestments. The industries included in the analysis out of a total of 114 ICB sub-sectors are selected based on industry size measured by number of active companies and data availability to calculate announcement returns. The time period for the analysis are the 10 years from 1998 to 2007.

Figure 2.5 shows the M&A activity and return results for European acquirers by industry. The average activity measured by share of industry companies that completed an acquisition between 1998 and 2007 has an industry average of 27.00% with a standard deviation (StDev) of 7.88%. The maximum activity is observed in the Life Insurance Industry (ICB 8575) with 46.34% of companies completing a major transaction in this 10 year period. The minimum of 8.45% is found in Conventional Electricity (ICB 7535). These findings are consistent with the results from various previous studies that examine industry dynamics as a driver of M&A activity (e.g., Mitchell and Mulherin 1996; Andrade and Stafford 2004).

Cross industry value creation also exhibits large differences. The industry average shows a positive CAR of 0.95% with a StDev of 0.95%. Highest announcement returns were achieved in Computer Hardware (ICB 9572) with 3.29% while the lowest level was realized in Paper (ICB 1737) with -0.75%.

The results for divestments in Figure 2.6 also propose significant variation in M&A activity and success across industries. The average divestment activity level is 16.76% (StDev 6.13%) of active industry sellers. The most active industry was Automobiles (ICB 3353) with a rate of 30.61%. The lowest activity level can be observed in Life Insurance (6.57%) which is in turn the most active acquiring industry. From a value perspective the industry average lies at CAR 1.02% with a StDev of 1.62%. The highest average announcement returns to asset sellers was also achieved in Automobiles (6.42%), the most actively divesting industry. On the other hand, the lowest returns were realized among sellers in the Hotels sector (ICB 5753) with CAR of -1.90%.

The industry perspective also reveals large differences in activity and value creation across European industries. Especially value creation varies from significant value destruction for shareholders of sellers and acquirers to large gains in shareholder value. Based on these insights an in-depths analysis of industry determinants of M&A value creation is conducted in Chapters 6 and 7 of this thesis. Based on recent research, the main predictions are that changes in industry performance and productivity as well as industry structure have significant power to explain the variations in M&A activity and value creation of acquisitions and divestments.

The initial descriptive analysis of corporate restructuring activity in Europe clearly shows that large variations in value creation exist over time and across industries. This result, however, requires further investigation of the determinants of performance deviations. Based on recent research on market and industry effects of corporate restructuring success, Sections A. (Chapters 4 and 5) and B. (Chapters 6 and 7) develop an approach to identify the determinants of corporate restructuring success in Europe.

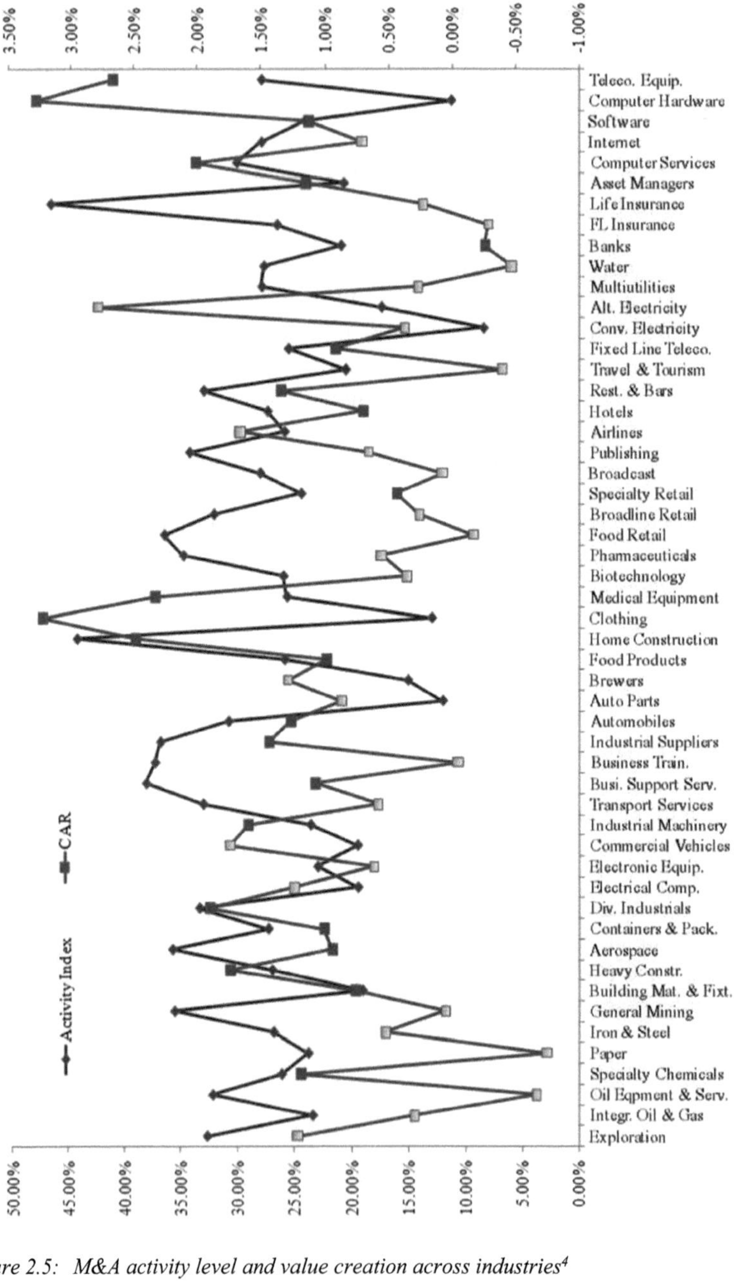

Figure 2.5: M&A activity level and value creation across industries[4]

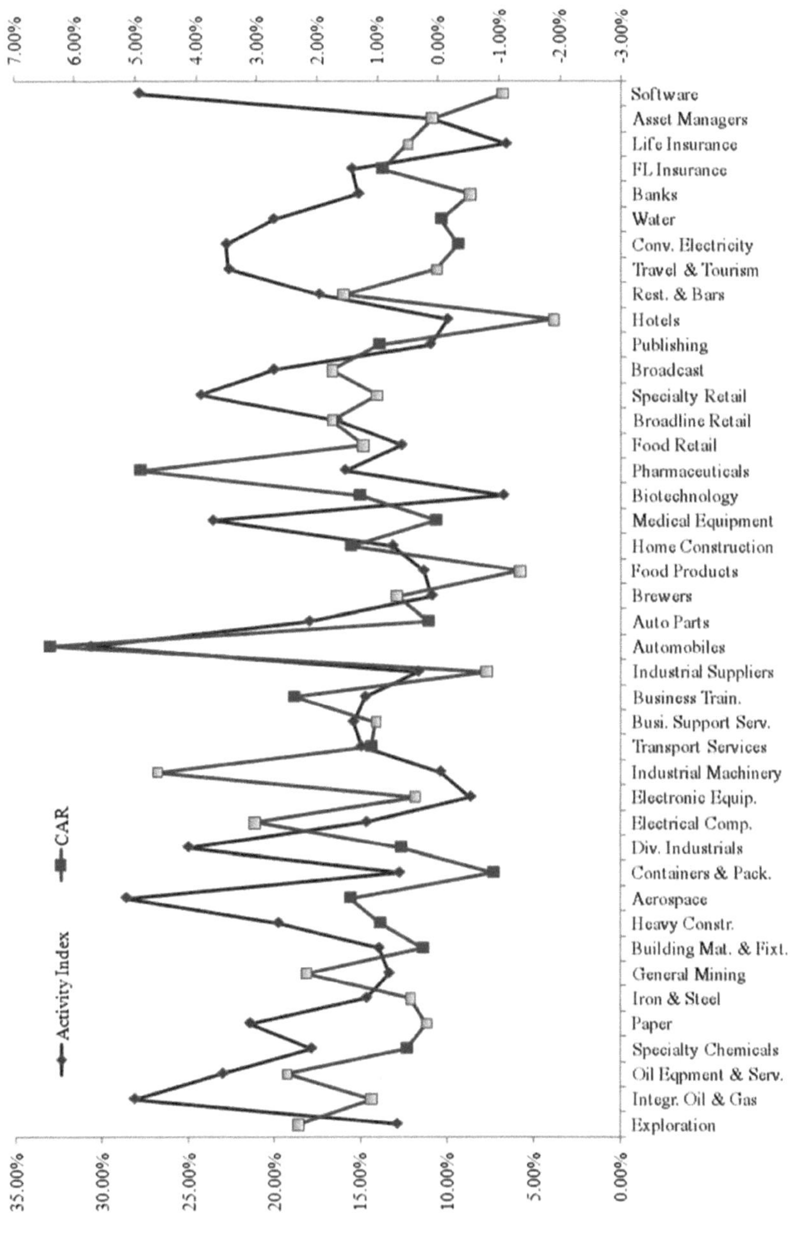

Figure 2.6: Divestment activity level and value creation across industries[5]

4 The relative acquisition activity is measured as share of companies within one of 52 ICB sub-sectors that are involved in an acquisition as acquirer during the 10 years between 1998 and 2007. 52 ICB sub-sectors out of a total of 114 are included in the analysis. Sub-sectors are selected when at least 10 acquirer CAR could be calculated and at least 10 companies were active between 1998 and 2007. The short-term abnormal announcement returns (CAR) per year are aggregated by industry. CAR are calculated for three days around the announcement [-1/+1] using the Market Model as proposed by Brown and Warner (1980 and 1985). The Market Model factors are estimated based on an OLS regression of an observation period of 180 trading days prior to a 41-day event period around announcement [-20/+20]. The statistical significance of the results are tested with a t-statistic. All results with a confidence level below 10% are marked as filled data points in the chart while insignificant data points show gradient fillings. Transactions are included in the analysis when (i) the acquirer has its headquarter in a country of the European Union, non-EU member countries in Eastern Europe, Switzerland, or Russia at the time of transaction announcement; (ii) the transaction value was reported and larger than EUR 10 mn; (iii) the transaction value exceeded 1% of the acquirers market capitalization at the end of the months preceding the transaction date; (iv) more than 50% of the targets ownership rights were transferred to the acquirer. Transaction data was received from Thomson Reuters' SDC Platinum database. Capital market data was downloaded from Datastream. The data shown include all M&A transactions with reported transaction values of at least EUR 10 mn.

5 The relative divestment activity is measured as share of companies within one of 42 ICB sub-sectors that are involved in a divestment as seller during the 10 years between 1998 and 2007. 42 ICB sub-sectors out of a total of 114 are included in the analysis. Sub-sectors are selected when at least 10 seller CAR could be calculated and at least 30 companies were active between 1998 and 2007. The short-term abnormal announcement returns (CAR) per year are aggregated by industry. CAR are calculated for three days around the announcement [-1/+1] using the Market Model as proposed by Brown and Warner (1980 and 1985). The Market Model factors are estimated based on an OLS regression of a observation period of 180 trading days prior to a 41-day event period around announcement [-20/+20]. The statistical significance of the results are tested with a t-statistic. All results with a confidence level below 10% are marked as filled data points in the chart while insignificant data points show gradient fillings. Transactions are included in the analysis when (i) the acquirer has its headquarter in a country of the European Union, non-EU member countries in Eastern Europe, Switzerland, or Russia at the time of transaction announcement; (ii) the transaction value was reported and larger than EUR 10 mn; (iii) the transaction value exceeded 1% of the acquirers market capitalization at the end of the months preceding the transaction date; (iv) more than 50% of the targets ownership rights were transferred to the acquirer. Transaction data was received from Thomson Reuters' SDC Platinum database. Capital market data was downloaded from Datastream. The data shown include all M&A transactions with reported transaction values of at least EUR 10 mn.

3. Research Foundation

This Chapter introduces the basic concepts that constitute the foundation of the analyses conducted in Chapters 4 to 7. First, a brief definition of mergers and acquisitions (M&A) as well as corporate divestiture is given in order to establish the use of these terms throughout my thesis. Second, the basic approaches and methodologies of analyzing value creation of M&A and corporate divestiture are introduced and discussed.

3.3 Corporate restructuring, M&A, and corporate divestiture

Focus of the presented analyses is corporate restructuring by the means of mergers and acquisitions (M&A) and corporate divestiture. Corporate restructuring in general is a broad term that can be applied for various changes in organization, ownership structure, and corporate control throughout the life cycle of a corporation. The understanding of corporate restructuring in this thesis is more specific and pertains to the reconfiguration of the corporate portfolio by expansionary M&A or by the disposal of firm assets through divestments (Copeland and Weston 1988). Furthermore, the understanding of corporate restructuring focuses on changes in ownership of firm assets that result in the transfer of control, i.e., the majority of public or private equity from a seller to a buyer. The interaction between seller and buyer, thus, form a market for corporate control (Jensen and Ruback 1983). The two forms of corporate restructuring addressed by this study, M&A and corporate divestiture, are defined below:

Mergers and acquisitions (M&A) is a widely used term that comprises a number of corporate ownership and control transfers. In a narrower understanding, M&A is an expansionary process in which two or more entities are combined to one (Weston and Chung 1990). Mergers and acquisitions in this narrower sense can be distinguished based on the future legal status of the target and the degree of codetermination from the target's perspective into acquisitions and mergers. The differentiation is mainly determined from a legal perspective. In a merger, both involved management boards agree to combine their two firms and propose the combination jointly to their respective shareholders. The individual companies cease to exist and establish a new corporate entity in which the former shareholders share ownership and control (Damodaran 2004). Acquisitions, on the other hand, are combinations of two entities in which the legal status of both parties remains unchanged. Two general modes of acquisitions exist. First, acquirers can choose to tender for the shares of a target company (share transactions) or directly buy corporate assets such as subsidiaries or business units (asset transactions).

The definition of M&A as used throughout this study can be more simply summarized as the transfer of a majority equity stake and subsequently control rights of an acquisition target from unrelated sellers to buyers. Mergers are classified in this logic when shareholders of one merging party receive the majority of equity in the joint organization. The terms mergers and acquisitions, M&A, takeovers, and corporate acquisitions are used interchangeably and refer to the narrow definition of M&A as described above.

In a wider sense, M&A also comprises disposal of ownership and control of a seller to a buyer. The decision to divest assets is therefore reciprocal to the narrower definition of acquisitions introduced above. The understanding of divestments in this thesis follows Hillier et al. (2009) who define divestments as the disposal of subsidiaries, divisions, or other combinations of fixed assets that result in a direct transfer of ownership between two unrelated corporate entities.

The terms corporate divesture, divestments, corporate sell-offs, asset disposals, and asset sales are used synonymously and refer to the preceding definition.

3.4 Previous research

The presented study of corporate restructuring is based on a broad body of theoretical and empirical work on value creation of M&A and corporate divestiture. Sections A (Chapters 4 and 5) and B (Chapters 6 and 7) provide a detailed discussion of previous research in the context of market cycles and from an industry perspective respectively. To avoid duplication the author refers to the respective chapters for an overview of related research.

3.5 Measuring success of corporate restructuring

Corporate restructuring success is one of the most intensively and controversially discussed fields in corporate finance. Different approaches and perspectives on how to determine success and value creation of corporate restructuring have evolved in this discourse. Bruner (2002) provides in his summary of research on M&A value creation four general approaches: event studies, accounting studies, surveys of executives, and clinical studies. The focus of this study is on event studies and accounting studies.

This chapter introduces the most commonly used applications of event and accounting studies. It also discusses their limitations of measuring value creation and success. The following pages do not provide an in depth description of the technicalities of the different methods. The goal is to provide a brief, comprehensive introduction to the empirical approaches underlying this study. A detailed description of the respective models is given in the methodology chapters of the respective content sections.

3.5.1 Event studies

Event studies are arguably the most frequently applied method to analyze M&A success (and, to a smaller extent, corporate divestiture returns).

Event studies examine stock market returns that are related to corporate events. They focus on value creation from a company's shareholder perspective. Event studies are applied for a large number of different corporate events that may influence the value of a firm. Common fields in which event studies are used comprise, e.g., seasoned equity offerings (SEO), stock splits, and earnings reports, but also announcements of various strategic company decisions. Corporate restructuring by the means of M&A and corporate divestiture has been a main research field of event studies over the last decades. Since the 1970s event studies and, hence, the shareholder value view have dominated the field of measuring corporate restructuring success (Bruner 2002). The basic methodology, although many variations exist in the exact specifications, relies on the comparison of observed stock market returns after a corporate event with expected returns in the absence of this event. Thus, event studies aim at identifying abnormal returns that relate to a specific event (Kothari and Warner 2007).

An important aspect of the event study approach is the application of different time horizons to determine shareholder value creation. Event study research frequently distinguishes between short- and long-term value creation. The two time horizons have different implications for the interpretation of results and are exposed to a number of challenges that need to be considered. The remainder of this chapter discusses event studies from these two perspectives.

Short-term event studies analyze stock market reactions within a few days around the announcement of a transaction. In a corporate context, abnormal performance at the time of an event announcement provides a measure of the impact an unexpected event has on the value of a company. The foundation of this view is the efficient market hypothesis (EMH). EMH assumes that capital markets, i.e. investors, incorporate new information that is disclosed by companies or becomes public at a certain point in time and impacts future company performance is immediately and correctly incorporated in firm valuations (Bruner 2002). The magnitude of the announcement returns indicate, thus, the changes in firm value related to a specific event. Changes in value related to an event are only consistent with EMH when investors could not anticipate the event in advance (Brown and Warner 1985).

The challenge for researcher is to separate valuation effects that relate to a specific event from other factors that influence company value at the time of the announcement. Brown and Warner (1980) argue that abnormal returns can only be identified in comparison to an adequate benchmark. Hence, it is necessary to identify ex ante normal returns to which ex post actual returns can be compared. At least for announcement effects, a widely accepted approach has established that applies the one-factor capital asset pricing model (CAPM) (Black 1972). The Market Model (Brown and Warner 1980) is the dominant application of CAPM for event studies. The model estimates expected return of a stock based on the linear relation between market returns and individual company returns. The two factors applied to establish this linear relationship are unsystematic (unrelated to market returns, α) and systematic (related to market returns, β) company returns. These factors are typically estimated based on daily stock returns before the announcement of an event. Brown and Warner (1980 and 1985) provide evidence that this approach is at least equally powerful to estimate an adequate benchmark as more complex multi-factor models. They also show that Market Model results are robust with regard to autocorrelation and changes in variance.

The effectiveness of the Market Model relies heavily on two major assumptions. The first is efficiency of capital markets (EMH) that implies the ability of investors to correctly assess the future value implications of corporate events. The second assumption implies no material restriction on arbitrage that would prohibit full stock price adjustments as reaction on new information. Due to the reliance on efficient capital markets, event studies also serve the purpose of testing market efficiency. Abnormal returns that are persistently different from zero after a corporate event are inconsistent with the market efficient view (Brown and Warner 1980). Recent research results have increasingly challenged EMH by showing that company returns continue to show abnormal return patterns over longer time periods after announcement. These results challenge the assumption that investors are able to fully assess all value implication at announcement.

In addition to widely used announcement return studies that rely on efficient capital markets to assess M&A success, various long-term approaches have increasingly gained acceptance. The increasing importance of long-term studies is mainly owed to doubts about the EMH. These doubts have led to the rapid evolution of the behavioral finance field in recent years (Loughran and Ritter 2000).

Long-term studies typically focus on abnormal returns from one up to five years after the event. Compared to short-term methodologies, long-term approaches are, however, numerous and controversially discussed among researchers. The main challenge associated with detecting long-term abnormal returns is the identification of expected returns and risk adjustment to form an adequate benchmark. Kothari and Warner (2007) show that the power of the relatively simple CAPM adjusted method (Market Model) to detect abnormal returns in a few days around announcement is little affected by misevaluation of α and β because the affected daily returns are very small (approx. 0.05% on average) compared to the size of announcement returns (often around 1% on average). A small misevaluation of risk adjustment can, however, accumulate to large differences in returns over longer time periods. Adequate benchmark construction is, thus, essential in long-term event studies.

Due to this fact, some controversy with regard to model choice has evolved in financial research (Loughran and Ritter 2000, Mitchell and Stafford 2000). Two general approaches have gained dominant positions in recent research. One is an analysis of abnormal returns in event-time applying character based matching to form a benchmark. The other examines abnormal returns based on a calendar-time portfolio. Both methods will be briefly discussed based on the most frequently applied model.

Buy-and-hold abnormal returns (BHAR) represent the most commonly used methodology in determining long-term performance in event-time (see, e.g., Barber and Lyon 1997, Lyon et al. 1999, Loughran and Ritter 2000). BHAR is determined by comparing an event firm (e.g., an acquirer) to a non-event benchmark. The matching is based on specific characteristics that are shared by event company and benchmark. Most frequently book-to-market valuation and size are used for matching purposes (Lyon et al. 1999). The benchmark is then constructed as a portfolio of similar non-event firms or a single firm that best matches the event-firm. In order to measure abnormal returns the differences in buy-and-hold investment returns are compared. This approach mimics the experience of an investor that invests in both stocks (or portfolio of stocks). BHAR is exposed to a number of methodological pitfalls. The new listing bias, the rebalancing bias, and skewness of returns (Lyon et al. 1999) can be mitigated by applying careful matching and benchmark construction as well as by advanced statistical tests on a large enough sample. The joint-test problem, however, remains. It pertains to the assumption that the matching non-event benchmark differs in performance only due to the event and not because of other idiosyncratic factors and cross-correlation of returns. Cross-correlation of returns in event-time, especially due to not randomly selected matching samples, is an often reported bias of this method (Mitchell and Stafford 2000).

The Fama-French-3-Factor-model (FF3F) and increasingly the Carhart (1997) Fama-French-4-Factor-model (FF4F) are common representatives of the calendar-time portfolio approach. FF4F eliminates the cross-correlation problem by constructing a continuously rebalanced portfolio of event-firms. Risk adjustment is conducted with a multifactor model. The FF4F model uses for this purpose market, size, market-to-book, and momentum factors that are regressed with the event-portfolio return. The regression returns an α that represents factor adjusted abnormal returns.

Loughran and Ritter (2000) argue that the calendar time approach has less power to detect abnormal returns because it averages over time periods and, thus, does not account for managers' timing decision. They, instead, argue in favor of equally weighted company returns (BHAR) instead of equally weighted time periods (FF3F/FF4F).

3.5.2 Accounting studies

A second group of studies that is commonly applied to analyze the success of corporate restructuring are accounting studies. In contrast to event studies that examine stock market returns and, thus, focus on shareholder value, accounting studies look at effects from corporate restructuring on actual company performance. Healy et al. (1992) argue that event studies that rely on stock market performance are unable to identify the real economic gains that relate to corporate restructuring. Event studies rely on the efficiency of capital markets - an assumption that is often challenged in recent literature. Another aspect is the inability of event studies to identify the actual source of abnormal performance. Valuation gains are a somewhat nebulous measure as they are, in principle, determined by the market anticipation of future cash flows to the firm. This implies two potential sources of valuation gains. The first is actual improvements in the productivity of assets through synergies or removal of dis-synergies. The second source is future growth of cash flows. Corporate restructuring can address both sources. Hence, accounting studies add a perspective on the sources of corporate restructuring gains that helps interpreting the event study results.

The performance indicators analyzed in accounting studies differ largely in recent literature. Most common indicators of operative performance are, however, measures based on return on assets (ROA). Returns are most frequently defined as a measure or proxy of company cash flows. Typical studies refer to earnings before interest, tax, depreciation, and amortization (EBITDA) to proxy operative cash flows (Martynova et al. 2006, Bouwman et al. 2009, Hillier et al. 2009). In order to identify abnormal accounting effects that are caused by the examined event, two general strategies are commonly applied in recent studies. The first perspective is a comparison of operative performance measures pre and post transaction to identify changes that can be attributed to merger synergies (Healy et al.

1999, Harford 2005). A second perspective pertains to abnormal performance developments in the years after a transaction compared to an adequate benchmark (Bouwman et al. 2009, Laabs and Schiereck 2010). Benchmarks in accounting studies are usually constructed based on a characteristic based matching of firms that have not been exposed to the corporate event analyzed.

Accounting studies provide a tangible and credible assessment of firm performance after corporate restructuring transactions. However, a number of weaknesses accompany this perspective. Bruner (2002) argues that accounting studies are affected by different accounting standards across countries and companies as well as changes in reporting practice over time. He furthers identifies the backward looking nature of accounting studies that ignore future growth prospects as a weakness of this approach.

3.5.3 Research approach

The following analyses aim at providing empirical evidence for the success of corporate restructuring transactions based on a large European transaction sample. Given this objective, the empirical approach applies event studies which are complemented by an analysis of accounting effects. The analysis omits the use of executive surveys and case studies to focus on a comprehensive quantitative analysis of corporate restructuring. Especially with regard to European transactions, empirical analyses of large transaction samples are very rare in particular when compared to the multitude of US-focused research. Possible reasons for this observation are the fragmentation of European markets that only within the last two decades started to integrate. Another factor is a more limited availability and less ease of use of European financial information compared to widely available and well processed US market and company data (Martynova et al. 2006, Ince and Porter 2006). Therefore, the presented analysis does not only aim at shedding light on the effects of market cycles and industry factors on corporate restructuring, but also provides a complete analysis of European corporate restructuring over the last two decades.

The discussion of different empirical methods and their limitations has led to the conviction that a comprehensive analysis of corporate restructuring needs to entail different approaches in order to yield a complete picture of corporate restructuring success. Therefore, all commonly used methods to determine abnormal stock market returns are applied in this study. The approaches entail analyses of Market Model adjusted abnormal announcement returns as the dominant short-term methodology as well as both event-time and calendar-time analyses of long-term abnormal returns. For the different research questions in Sections A and B the approaches are slightly altered with regard to the benchmark definition in order to apply the best fitting model for the respective research interest (e.g., from a single, best matching benchmark company to industry specific benchmark portfolios). In Section A a study of operating returns is added to examine corporate restructuring decisions from a capital market view as well as from an accounting perspective. This approach follows Healy et al.'s (1992) argument that it is difficult to rely on a stock market view alone for the interpretation of abnormal returns. Accounting studies add an indication on the economic sources of stock price returns.

Based on previous findings it is expected that results will differ depending on the applied methodology. This expectation has two implications for the interpretation of the results. First, the application of different methods within the same time horizon serves as a robustness check for the respective outcomes. This is in particular relevant when comparing relative long-term abnormal returns between sub-samples. Loughran and Ritter (2000) argue that the magnitude of abnormal returns across methods is expected to, and even should, differ due to different risk adjustments. Their view, however, leads to the assumption that relative return differences between sub-samples are more likely to persist under different methods than the level of abnormal returns. Based on this consideration the presented study focuses on these relative differences when analyzing the determinants of value creation. The second implication is that variations in results for different time horizons can serve as an additional source of insight with regard to the level of potential mispricing for different transaction types.

A detailed description of the applied methods can be found in the respective chapters within the content sections.

Section A

Wealth Creation of Corporate Restructuring across Market Cycles

4. Wealth Creation of Mergers in Downturn Markets

4.1 Introduction

Empirical evidence shows a positive relation between merger and acquisition (M&A) activity and market valuation level (Mitchell and Mulherin 1996, Lambrecht 2004, Jovanovic and Rousseau 2008). The experience of the last two decades strongly supports this view. The amount and volume of M&A have reached the highest levels in history during the boom years of 1998/99 and 2006/07. With the collapse of stock markets in 2001 and 2008, M&A activity also declined steeply compared to the last year of the stock market boom: -58% (2001) and -55% (2008) measured by total transaction value and -35% (2001) and -32% (2008) by number of transactions.[6]

Less evident is the value effect of acquisitions in strong and weak markets for acquirers' shareholders. Merger waves in booming stock markets are often considered rational reactions to industry shocks caused by new technologies, changes in factor costs or deregulation. Using M&A to encounter such changes and to quickly adapt to a new market situation can be value creating (Mitchell and Mulherin 1996, Harford 2005). However, a growing body of literature argues from a behavioral perspective that boom markets rather generate agency costs instead of shareholder value. In this view, high valuations in strong markets lead managers to pursue transactions motivated by self-interest that reduce firm value (Jensen 2005, Gorton et. al 2009, Goel and Thakor 2010). Some recent takeovers provide anecdotal evidence for the behavioral argument. Transactions like the AOL-Time Warner merger in 2000 or ABN Amro's acquisition by Fortis, RBS, and Banco Santander in 2007 were announced at the very peak of stock markets. Retrospectively, they are very likely considered ill-fated by shareholders of the acquiring companies. Weak markets, on the other hand, may offer a favorable environment for M&A. Low valuations, reduced competition for acquisition targets, and troubled companies that are willing to sell attractive but non-core subsidiaries can make takeovers profitable in lean times. However, M&A can also pose a challenge that may prove too big to handle when company sales fall and inventories grow. Additional complexity from integration and the need to finance a large M&A investment when financial resources become scarce is a risky decision and can lead to failure.

This analysis contributes to the discussion by providing current empirical evidence from a European perspective on value creation of M&A in different market

6 Based on European M&A data from Thomson Reuters' SDC Platinum Database.

phases. The examination builds on and adds to Bouwman et al. (2009) who suggest that US transactions created less long-term value when announced in markets with high valuation levels. This thesis focuses on value creation in weak markets. First, value creation in dependence of market valuation is determined. Second, specific differences in transaction characteristics of acquisitions in high and low markets are analyzed. In order to gain a comprehensive view on value creation for acquirers' shareholders, different perspectives on M&A success are taken. The short-term value effect is addressed with an analysis of abnormal stock returns at transaction announcement. Long-term returns are determined in event-time using buy-and-hold abnormal returns and in calendar time by applying a 4-factor market model. In addition, an analysis of operational improvements is conducted. The analysis is based on a data sample of 2'002 transactions completed by European acquirers that were announced between January 1st, 1989 and December 31st, 2006.

This study shows, in accordance with results from Bouwman et al. (2009), that transactions in strong markets outperform acquisitions in low valuation markets in the days around announcement. In the long run, however, acquisitions in low markets generate more value for bidders' shareholders than M&A transactions in booming markets. Cash transactions perform better than stock paid transactions in all market environments. The positive differential to stock transactions, however, is highest in low valuation markets where share payment leads to significant value destruction. In particular, smaller sized acquisitions with lower complexity and financing requirements create value for shareholders in weak markets driving long-term outperformance compared to transactions in strong market phases. Takeovers of firms in financial distress, on the other hand, destroy shareholder value in depressed markets. The results suggest that M&A during downturns is less exposed to agency problems and benefits from reduced competition for attractive targets as long as integration complexity is limited.

The remainder of this paper is structured as follows. Chapter 4.2 gives an overview of the related research and develops the underlying hypotheses for this study. Chapter 4.3 describes the data sample and introduces the applied methodology. In Chapter 4.4 the results are discussed in detail and finally a summarizing conclusion is drawn in Chapter 4.5.

4.2 Literature and hypotheses

In this section related research is briefly introduced based on which specific prediction for the examination are deducted.

4.2.1 Related literature

The presented analysis of market effects on M&A success builds on results from studies of merger waves and on insights from studies of M&A value creation. This chapter provides an overview of main results from these two groups of studies starting with the first group leading to the second. This overview provides the foundation for developing specific hypotheses by combining learnings from both research topics.

The effects of market conditions on M&A activity have been topic of numerous studies over the last decades.[7] Already Gort (1969) identifies, among other drivers, differences in perceived valuation between buyer and seller and economic disturbances that lead to these differences as possible reasons for increased merger activity. Later, Mitchell and Mulherin (1996) argue that industry shocks are main drivers of M&A activity based on their findings from an analysis of the 1980s merger wave. Harford (2005) adds that besides industry shocks, capital liquidity is necessary to cause a takeover wave (see also Eisfeldt and Rampini 2006). Both studies also acknowledge the positive relation between market valuation, industry shocks, and merger activity. Mitchell and Mulherin (1996) find that the most robust results of their analysis is the positive correlation of stock market performance and M&A activity. Later, Maksimovic and Phillips (2001) and Lambrecht (2004) provide evidence that the merger waves of the 1990s are also pro-cyclical in strong markets. They constitute that sellers are more likely to sell and buyers more likely to buy when their markets perform strongly. Lambrecht (2004) points out that especially mergers that are motivated by economies of scale drive activity in growing markets. Shahrur and Venkateswaran (2009) propose that firms may increasingly engage in diversifying M&A transactions when their core business segments experience an adverse shock. Lubatkin and Chatterjee (1991), on the other hand, argue that in bear markets, managers and shareholders become more reserved towards M&A.

The preceding explanations for merger activity follow a neo-classical, synergistic perspective implying that M&A activity is motivated by an optimal allocation of productive assets especially when industries undergo fundamental change. An alternative perspective is provided by studies focusing on behavioral aspects such as hubris and empire building of managers, which can be enforced by high market valuation levels. Roll (1986) first introduces management hubris as a potential explanation for the pursuit of transaction even when the rationally expected gains do not justify the offered price. Gorton et al. (2009) identify the fear of

7 For a detailed discussion of the past merger waves please refer to, e.g., Brealey and Myers (2003) or Weston and Chung (1990).

managers to lose their position after a takeover as a driver of M&A activity. Managers try to protect themselves by following an "eat or be eaten" approach. Goel and Thakor (2010) introduce envy as an additional cause of merger waves to the behavioral discussion. They built a model in which merger waves are induced by envy with regard to differences in compensation between managers of larger and smaller firms. Behavioral explanations for M&A activity imply agency costs and, hence, negative economic effects from a buyer's shareholder perspective. Jensen (2005) argues that agency conflicts are particularly strong when companies are overvalued. High valuation markets can provoke selfish management decisions regarding M&A. Goel and Thakor (2010), therefore, suggest that transaction synergies in bull markets are generally lower than in depressed market environments.

Shleifer and Vishny (2003) provide an explanation of merger activity that includes aspects of both neo-classical and behavioral views. They propose that managers do not act irrationally but rather react rationally to inefficient markets. The conclusion drawn from their model implies that managers will conduct stock paid transactions when valuation levels are high and their equity is likely to be overvalued. Returns from these share acquisitions are, thus, higher than from cash acquisitions, because they exploit market misevaluation in favor of bidders' shareholders, at least in the short term. In addition, Rhodes-Kropf and Viswanathan (2004) argue that in times of high market valuation shareholders of acquisition targets tend to accept overvalued shares as acquisition currency because they underestimate the relative misevaluation of the bidder's equity. Consequently, they argue, high valuation markets drive merger activity. Rhodes-Kropf et al. (2005) provide empirical evidence for this argument. They show that acquirers are significantly higher priced than their targets and that highly overvalued buyers make up for a disproportionately high share of acquisitions. These results are also supported by findings from Ming et al. (2006), Ang and Cheng (2006), and Brown and Fung (2009). Baker at al. (2009) extend the over-valuation perspective to cross-border direct investments and M&A. They find that high market valuations in the acquirer country positively affects cross-border activity. They also test for the effect of under-valuations in the target markets and conclude that low asset prices and fire sales in weak markets do not have a significant effect.

A continuously growing body of literature analyzes different aspects of value creation of acquisitions. Despite large variations in results, in general, a positive value effect for shareholders of targets has been observed while acquirers' shareholders on average do not profit from M&A (see e.g. Bruner 2002 or Jensen and Ruback 1983 for a still valid overview of older studies). The results of operational improvements following acquisitions remain inconclusive. Some studies find a significant improvement of post-transaction performance (Healy et al. 1992,

Heron and Lie 2002), while others determine no significant or negative effects (Moeller et al. 2004).

Numerous studies have examined value creation of specific transaction types. Loughran and Vijh (1997) present negative announcement returns for share transactions while cash acquisitions yield positive returns (see also Wang and Chung 2009, Moeller et al. 2004). Heron et al. (2002) find, however, no effect of payment method on operational performance after transactions. Fuller et al. (2002) show that acquisitions of private companies and subsidaries result in higher announcement returns compared to acquisitions of public targets, regardless of paymement method. They also propose that increasing target size has a negative effect on returns of public takeovers and a positive effect on private transactions. Cooney et al. (2009) validate these findings and propose that underpricing of private target is related to increased uncertainty regarding private company valuations.

With regard to global and industrial diversification, evidence from prior research shows that acquisitions of businesses in new industries create less value than core industry transactions (Hyland and Nail 2006, Maquieira et al. 1998, Berger and Ofek 1995). Devos et al. (2009) argue that operative synergies are the main source of merger value creation. They provide evidence that operative synergies are realized mainly in intra-industry transactions. Value creation is, hence, larger for M&A transactions in core industries. Hoberg and Philips (2010) come to similar results using a text-based analysis of product market similarity. They propose that the combination of companies with very similar characteristics yield higher announcement returns and operational improvements. Custodio and Metzger (2010) present evidence that industry experience of senior managers positively affects value creation of M&A transactions. Shahrur and Venkateswaran (2009) add that diversifying transactions potentially reveal negative prospects of the acquirer's core-industry and, thus, show negative value effects on industry peers.

Cross-border transactions are another frequently discussed characteristic. The value creation potential of cross-border transaction for shareholders of the bidder remains, however, unclear. Studies report positive value effects of cross-border acquisitions (Gleason et al. 2002, Chari et al. 2010 for emerging market targets) neutral effects (Gregory and McCorriston 2005), and negative effects (Aw and Chatterjee 2004, Ferreira et al. 2010).

Carapeto et al. (2010) analyze acquisitions of distressed targets. They find that the share of bankrupt and financially distressed acquisition targets increases in weak markets. Their results indicate that capital markets, in general, expect positive value effects from distressed transactions based on abnormal announcement returns. The performance improvements after the transactions, however, show decreasing operative performance of acquirers. Clark and Ofek (1994) also argue that companies on average do not succeed to turn around distressed acquisition targets.

Interest of this study is the discussion of value creation in different market phases. Prior research on this topic has mostly focused on relative overvaluation on individual firm level. Lin and Fu (2008) examine value creation of acquisitions by overvalued firms using short- and long-term abnormal returns to shareholders. They conclude that overvalued companies destroy value both at announcement and in the years following the transaction. They also find that cash transactions outperform share transactions of overvalued companies supporting Jensen's (2005) agency cost argument. Contradictory evidence, however, is provided by Savor and Lu (2008) who find that the long-term buy-and-hold returns favor shareholders of overvalued firms after a share transaction.

Transaction performance from a market level perspective has seen little attention so far. Chidambaran et al. (2010) examine M&A transactions in "hot and cold" merger markets measured by transaction activity with a focus on transactions in hot, active markets. Analyzing 2'510 US transactions between 1988 and 2005 they find that hot market acquirers prefer stock to cash payment and pay higher premiums. They also analyze short- and long-term returns to shareholders of the buyer. The results show that announcement returns in active markets are generally lower especially for stock financed transactions. Longer term capital market reactions over 12 months also show an under-performance of stock transactions.

Rhodes-Kropf and Viswanathan (2004) propose that better transaction decisions are made when markets are depressed. Bouwman et al. (2009) examine transactions during different market valuation phases and present supporting evidence for this prediction. They determine high, neutral, and low valuation phases based on relative price-earnings levels of the S&P 500 index. Based on the analysis of 2’944 transactions of US acquirers between 1972 and 2002 they argue that transactions under low market valuation levels create less value at announcement than boom market transactions. Low market transactions, however, outperform in the long run. Adding to previous behavioral hypotheses, Bouwman et al. (2009) identify managerial herding as a possible explanation for weak performance of high market M&A. They argue that managers engage in M&A imitating their successful peers to repeat the success of prior transactions despite declining value creation potential of the available takeover opportunities. These findings support Jensen's (2005) view on agency costs of highly valued stock.

This paper contributes to the discussion of acquisition quality in different market valuation phases by adding an analysis of transaction characteristics with a focus on M&A in weak markets. This thesis takes a European perspective, adding to the US-focused analysis of Bouwman et al. (2009) and introduces some adjustments in the design to, e.g., account for industry specific valuation levels. The data also includes the most recent merger wave of the last decade, which has been strongly influenced by high capital liquidity in contrast to previous shock induced waves.

4.2.2 Specific predictions

Previous research provides different theories with regard to the impact of market valuation levels on M&A's value creation. Following a neo-classical view, the expected long- and short-term return of M&A regardless of market phase should be positive. High market valuations indicate changes in industry dynamic and should enable companies to take advantage of new opportunities through M&A. Hence, these acquisitions should be especially value enhancing (Mitchell and Mulherin 1996). From a behavioral perspective, investor induced stock market overvaluation generates agency costs which are value destroying for bidders' shareholders (Jensen 2005). Weak market transactions on the contrary should display a number of positive effects on value creation. First, these transactions should be less exposed to agency costs. Second, bidder competition for targets may be smaller than in strong markets because potential strategic investors are focused on internal operational improvements and struggle to free up sufficient financing for M&A. Results from the European Central Bank (ECB) show that companies reduce investments when their financial situation worsens. Gell et al. (2008) propose that companies apply better target selection when investment decisions have to be thoroughly examined in uncertain market environments. Thus, higher value creation for shareholders of weak market acquirers is expected compared to boom market transactions.

4.H1: M&A transactions in low valuation markets create more value for bidders' shareholders and lead to higher operative performance improvement than takeovers in booming markets.

Market valuation levels are expected to affect the choice and value creation potential of different transaction types. Specific predictions are made with regard to payment methods and target characteristics across market valuation phases. The payment method is predicted to have a significant influence on M&A performance in different markets. Shleifer and Vishny (2003) argue that overvalued shares used as transaction currency to acquire real assets benefits bidders' shareholders in boom markets, at least from a short-term perspective, when a valuation differential can be exploited. Therefore, transaction payment should be more frequently in shares during high valuation markets than during weak markets. Ang and Cheng (2006) provide empirical evidence for the value effect of share transactions of highly valued companies. They find that overvalued firms that acquire relatively lower valued targets generate sustained wealth gains for shareholders of buyers in the short- and long-term. Assuming a market induced part of firm overvaluation as proposed by Rhodes-Kropf and Viswanathan (2004), this leads to the prediction that takeovers using shares as payment method are more favorable for shareholders of the acquirer in strong markets. During weak markets, cash transactions should be more favorable.

4.H2: Share transactions perform weakly when market valuations are low.

The decision to diversify is also predicted to affect M&A success in different market environments. In general, focused transactions aim at realizing operative synergy while diversifying transactions often seek financial synergy through risk reduction. Recent studies document that conglomerate transactions create less value for shareholders of bidders (Devos et al. 2009, Hoberg and Philips 2010). A possible explanation, besides larger synergies of intra-industry takeovers, is increased complexity of acquisitions in non-core segments. In a challenging business environment, additional complexity should have the strongest adverse effect on M&A success. Based on the predictions from Shleifer and Vishny (2003), conglomerate transactions are expected to be more common and more successful in higher valuation markets. With regard to geographic diversification a similar argumentation is followed. Baker et al. (2009) find a positive effect from high market valuations on cross-border activity. They propose that multinational companies act as arbitrageurs as suggested by Shleifer and Vishny (2003). The general value effect from these cross-border acquisitions remains, however, uncertain due to contradictory results from previous research. Potential value drivers for cross border transactions are international risk diversification, exchange rate differentials, and operative synergies, e.g., through access to new markets (Danbolt 2004). Opposed to synergies, a number of challenges are associated with foreign M&A investments. Aw and Chatterjee (2004) propose cross cultural differences and loss of control in cross border transaction as reasons for a potential under-performance. The higher complexity of cross border integration is expected to negatively affect value creation and operational performance especially in weak markets. Therefore, an outperformance of domestic transactions is predicted for weak markets.

4.H3: Industrial and international diversification through M&A creates less value in weak market environments.

The effect of relative transaction size on value creation has seen little attention so far. However, in connection with different market environments this factor appears relevant. In general, larger acquisitions are more likely to create sufficient synergies affecting capital market and operational performance of the combined company (Martynova et al. 2006, Devos et al. 2009). Larger acquisitions, however, also create more integration risk. In weak markets, smaller targets relative to buyers' size appear more attractive because they generate less uncertainty in terms of integration success and financing. When companies struggle with internal problems in difficult markets, M&A poses additional complexity that can harm overall performance. Therefore, investors are expected to react cautiously to the announcement of large transactions in weak markets. Smaller, less complex transactions are expected to outperform larger transactions in down-markets.

4.H4: In weak markets, smaller transactions create more value for shareholders of buyers than large transactions.

The public status of targets has been found to have a large effect on value creation for bidders' shareholders in prior research (Fuller et al. 2002, Moeller et al. 2004). Private transactions usually outperform public ones. In general, acquisitions of divested subsidiaries and parts of companies generate the highest value for bidding companies. Possible explanations are lower liquidity of private targets (Fuller et al. 2002) and information asymmetry (Custodio and Metzger 2010) that both lead to discounts for private targets and subsidiaries benefiting acquirers' shareholders. In weak markets, information asymmetry can have a particularly strong effect due to uncertain market outlooks. An outperformance of private and subsidiary transactions compared to public takeovers is expected for all market valuation phases. In down markets, subsidiaries are anticipated to be most attractive due to the higher quality of assets that are for sale in down-markets. Parent companies may be willing to sell attractive non-core businesses to generate additional cash in order to weather bad market conditions.

4.H5a: Acquisitions of private targets outperform public targets regardless of prevailing market valuation level. 4.H5b: In weak markets, divested parts of companies are particularly attractive and generate more value than other types of transactions.

Distress transactions are expected to be more frequent when markets perform weakly. The probability of turning around a troubled target, however, is predicted to be lower when markets are declining. Clark and Ofek (1994) and Carapeto et al. (2010) come to the result that operative performance decreases after distressed takeovers. Due to the additional operational challenges posed by the integration of weak targets, the value effect is expected to be especially negative compared to non-distressed transactions in downturn markets.

4.H6: Distress related M&A is more frequent in down-markets but with lower value creation potential than in stronger market environments.

4.3 Data and methodology

In this section the data sample is introduced and the empirical approach described.

4.3.1 Applied data

The applied M&A data is based on completed transactions included in Thomson Reuters SDC Platinum database. All European transactions announced between January 1st, 1989 and December 31st, 2006 have been considered. Transactions with the following characteristics have been selected for analysis:

- The buyer is based in Europe with headquarters in one of the European countries including the Eastern European states and Russia. The buyer is also listed on a European stock exchange.
- Transaction value equals or exceeds EUR 10 mn and constitutes at least 1% of the acquirer's market capitalization at the day of announcement.
- The acquirer owns more than 50% of the target's equity after completion of the transaction.
- The buying firm belongs to the 200 largest companies of one of the industry sectors classified by the Industry Classification Benchmark (ICB) measured by market capitalization on December 31st, 2008.[8]
- Financial institutions including real estate and private equity companies (ICB sector Financial Institution) are excluded from the analysis to fully focus on strategic M&A.[9]

---

8 The results remain robust when applying the 100, 150, 220 largest companies per industry.

9 The Industry Classification Benchmark (ICB) is published and maintained by Dow Jones und Financial Times Stock Exchange (FTSE). It classifies companies based on their main sources of revenue in 10 industries with 114 sub-sectors. The considered industries are (i) Oil and Gas (0001), (ii) Basic Materials (1000), (iii) Industrials (2000), (iv) Consumer Goods (3000), (v) Health Care (4000), (vi) Consumer Services (5000), (vii) Telecommunication (6000), (viii) Utilities (7000), and (ix) Technology (9000). Financial Institutions (8000) including real estate and private equity companies are not considered due to often unclear differentiation between strategic acquisitions and trade sales as well as for the special properties of the applied financial ratios (see Martynova et al. 2006).

All financial information including capital market, balance sheet, and income statement data is obtained from Datastream, Thomson Financial, and Worldscope databases. Studies show that Datastream share prices have to be handled with care due to a number of data errors (Ince and Porter 2006, Espenlaub et al. 2009). Ince and Porter (2006) provide evidence that Datastream share information contains a considerable share of security misclassification and incorrect share returns mainly for small firms. The focus on larger industry constituents mostly mitigates this potential pitfall. All analysis results are adjusted for outliers by trimming 1% of extreme values and manually checked for illogical data entries. After cleaning the data, 2‘002 transactions remain for which all required financial information is available and suitable control firms for BHAR and abnormal return on assets (AROA) analyses could be identified. Table 4.8 (Appendix) provides an overview of the applied data sample.

4.3.2 Classification of market valuation levels

In order to analyze M&A value creation in different market phases, the European stock market is classified on the basis of valuation levels. The chosen approach builds on the methodology developed by Bouwman et al. (2009). Periods of high, neutral, and low market valuation are determined using trailing price-to-earnings (P/E) multiples. Due to a general upward trend in P/E ratios and extreme valuation spikes in 2000 and 2001, the P/E multiples are de-trended by removing the best straight line fit of the classified month and the preceding five years. The de-trended P/E multiples are then divided at their median. The top half of the above median months are classified as high valuation markets, the lower half of the below median months as low markets, and the rest as neutral markets.[10] In addition to Bouwman et al. (2009) this analysis is performed based on index P/Es for the nine considered ICB industries. This approach is chosen because valuation phases were found to differ significantly between industries. An overall market perspective would falsly classifiy industries with less volatile or unaffected P/E levels. Figure 4.1 illustrates the market classification for the European DS-Total Market index from Datastream.

10 Bouwman et al. (2009) discuss and contrast in depth different methodologies of classifying market valuation levels. Besides P/E ratios they examine market-to-book (M/B) and overall index levels of the S&P 500. They also test the robustness of their approach to changes in de-trended period and changes in the classification window from month to quarters.

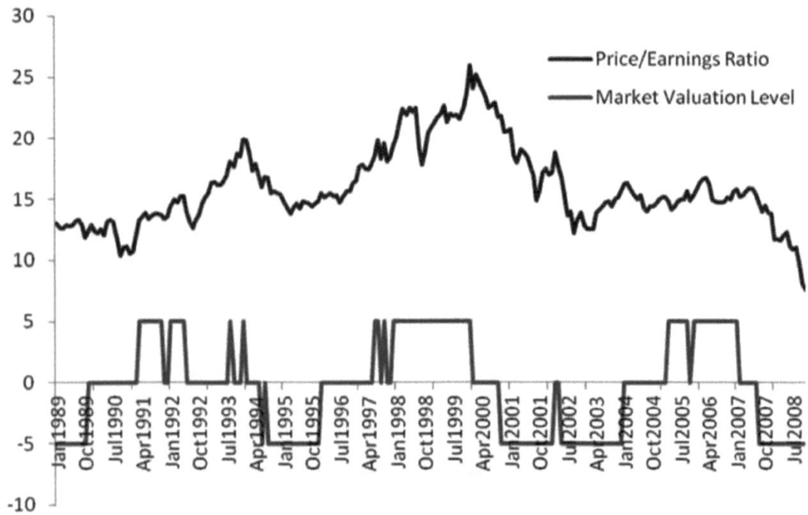

Figure 4.1: P/E multiples and valuation levels of the European DS-Total Market index

The classification of the applied data samples yields 423 transactions in low markets, 919 in neutral markets, and 660 in high valuation markets. The summary statistic in Table 4.8 (Appendix) gives a detailed overview of the classification result.

4.3.3 Approach to determine quality of M&A transactions

In order to determine the value effect of M&A for acquiring companies in different valuation phases, multiple perspectives are applied. First, an univariate analysis of value creation and performance improvement is conducted. From a capital market perspective, abnormal announcement returns (CAR) are used to examine short-term value effects. Buy-and-hold returns (BHAR) are applied to analyze longer-term value creation. In addition to the event-time view, a calendar-time perspective using a 4-factor model based on Fama and French (1993) and Carhart (1997) is added to the long-term perspective (FF4F). To assess the operative impact of M&A transactions, excess operative returns (AROA) are included. In a second step, based on the univariate results, a multivariate regression model is estimated. CAR, BHAR, and AROA outcomes are regressed using different transaction characteristics as independent variables to test the determinants of M&A performance in different market environments.

4.3.3.1 Methodology for assessing short-term value creation

To determine the short-term value effect of acquisitions for shareholders of the acquiring company, the cumulative abnormal returns around the announcement date (CAR) are calculated. The examined event window consists of 41 days reaching from 20 days before to 20 days after the announcement day of the analyzed transactions. To determine the short-term abnormal return the Market Model as proposed by Brown and Warner (1980 and 1985) is applied (Equation (4.1)).

$$AR_{it} = R_{it} - (\alpha_i + \beta_i \cdot R_{mt}) \tag{4.1}$$

R_{it} represents the stock return of company i in period t while R_{mt} describes the return of the specific European industry index of the acquiring company's industry as classified by ICB. The market model parameters are calculated using Ordinary Least Squares (OLS) regression over a period of 180 trading days prior to the analyzed event window. Cumulative abnormal returns (CAR) are then calculated by summing the abnormal returns over different event windows (Equation (4.2)).

$$CAR_{EventWindow(m1,m2)} = \sum_{m1}^{m2} AR_{it} \tag{4.2}$$

To test the statistical significance the parametric cross-sectional z-Test (BMP) proposed by Boehmer et al. (1991) is applied . The test statistic accounts for a potential increase in stock return volatility around the announcement period of a transaction. The cross-sectional test combines return variance during the event and estimation periods. Equation (4.3) provides the applied test statistics as outlined by Boehmer et al. (1991).

$$t = \frac{\frac{1}{N}\sum_{t=1}^{N} SAR_{it}}{\sqrt{\frac{1}{N(N-1)}\sum\left(SAR_{it} - \sum_{i=1}^{N}\frac{SAR_{it}}{N}\right)}} \tag{4.3}$$

Equation (4.3a) illustrates the standardization procedures using the estimation period variances.

$$SAR_{it} = \frac{CAR_{ie_1-e_2}}{SD_{Eit}}; \text{ with } SD_{Eit} = SD_{it}\sqrt{1 + \frac{1}{T} + \left(\frac{(R_{Mt} - R_M)^2}{\sum_{j=1}^{T}(R_{Mj} - R_M)^2}\right)} \tag{4.3a}$$

SAR_{it} represents the standardized abnormal return for company i on day t within the event period. SD_{Eit} is the standard error of the event period for company i on day t. The SD_{it} variable, in turn, is the standard error within the estimation period. T stands for the number of days in the estimation period. R_{Mt} is the market return on day t of the event period, R_{Mj} the return on day j of the estimation period, and R_M the average return of the Market in the event period.

In addition, the non-parametric generalized sign test (GST) introduced by Cowan et al. (1990) is calculated. Bartholdy et. al (2007) show that non-parametric tests have larger power to detect abnormal returns especially for thinly traded stocks. The GST tests the share of positive abnormal returns within the sample compared to an expected share of positive results. The expected share of positive observations is estimated based on abnormal returns observed in the estimation period. Equations 4.4 and 4.4a show the computation of the GST as proposed by Cowan et al. (1990).

(4.4) $$z = \frac{N*P - E(N*p')}{\sqrt{N*p'*(1-p')}}$$

In Equation (4.4), N stands for the number of companies within the data sample. P is the observed percentage of positive observations. The expected percentage of positive observation for the sample is represented by p'. It is defined as provided in Equation (4.4a).

(4.4a) $$p' = \frac{1}{n}\sum_{i=1}^{n}\frac{1}{180}\sum_{t=e_1}^{e_{180}} S_{it}$$

S_{it} indicates whether a company's abnormal return within the estimation period was positive or negative. S_{it} takes the value 0 if abnormal returns are below zero or 1 when above.

4.3.3.2 Methodology for assessing mid- to long-term value creation

The approach to determine longer-term capital market returns of M&A transactions is two-fold. In order to address the often discussed statistical challenges that accompany the calculation of long-term abnormal stock performance, both commonly used methodologies, the calendar-time approach proposed by Fama and French (1993) including Carhart's (1997) momentum factor (FF4F) and the buy-and-hold abnormal return (BHAR) in event-time proposed by Barber and Lyon (1997) and Lyon et al. (1999), will be pursued.[11]

11 Mitchell and Stafford (2000) discuss and contrast the BHAR and FF3F approach for different applications in event studies. Their results favor FF3F. Other studies, however,

First, BHAR of acquiring companies are determined following the matching control firm approach, e.g., applied by Brown and Fung (2009). To measure abnormal performance of acquirers, non-merging control firms with comparable characteristics are selected as benchmarks. As proposed by Lyon et al. (1999), market-to-book ratios (M/B) and the size measured by market value are used to select control firms. In addition to the common approach, special attention is put on finding control companies with matching industry specific characteristics. The following steps are applied:

- End of June market values and previous fiscal year's M/B ratios are determined for all European companies included in the data sample for every year.
- For each acquiring firm, all non-merging firms within the same ICB subsector (114 sub-sectors) and with market values between 70% and 130% of the bidder's market value at announcement day are identified. If less than three matching firms could be found, companies within the same 3-, 2-, and 1-digit ICB codes are considered consecutively.
- From the list of similar sized firms the one with the smallest absolute difference in M/B value is selected as control firm.

By selecting control firms within the same industry sub-sectors and with comparable relative market valuations, effects from potential individual firms misevaluation (as found, e.g., by Ang and Cheng 2006, Brown and Fung 2009) are mitigated. The identified control firms for each transaction are used as a benchmark to calculate the buy-and-hold abnormal returns of each acquirer in the corresponding sample. Equation (4.5) describes the computation of the BHARs.

(4.5)
$$BHAR_{iT} = \prod_{t=s}^{s+T}(1+R_{it}) - \prod_{t=s}^{s+T}(1+R_{controlfirm,t})$$

R_{it} and $R_{controlfirm,t}$ describe the monthly returns of the bidder and the control firm respectively. The BHARs are calculated for a 12-, 24-, and 36-month period. The statistical significance is tested using a t-test. The analysis focuses on equally weighted BHAR to reflect returns to investors allocating funds equally among investment choices. To account for potential effects from acquirer size, a value-weighted perspective is provided in Table 4.9 (Appendix). Appendix 4.6.2 also includes a description of the weighting approach.

The second long-term approach follows the calendar time methodology introduced by Fama and French (1993). The 4-factor model (FF4F) addresses some of

---

argue in favor of BHAR finding that FF3F has less power to identify abnormal returns (e.g., Loughran and Ritter 2000).

the shortcomings of the BHAR methodology, e. g., the cross-sectional correlation of firms in event-time (Mitchell and Stafford 2000). It, however, is potentially exposed to other pitfalls, e.g., heteroscedasticity. The 4-factor model determines excess returns of a portfolio of sample firms by regressing the time series of (i) the market excess return, (ii) the differences in return between small and big firms, (iii) the excess returns of high vs. low book-to-market (B/M) companies, and (iv) the Carhart momentum factor. The model takes the form of Equation (4.6).

$$(4.6) \qquad R_{pt} - R_{ft} = a_p + b_p\left(R_{mt} - R_{ft}\right) + s_p SMB + h_p HML + m_p PR1YR + e_{pt}$$

R_{pt} is the return of a continuously changing portfolio of companies or subgroups of these companies that conducted acquisitions within the preceding 36 months. The acquirer portfolio is re-constructed on a monthly basis when new bidders are included and inactive companies leave after the 36-month period. R_{mt} - R_{ft} represents the market factor, calculated by subtracting the risk free rate (three months Euribor after 1999, Libor until 1999) from the value waited market portfolio (Europe DS-Total Market index). SMB is the size factor. The companies of the Europe DS-Total Market index are ranked based on their market value on the last trading day of June each year. The median is used to split the companies into big (B) and small (S) portfolios. HML is the book-to-market factor which is formed by subtracting high B/M value stocks and low B/M growth stocks. The portfolios are formed by ranking the companies according to their B/M level and distributing the top and bottom 30% to the respective portfolios (H and L) and the remaining 40% in a medium portfolio (M). Six portfolios are created each year (S/L, S/M, S/H, B/L, B/M, and B/H). The SMB portfolio is supposed to replicate the risk factor in returns related to size. It is calculated using the average of the monthly returns on the three small (S) portfolios minus the three big (B) portfolios. The HML portfolio mimics the risk factor related to book-to-market valuation and is calculated in the same way using the two high (H) and the two low (L) portfolios. Due to simple averaging of the portfolios the factors should be largely free of the other factor's effect.

In addition, a momentum factor is included to account for portfolio momentum effects as proposed by Carhart (1997). PR1YR is the return differentials of two equally weighted portfolios constructed out of firms with the highest and lowest 30% of eleven months returns prior to the announcement month. The coefficients b_p, s_p, h_p, and m_p determine the loading of the respective factor indicating the composition of the sample portfolio and the factor's effect on returns. The a_p coefficient finally represents the monthly return of the sample portfolio over a 36 months period that cannot be explained by the four factors. The sum of the error terms e_{pt} is assumed to be zero. The statistical significance is tested using a t-test.

In addition to the capital market perspective applied so far, an analysis of the operative performance development of bidders after a transaction is conducted. The methodology applied is based on Healy et al. (1992). However, the focus of this study is not on a pre-transaction vs. post-transaction comparisons but on relative performance variations after acquisitions in different market valuation phases. The chosen approach follows the methodology applied by Bouwman et al. (2009) and Wang and Chung (2009). In order to measure abnormal operative performance (AROA), earnings before interest, tax, depreciation, and amortization (EBITDA) are analyzed over a 3-year period after the transaction excluding the year of announcement. EBITDA is normalized by average total assets. To determine abnormal performance, control firms are selected for every transaction following the approach applied for the BHAR analysis again focusing on closest industry-specific (4-digit ICB) matches. The control firm matching is conducted using comparable firm sizes and the smallest absolute difference in pre-transaction EBITDA over average total assets instead of market-to-book ratios to select companies with similar operative performance. AROA is then calculated as the difference in normalized operative result between acquirer and non-merging control firm. Significance is tested using a t-test.

4.4 Empirical results

4.4.1 Overall value creation in different market environments

Results of the announcement effects (CAR) are summarized in Table 4.1. Panel A. shows the result for the whole sample of 2'002 transactions independent of market valuation levels. The overall effect of takeover announcements is found to be significantly positive between 0.67% and 0.90%. The positive result is not consistent with the majority of prior event studies. Bruner (2002) finds that on average M&A transactions are value neutral or even value destroying. He, however, also reports a large variance in results. The assessment of the positive value effect should take into account that the acquirers selected were active at the end of 2008. Hence, a survivorship bias is expected to positively skew the results. Since the focus of this study is on relative performance of transactions in different market environment this bias should not affect the results of such a comparison.

Of special interest is the performance difference between high and low market announcements. Panel B. in Table 4.1 reports significantly positive announcement returns for high market acquisitions between 0.87% and 1.18%. Abnormal announcement returns in weak markets are mostly not significantly different from zero except for the smallest 3-day window, which displays a slightly positive announcement effect. The difference in means shows a significant over-performance of high market transactions of between 0.71% and 1.52%. Assuming efficient capital markets, M&A in lean times seems to be less attractive than boom market transactions. This result underlines the hypothesis that industry shocks that correlate with high valuation markets present value creating M&A opportunities as argued, e.g., by Mitchell and Mulherin (1996). This outcome is also consistent with Bouwman et al. (2009). Another finding in the announcement effects of low market transactions is that the returns on announcement day are positive on average. The market reactions in larger event windows around announcement, however, are increasingly negative. Although the variance of the CAR increases over larger windows, the downward trend appears significant and is only observed in low valuation markets.

A possible explanation could be the adaption of rumors prior to the announcement (leakage) and further information gathered after the announcement by existing shareholders that react more slowly to the transaction than the overall market (e.g., Schwert 2006; Shahrur 2005). Another possible explanation along these lines is a general under-reaction to transaction announcement in times when investors have to process a multitude of information which is likely to apply in uncertain market environments (Hirshleifer 2009). Thus, the decrease in CAR suggests a pessimistic evaluation of low market transactions by existing shareholders.

Table 4.1: Short-term CAR of M&A transactions under different market valuation levels

A. All Market Valuations						N = 2'002
Event-time	CAR	median	z-test BMP[1]	p-value	GST[2]	p-value
[-10, +10]	0.67%	0.46%	5.15	<0.01[a]	3.51	<0.01[a]
[-5, +5]	0.90%	0.63%	6.72	<0.01[a]	5.52	<0.01[a]
[-3, +3]	0.83%	0.64%	7.03	<0.01[a]	5.66	<0.01[a]
[-1, +1]	0.73%	0.43%	7.75	<0.01[a]	6.33	<0.01[a]
B. High Market Valuations						N = 660
Event-time	CAR	median	z-test BMP[1]	p-value	GST[2]	p-value
[-10, +10]	0.87%	0.43%	3.17	<0.01[a]	2.64	<0.01[a]
[-5, +5]	1.18%	0.79%	4.33	<0.01[a]	4.12	<0.01[a]
[-3, +3]	1.04%	0.67%	4.59	<0.01[a]	4.43	<0.01[a]
[-1, +1]	0.87%	0.47%	4.77	<0.01[a]	4.12	<0.01[a]
C. Neutral Market Valuations						N = 919
Event-time	CAR	median	z-test BMP[1]	p-value	GST[2]	p-value
[-10, +10]	1.14%	0.96%	5.08	<0.01[a]	3.92	<0.01[a]
[-5, +5]	1.00%	0.63%	5.22	<0.01[a]	4.32	<0.01[a]
[-3, +3]	0.92%	0.68%	5.38	<0.01[a]	4.65	<0.01[a]
[-1, +1]	0.72%	0.44%	5.42	<0.01[a]	5.37	<0.01[a]
D. Low Market Valuations						N = 423
Event-time	CAR	median	z-test BMP[1]	p-value	GST[2]	p-value
[-10, +10]	-0.65%	-0.75%	-0.31	0.38	-1.43	0.08[c]
[-5, +5]	0.26%	0.24%	1.37	0.09[c]	0.51	0.30
[-3, +3]	0.33%	0.04%	1.43	0.08[c]	0.07	0.47
[-1, +1]	0.56%	0.25%	2.81	<0.01[a]	0.71	0.24

E. Difference between Neutral and Low Market Valuations			
Event-time	CAR	t-value[3]	p-value
[-10, +10]	1.78%	3.13	<0.01[a]
[-5, +5]	0.74%	1.66	0.09[c]
[-3, +3]	0.59%	1.52	0.13
[-1, +1]	0.16%	0.59	0.56
F. Difference between High and Low Market Valuations			
Event-time	CAR	t-value[3]	p-value
[-10, +10]	1.52%	2.50	0.01[b]
[-5, +5]	0.91%	1.92	0.06[c]
[-3, +3]	0.71%	1.76	0.08[c]
[-1, +1]	0.31%	1.06	0.29

This table shows the results from a short-term event-time analysis of the cumulative abnormal returns (CAR) in different time windows around the transaction announcement. All transactions between January 1st, 1989 and December 31st, 2006 are included for which all required acquirer information is available until December 31st, 2009. 1) Standardized cross-sectional test as proposed by Boehmer et al. (1991). 2) Generalized Sign Tests (GST) as in Cowan et al. (1990). 3) To test the difference in means between sub-samples the standard t-test for mean differences is applied. The p-values resulting from z- and t-statistics are marked with "a" if significance is in 1% area, with "b" in 5% area, and with "c" in 10% area.

Table 4.2: Long-term BHAR and long-term AROA – M&A

	1. Abnormal Long-term Capital Market Returns (BHAR)				2. Abnormal Long-term Operative Performance (AROA)			
				A. All Market Valuations				N = 2'002
Period	BHAR	Median	t-value[1]	p-value	AROA	median	t-value[1]	p-value
12 months	2.36%	3.26%	2.11	0.04[b]	-0.05%	0.03%	-0.26	0.79
24 months	3.22%	2.79%	2.19	0.03[b]	-0.61%	-0.46%	-3.02	<0.01[a]
36 months	2.38%	-0.90%	1.33	0.19	-0.76%	-0.43%	-3.73	<0.01[a]
				B. High Market Valuations				N = 660
Period	BHAR	Median	t-value[1]	p-value	AROA	median	t-value[1]	p-value
12 months	-1.34%	-1.78%	-0.71	0.48	-0.42%	-0.10%	-1.19	0.23
24 months	-1.59%	-0.33%	-0.60	0.55	-0.62%	-0.25%	-1.70	0.09[b]
36 months	-1.47%	-2.18%	-0.45	0.65	-0.88%	-0.41%	-2.33	0.20[b]
				C. Neutral Market Valuations				N = 919
Period	BHAR	Median	t-value[1]	p-value	AROA	median	t-value[1]	p-value
12 months	3.88%	3.73%	2.25	0.02[b]	0.12%	-0.19%	-0.43	0.67
24 months	6.34%	3.38%	2.95	0.01[b]	-0.71%	-0.64%	-2.65	<0.01[a]
36 months	1.74%	0.61%	0.63	0.27	-0.80%	-0.59%	-2.74	<0.01[a]
				D. Low Market Valuations				N = 423
Period	BHAR	Median	t-value[1]	p-value	AROA	median	t-value[1]	p-value
12 months	5.94%	5.39%	2.07	0.02[b]	0.14%	0.21%	0.30	0.76
24 months	5.54%	4.68%	1.81	0.07[c]	-0.36%	-0.18%	0.72	0.47
36 months	6.70%	0.21%	2.27	0.02[b]	-0.49%	-0.20%	1.14	0.26
				E. Difference between Neutral and Low Market Valuations				
Period	BHAR	t-value[2]	p-value		AROA	t-value[2]	p-value	
12 months	-2.06%	-0.73	0.46		-0.01%	-0.03	0.97	
24 months	0.80%	0.26	0.79		-0.36%	-0.63	0.53	
36 months	-4.96%	-1.22	0.22		-0.31%	-0.59	0.75	
				F. Difference between High and Low Market Valuations				
Period	BHAR	t-value[2]	p-value		AROA	t-value[2]	p-value	
12 months	-7.28%	-2.49	0.01[b]		-0.56%	-0.97	0.33	
24 months	-7.13%	-2.09	0.04[b]		-0.26%	-0.43	0.67	
36 months	-8.12%	-1.19	0.23		-0.39%	-0.68	0.50	

This table illustrates combined results from two long-term analyses of post-acquisition performance. (i) Long-term capital market returns in event-time (BHAR) are shown on the left side of the table for 12, 24, and 36 months. (ii) The right side of the table contrasts operative improvements (AROA) over one, two, and three years after the announcement year. All transactions between January 1st, 1989 and December 31st, 2006 are included for which all required buyer information is available until December 31st, 2009. 1) Significance is tested using a classical t-test. 2) To test the difference in means between sub-samples, the standard t-test for mean differences is applied. The p-values resulting from t-statistics are marked with "a" if significance is in 1% area, with "b" in 5% area, and with "c" in 10% area.

The long-term perspective provides evidence that challenges the efficient market view underlying the analysis of announcement returns. Table 4.2 summarizes the equally weighted results. Table 4.9 (Appendix) provides value weighted 24-month BHAR results. The overall sample exhibits significantly positive capital market returns 12 and 24 months after announcement of 2.36% and 3.22%. The positive effect is not robust to value weighting. Value weighted BHAR show a generally more negative outcome of between -8.44% and -9.67% indicating that larger acquirers engage in more value decreasing acquisitions. The comparison of high and low market returns reverses the announcement return findings. High market acquisitions result in insignificantly negative equally weighted BHAR while low market bidders significantly outperform their benchmarks by between 5.54% and 6.70%. The mean difference view emphasizes the over-performance of low market acquisitions of between 7.13% and 8.12% (8.28% and 9.13% value weighted) compared to boom-market transactions.

The abnormal operative performance (AROA) shows a constantly decreasing trend. The overall sample, high, and neutral markets indicate significant negative abnormal operative performance of acquiring companies two and three years after transaction announcement. Low valuation markets exhibit insignificant AROA. The mean difference view, however, shows only insignificant over-performance of low market transaction compared to high and neutral market acquirers. The overall finding indicates that integration efforts negatively influence operative performance post-transaction.

In addition to the event-time view a 4-factor calendar-time regression (FF4F) is estimated to test abnormal long-term capital market performance. The findings are shown in Table 4.3. The calendar-time results differ in some aspects from the event-time results. The “a” coefficient of the FF4F regression that constitutes the monthly abnormal return is insignificantly positive for the full sample and the neutral market sample of acquiring firms.

High market acquirers (Panel B.) show monthly excess returns of 0.15% (5.38% over 36 months) significant within the 10% confidence interval. Low valuation-market bidders realize monthly excess returns of 0.37% (13.45% over 36 months) significant within the 1% confidence interval. Low market transactions clearly outperform from a calendar-time perspective underlining the intuition that acquisitions conducted in difficult environments are more value creating from a shareholders' perspective than takeovers in stronger markets.

The results indicate that markets do not reflect the entire value creation of a transaction at announcement. The long-term under-performance of high market acquisitions also supports the view that high valuation levels and increased transaction activity generate agency costs that destroy value for shareholders of acquiring companies compared to low market transactions (Jensen 2005). The higher long-term performance of down market transaction proposes that these agency costs are absent in lean times. The results also suggest that managers apply better target selection when the market environment is challenging. Possible explanations are, e.g., a sounder investment decision process when financing is harder to secure amid uncertain market outlooks and potentially more attractive takeover opportunities when companies manage their asset portfolio to increase liquidity to weather bad market conditions.

Based on the result Hypothesis 4.H1 is supported for long-term value creation of down market takeovers.

Table 4.3: Monthly calendar-time return regressions (FF4F) M&A

	a	t-value	b	t-value	s	t-value	h	t-value	m	t-value
A. All Market Valuations										
Coef	0.07%	1.24	1.03	**91.72[a]**	-0.42	**-13.79[a]**	-0.03	1.46	-0.08	**-6.56[a]**
			$R^2_{adjusted} = 0.979$					F = **2'825.78[a]**		
B. High Market Valuations										
Coef	0.15%	**1.86[b]**	1.00	**57.40[a]**	-0.49	**-10.11[a]**	0.06	1.53	-0.11	**-5.48[a]**
			$R^2_{adjusted} = 0.955$					F = **1'128.96[a]**		
C. Neutral Market Valuations										
Coef	0.05%	0.63	1.04	**62.48[a]**	-0.34	**-7.63[a]**	-0.03	-0.91	0.08	0.41
			$R^2_{adjusted} = 0.958$					F = **1'270.05[a]**		
D. Low Market Valuations										
Coef	0.37%	**3.54[a]**	1.06	**47.52[a]**	-0.37	**-5.88[a]**	-0.16	**-3.53[a]**	-0.04	**-1.70[c]**
			$R^2_{adjusted} = 0.952$					F = **786.49[a]**		

This table presents results from 4-factor (FF4F) portfolio regressions. The intercept "a" represents the monthly abnormal return of a continuously adapted portfolio of acquiring companies that bought within the 36 months preceding the respective month. The analysis is conducted for portfolios of all, low, neutral, and high market acquirers between January 1st, 1989 and December 31st, 2006. The coefficients "b", "s", "h", and "m" represent the loadings of the regressed market factors. "b" is the classical beta coefficient of the market excess return. "s" expresses the composition of the acquirers' portfolio in terms of size distribution while "h" indicates the same for value vs. growth distribution. "m" indicates the effects of momentum within the market portfolio. The classic t-statistic is conducted to test significance. The statistical fit of the model is indicated by the adjusted determination coefficient $R^2_{adjusted}$ and F-statistic. The test values are marked with "a" if significance is in 1% area, with "b" in 5% area, and with "c" in 10% area.

4.4.2 Transaction characteristics in different market phases

Based on the previous findings specific differences in takeover characteristics are examined between high, neutral, and low market transactions. Special attention is put on the specific characteristics of low market transactions compared to transactions in other market valuations phases. Table 4.4 provides a summary of transaction characteristics in different markets.

First, M&A activity in high valuation markets is 56% higher than in low valuation markets. This is consistent with the often-identified correlation between valuation levels and takeover activity (e.g., Maksimovic and Phillips, 2001). The transaction value does not decrease significantly between high valuation and low valuation markets. An expected increase due to higher valuations in up-markets, higher financing capacity, and the behavioral explanations of merger waves such as hubris, managerial herding, and envy is not observed.

The distribution of transaction size relative to acquirers' market capitalization is skewed towards relatively large transactions in all valuation phases with mean relative sizes between 17.09% in low and 19.43% in neutral markets. The median of relative transaction size differs between market phases. The median in strong markets is 10.41% compared to 5.09% in weak markets. This indicates a higher share of relatively large acquisitions in high valuation markets.

Capaldo et al. (2009) proposes that weak market transactions are often express deals with shorter periods between announcement and completion. This view cannot be confirmed. The days to completion remain fairly stable between 100 (70) and 107 (67) days in mean (median).

The payment method is identified as a major driver of transaction value creation in previous studies (e.g., Loughran and Vijh 1997). Existing evidence suggests that high market transaction see a higher share of cash transactions (Shleifer and Vishny 2003, Rhodes-Kropf and Viswanathan 2004). However, the distribution of payment methods across different market valuation phases shows no such relation. The sum of hybrid and share transactions even increases in weak markets to 29.32% from 22.12% in high markets. Therefore, the prediction (4.H2) that fully or partially share-financed transactions have a more dominant role in high valuations markets is rejected for the presented European data sample.

The share of cross-border acquisitions is highest in weak (68.32%) compared to neutral (60.17%) and high (64.55%) valuation markets. The share of conglomerate transactions remains stable between high and low valuation phases in a 4- and 2-digit SIC code perspective. The conglomerate share is slightly higher in weak markets. However, the neutral market value exceeds the conglomerate share compared to the high and low market values from both perspectives. The argument that low market acquirers seek out less complex transactions in hard times is not supported by this data. The distribution of private, public, and divestment transactions across different market phases remains inconclusive. The portion of bankruptcy or restructuring related transactions is predicted to be higher in down-markets than in other market phases (Carapeto et al. 2010). However, the differential between neutral markets (6.52%) and low valuation markets (7.51%) is relatively small. The prediction that distress related transactions are more frequent when markets are weak (4.H6) is not supported by the data sample.

Table 4.4: Overview of transaction characteristics in different market valuation phases – M&A

Transaction characteristic	All valuations	High	Neutral	Low
Number of transactions	2'002	660	919	423
Mean (median) transaction value in EUR mn	644 (108)	738 (91)	560 (111)	677 (116)
Mean (median) relative size in %[1]	18.12 (5.79)	17.40 (10.41)	19.43 (5.44)	17.09 (5.09)
Mean (median) premium in %[2]	47.10 (34.81)	39.92 (32.62)	37.39 (34.76)	72.45 (36.50)
Mean (median) days to completion[3]	102 (68)	107 (67)	100 (70)	102 (69)
Payment method				
Transaction (value) share cash only in %	76.87 (42.90)	77.58 (35.74)	79.33 (53.33)	70.45 (36.32)
Transaction (value) share hybrid in %[4]	17.33 (39.12)	15.76 (57.43)	16.32 (27.14)	21.99 (29.52)
Transaction (value) share stock only in %	5.54 (17.97)	6.36 (6.82)	4.13 (19.51)	7.33 (34.15)
Target characteristic				
Transaction (value) share cross border in %[5]	63.34 (73.75)	64.55 (84.41)	60.17 (75.16)	68.32 (53.11)
Transaction (value) share diversifying 4SIC in %[6]	70.04 (58.50)	66.21 (38.84)	74.32 (71.84)	66.67 (67.92)
Transaction (value) share diversifying 2SIC in %[7]	42.72 (34.54)	39.33 (31.65)	44.56 (41.49)	42.86 (41.78)
Transaction (value) share of private in %[8]	30.42 (7.08)	33.79 (6.91)	28.84 (6.98)	28.61 (7.55)
Transaction (value) share of public in %[9]	22.68 (61.70)	20.61 (70.62)	24.59 (55.31)	21.75 (58.02)
Transaction (value) share of divestments in %[10]	43.36 (25.98)	41.67 (18.99)	43.63 (32.91)	45.39 (25.39)
Transaction (value) share of distressed in %[11]	5.89 (6.18)	4.68 (5.13)	6.52 (8.26)	7.51 (4.54)

This table summarizes the distribution of different transaction characteristics across the three market valuation phases high, neutral, and low measured based on the relative industry P/E ratio of the transaction month. The values displayed are the mean of the respective (sub)-sample cross-section. Median values are provided in brackets next to the mean values. 1) Relative size is measured based on deal value in relation to market capitalization of the acquiring company on announcement day. 2) The stock price premium paid by the acquirer is measured based on the stock price of the target four weeks prior to the announcement relative to the transaction value. Premiums are only available for listed target companies. 3) Days to completion is the number of days between first announcement of a takeover and its closing. Transactions which were announced only at closing are excluded from the numbers shown. Inclusion of these transactions leads to similar results. 4) Hybrid transactions are acquisitions in which the payment method is a mix of stock and cash or also includes other alternative payment methods. 5) Cross-border transactions opposed to domestic transactions are M&A transactions in which the country code of the acquirer differs from that of the target. 6&7) Diversifying transactions show a difference in primary 4-digit (or first 2-digit, respectively) figure of the Standard Industrial Classification (SIC) code between acquirer and target. 8, 9&10) All target companies classified in the public status field of the SDC data as private, public, or divestment. Public companies are listed at time of acquisition, while private companies are privately held, and divestments are purchases of company parts. 11) A transaction is classified as distressed when either marked as bankruptcy and restructuring related in the SDC database or when it had a negative operative cash flow in the quarter (respectively year if quarterly data is not available) preceding the announcement. Not all distressed transactions can be identified using this method due to limited availability of income data.

4.4.3 Value creation of different transaction sub-samples

The remainder of this section examines the value effect of different transaction types in low, neutral, and high valuation markets. Following the descriptive analysis a multiple regression model is estimated under 4.4.4. A short- and long-term perspective is taken to determine abnormal returns. As in Ferreira et al. (2010), short-term effects at announcement are measured using CAR both in a 3- and 21-day window around announcement as an additional robustness check and to account for the significant drift in announcement returns observed for low market transactions. Long-term capital market returns are determined by equally weighted 24-month BHAR. Value weighted BHAR results are provided in Table 4.9 (Appendix). Abnormal operational improvements are measured with AROA two years after the announcement year. First, the transactions are categorized in different sub-groups based on their characteristics. CAR, BHAR, and AROA are then calculated for every sub-group in high, neutral, and low valuation markets. Significant variations in performance between transaction characteristics and market valuation levels are analyzed by testing the mean differences. The following criteria based on the underlying predictions are applied: A. Payment method share or cash; B. Acquisitions in existing or new/diversifying fields based on the 4-digit SIC code of acquirer and target; C. Cross-border and domestic transactions based on SDC country code; D. Relative size of transaction value in relation to bidder's market capitalization at announcement divided at 5% based on the median relative size of transactions; E. Private, public, and divestment acquisitions corresponding to target status in SDC. F. Acquisitions of targets in financial distress or bankruptcy based on labeling in SDC and negative operative performance in the quarter (year if no quarterly data is available) before announcement. Tables 4.5 and 4.6 summarize the results for high, neutral, and low valuation markets.

The effect of payment methods on value creation in different market environments is shown in Panel A. of Table 4.5 for CAR and Table 4.6 for BHAR and AROA. Abnormal announcement returns of cash transactions in high valuation markets are significantly positive between 0.96% and 1.21%. Short-term abnormal returns of share transactions, however, are insignificant. With a significant mean difference of 4.39% in the 21-day window between cash and share transactions. A negative effect of share transactions at announcement cannot be observed in neutral or low valuation markets. This finding is consistent with behavioral explanations of M&A activity. It indicates that investors anticipate agency costs of share-financed takeovers when valuation levels are high. The finding corresponds with results from Lin and Fu (2008) on individual firm level. Cash transactions in high and neutral markets show significant, positive mean differences in announcement return compared to low market cash transactions. This results proposes that investors react cautiously when companies invest cash during times when liquidity may be a concern. The long-term BHAR results in Panel A. of Table 4.6 show a consistent under-performance of share transactions across all market phases. The highest value differential is found in low markets with a mean difference of 46.63% (62.93% value weighted) between cash and share transactions.

The mean difference between market phases amounts to 29.99% (42.33%) compared to neutral market transactions and 14.50% (48.31%) compared to high market takeovers. The results indicate that low valued shares used as acquisition currency in weak markets destroy shareholder value. Cash transaction, on the other hand, significantly outperform compared to high valuation markets with a mean difference of 9.42% (16.70%). The operative improvements indicate a lower level when the payment method is shares. The mean differences, however, remain insignificant. Hypothesis 4.H2 is, hence, supported with regard to the prediction that share transactions under-perform in weak markets in the long-term.

Panel C. in Tables 4.5 and 4.6 illustrates the value effect of cross-border and domestic transactions. Cross-border acquisitions create more value in weak markets. The finding indicates that international diversification is favorable from a capital market perspective when local markets deteriorate. This effect applies despite higher integration complexity of cross-border transactions. The predicted adverse effect of more complex diversifying transactions in weak markets is not observed (4.H3).

Table 4.5: CAR of different transaction characteristics in high, neutral, and low valuation markets – M&A

	1. High Markets			2. Neutral Markets			3. Low Markets			4. Mean Differences Neutral - Low		5. Mean Differences High - Low	
	N	$CAR_{[-1/+1]}$	$CAR_{[+10/-10]}$	N	$CAR_{[-1/+1]}$	$CAR_{[+10/-10]}$	N	$CAR_{[-1/+1]}$	$CAR_{[+10/-10]}$	$CAR_{[-1/+1]}$	$CAR_{[+10/-10]}$	$CAR_{[-1/+1]}$	$CAR_{[+10/-10]}$
A. Payment Method													
Cash Transactions	512	0.96%	1.21%	72[illegible]	0.83%	1.34%	298	0.66%	-0.59%	0.17%	1.93%	0.30%	1.80%
		(5.15[a])	**(3.62[a])**		**(5.78[a])**	**(5.22[a])**		**(2.73[a])**	(-0.40)	(0.58)	**(3.08[a])**	(1.00)	**(2.76[b])**
Share Transactions	42	0.09%	-3.17%	38	1.21%	1.07%	31	1.21%	1.28%	0.00%	-0.22%	-1.13%	-4.46%
		(0.57)	(-1.16)		**(1.50[c])**	**(1.71[b])**		(0.86)	(0.39)	(0.00)	(-0.11)	(-0.79)	(-1.50)
Mean Difference		0.88%	4.39%		-0.38%	-0.28%		-0.55%	-1.87%				
Cash - Shares		(0.96)	**(2.43[b])**		(-0.67)	(-0.34)		(-0.48)	(-0.76)				
B. Industry Focus of Transaction[1]													
Same Industry	223	0.67%	0.09%	23[illegible]	0.86%	0.72%	141	0.54%	-0.84%	0.33%	1.80%	0.14%	1.16%
Transactions		**(1.96[b])**	(0.57)		**(2.80[a])**	**(2.23[b])**		**(1.67[b])**	(-0.98)	(0.62)	**(1.76[c])**	(0.25)	(1.06)
Diversifying	437	0.97%	1.29%	58[illegible]	0.67%	1.28%	282	0.57%	-0.11%	0.10%	1.71%	0.41%	1.72%
Transactions		**(4.57[a])**	**(3.54[a])**		**(4.67[a])**	**(4.58[a])**		**(2.26[b])**	(-0.18)	(0.31)	**(2.48[b])**	(1.20)	**(2.35[b])**
Mean Difference		-0.30%	-1.20%		0.20%	-0.55%		-0.03%	-0.73%				
Same - Diversifying		(-0.72)	(-1.50)		(0.54)	(-0.84)		(-0.14)	(-0.69)				
C. Geographic Focus of Transaction[2]													
Domestic	234	1.17%	1.45%	36[illegible]	0.73%	1.25%	134	0.11%	-1.21%	0.62%	2.46%	1.06%	2.67%
Transactions		**(2.86[a])**	**(2.10[b])**		**(3.82[a])**	**(3.59[a])**		(0.62)	(-0.29)	(1.24)	**(2.22[b])**	**(1.91[c])**	**(2.17[b])**
Cross-Border	426	0.71%	0.57%	55[illegible]	0.71%	1.06%	289	0.76%	-0.38%	-0.06%	1.44%	-0.05%	0.95
Transactions		**(3.88[a])**	**(2.40[a])**		**(3.87[a])**	**(3.60[a])**		**(3.08[a])**	(-0.16)	(-0.17)	**(2.19[b])**	(-0.16)	(1.40)
Mean Difference		0.46%	0.88%		0.03%	0.19%		-0.65%	-0.83%				
Primary - Secondary		(1.14)	(1.10)		(0.08)	(0.32)		(-1.28)	(-0.72)				
D. Relative Size of Target[3]													
Larger Transactions	333	1.25%	1.50%	49[illegible]	1.11%	1.64%	223	0.63%	-0.99%	0.49%	2.63%	0.62%	2.49%
(>5% of Acquirer Value)		**(3.69[a])**	**(2.81[a])**		**(4.54[a])**	**(4.71[a])**		**(2.41[a])**	(-0.88)	(1.14)	**(2.94[a])**	(1.33)	**(2.62[a])**
Smaller Transactions	327	0.49%	0.25%	42[illegible]	0.26%	0.56%	200	0.48%	-0.26%	-0.22%	0.83%	0.01%	0.51%
(<5% of Acquirer Value)		**(3.22[a])**	**(1.59[c])**		**(3.13[a])**	**(2.11[b])**		**(1.47[c])**	(-0.51)	(-0.67)	(1.22)	(0.02)	(0.70)
Mean Difference	512	0.77%	1.25%		0.85%	1.50%		0.15%	-0.73%				
Larger - Smaller		**(2.11[c])**	**(1.76[c])**		**(2.89[a])**	**(1.90[c])**		(0.33)	(-0.75)				

Continued on next page

	1. High Markets			2. Neutral Markets			3. Low Markets			4. Mean Differences Neutral - Low		5. Mean Differences High - Low	
	N	$CAR_{[-1/+1]}$	$CAR_{[+10/-10]}$	N	$CAR_{[-1/+1]}$	$CAR_{[+10/-10]}$	N	$CAR_{[-1/+1]}$	$CAR_{[+10/-10]}$	$CAR_{[-1/+1]}$	$CAR_{[+10/-10]}$	$CAR_{[-1/+1]}$	$CAR_{[+10/-10]}$
E. Target Public Status[4]													
Private Target	223	0.92%	1.28%	265	0.84%	0.76%	121	0.82%	-0.75%	0.02%	1.50%	0.10%	2.02%
		(3.22^{a})	**(2.78^{a})**		**(3.45^{a})**	**(1.96^{b})**		**(1.76^{b})**	(-0.04)	(0.03)	(1.43)	(0.17)	**(1.85^{c})**
Public Target	136	0.33%	-0.36%	226	-0.05%	-0.16%	92	0.16%	-0.95%	-0.21%	0.80%	0.18%	0.59%
		(0.39)	(-0.44)		(-0.22)	(-0.40)		(1.06)	(-0.46)	(-0.33)	(0.63)	(0.25)	(0.43)
Subsidiary/Divestment	275	1.09%	1.27%	401	1.05%	2.14%	192	0.73%	-0.26%	0.32%	2.40%	0.36%	1.53%
		(4.03^{a})	**(2.69^{b})**		**(5.21^{a})**	**(5.58^{a})**		**(2.52^{a})**	(-0.19)	(0.87)	**(2.84^{a})**	(0.90)	(1.63)
Mean Difference		0.59%	1.64%		0.89%	0.91%		0.67%	0.21%				
Private - Public		(1.01)	(1.62)		**(2.00^{b})**	(1.10)		(0.95)	(0.15)				
Mean Difference		0.76%	1.64%		1.10%	2.30%		0.58%	0.69%				
Divestment - Public		(1.35)	(1.61)		**(2.60^{b})**	**(2.92^{a})**		(0.96)	(0.53)				
Mean Difference		0.17%	0.00%		0.21%	1.39%		-0.09%	0.49%				
Private - Divestment		(0.42)	(-0.01)		(0.63)	**(2.13^{b})**		(-0.17)	(0.41)				
F. Distress Related Transactions[5]													
Distressed Target	43	1.62%	-0.62%	43	-1.50%	-0.81%	32	-0.37%	-1.90%	-1.13%	1.19%	1.99%	1.28%
		(1.42^{c})	(-0.75)		**(-1.34^{c})**	(-0.11)		(-0.22)	(-0.81)	(-0.94)	(0.49)	(1.30)	(0.54)
Non-Distressed Target	437	0.82%	0.99%	849	0.83%	1.23%	282	0.63%	-0.54%	0.20%	1.77%	0.19%	1.53%
		(4.57^{a})	**(3.49^{a})**		**(5.79^{a})**	**(5.18^{a})**		**(2.96^{a})**	(-0.41)	(0.21)	**(1.91^{c})**	(0.19)	**(1.78^{c})**
Mean Difference		0.80%	-1.61%		-2.33%	-2.04%		-1.00%	-1.36%				
Distress - Non-Distress		(0.63)	(-0.92)		**(2.81^{a})**	(-1.29)		(-1.09)	(-0.80)				

The table shows short-term announcement returns (CAR) and mean differences for different sub-groups of M&A transactions in high, neutral, and low valuation markets. Statistic significance of CAR is tested with the standardized cross-sectional-Test as proposed by Boehmer et al. (1991). Corresponding z-values are provided in brackets. Significance of the mean differences is tested with a t-statistic for mean difference tests. Significant values are in bold and marked with "a" if significance is in 1% area, with "b" in 5% area, and with "c" in 10% area. 1) Diversifying transactions show a difference in primary 4-digit Standard Industrial Classification (SIC) code between acquirer and target. 2) Cross-border transactions involve acquirers and targets with different countries of residence. 3) Relative size is measured based on transaction value in relation to market capitalization of the acquiring company on announcement day. 4) All target companies classified as privately owned entities (private), public, or divestment based on the SDC database. 5) A transaction is classified as distressed when either marked as bankruptcy and restructuring related in the SDC database or when it had a negative operative cash flow in the quarter (respectively year if quarterly data is not available) preceding the announcement.

Panel D. of Tables 4.5 and 4.6 reports that relative transaction size affects M&A success across market phases. Announcement returns of transactions with high relative value are significantly higher for acquisitions in high and neutral markets while low markets exhibit an insignificantly negative effect of large takeover announcements. The positive implication of size is expected for stronger markets due to larger synergies (Devos et al. 2009). In low markets larger, more costly and complex transactions provoke a cautious reaction of investors. From a long-term perspective smaller acquisitions significantly outperform relatively large transactions when markets are weak. Compared to high valuation markets the BHAR of low market transactions are 11.50% (15.68% value weighted) higher. This result supports hypothesis 4.H4. In weak markets, larger financing requirements and integration complexity of large acquisitions negatively affect companies that simultaneously have to handle internal challenges. Small transactions, on the other hand, appear as value enhancing investment opportunities in times when competitors focus their attention on internal challenges and attractive targets are available. Table 4.10 (Appendix) tests the robustness of size effects to different relative and absolute size quintiles. The results support hypothesis 4.H4.

Panel E. provides evidence that acquisitions of private companies and of subsidiaries outperform public transactions in all market phases at announcement. This finding is consistent with results from Fuller et al. (2002) and Moeller et al. (2004). The long-run results indicate that especially divestments create value for shareholders in neutral and low valuation markets. The findings also propose that, in accordance with results from Gell et al. (2009), divestments generate excess value for acquirers' shareholders in weak markets compared to high valuation markets. This supports the hypothesis that especially in difficult market environments attractive business units are for sale posting good opportunities for potential buyers. Public transactions show a significantly negative effect on operational performance compared to private transactions across all market phases. Hypothesis 4.H5a and 4.H5b are mainly supported.

Panel F. shows that distressed transactions significantly destroy value in weak markets with a mean difference in BHAR of 26.81% (24.38% value weighted) compared to takeovers of healthy targets. In strong markets this relation is inversed with a long-term outperformance of distressed takeovers (9.40% equally weighted, 18.38% value weighted). Announcement returns are positive in high markets and negative respectively insignificant in neutral and low markets. A significant negative effect on operational performance can be observed only in neutral market environments. Hypothesis 4.H6 is supported by these findings.

Table 4.6: 24-month BHAR and AROA of different divestment types in high, neutral, and low valuation markets – M&A

	1. High Markets			2. Neutral Markets			3. Low Markets			4. Mean Differences Neutral - Low		5. Mean Differences High - Low	
	N	BHAR	AROA	N	BHAR	AROA	N	BHAR	AROA	BHAR	AROA	BHAR	AROA
A. Payment Method													
Cash Transactions	512	0.61%	-0.53%	729	6.66%	-0.55%	298	10.03%	0.21%	-3.37%	-0.76%	-9.42%	-0.75%
		(0.21)	(-1.38)		**(2.81[a])**	**(1.79[c])**		**(2.87[a])**	(0.41)	(-0.80)	(-1.27)	**(-2.05[b])**	(-1.16)
Share Transactions	42	-22.10%	-3.46%	38	-6.61%	-1.91%	31	-36.60%	-2.80%	29.99%	-0.99%	14.50%	-0.67%
		(-1.67)	(-1.55)		(-0.67)	(1.36)		**(-4.00[a])**	(-0.95)	**(2.23[b])**	(-1.43)	(0.90)	(0.29)
Mean Difference Cash - Shares		22.71%	2.93%		13.27%	1.36%		46.63%	1.87%				
		(1.67)	(1.26)		(1.31)	(0.94)		**(4.76[a])**	(0.76)				
B. Industry Focus of Transaction[1]													
Same Industry Transactions	223	-2.51%	-0.88%	236	5.92%	-0.28%	141	3.84%	-0.84%	2.08%	0.56%	-6.35%	-0.04%
		(-0.53)	(1.20)		(1.44)	(-0.54)		(0.73)	(-0.98)	(0.31)	(0.55)	(-0.90)	(-0.03)
Diversifying Transactions	437	-1.20%	-0.49%	583	6.48%	-0.86%	282	6.39%	-0.11%	0.09%	-0.99%	-7.59%	-0.38%
		(-0.38)	(1.21)		**(2.57[b])**	**(-2.75[a])**		**(1.80[c])**	(-0.18)	(0.02)	(-1.43)	(-1.60)	(-0.52)
Mean Difference Same - Diversifying		-1.30%	-0.39%		-0.56%	0.58%		-2.54%	-0.73%				
		(-0.23)	(-0.46)		(-0.12)	(0.94)		(-0.40)	(-0.69)				
C. Geographic Focus of Transaction[2]													
Domestic Transactions	234	0.76%	-0.21%	366	6.56%	-0.38%	134	2.00%	-1.25%	4.55%	0.87%	-1.24%	1.34%
		(0.17)	(-0.34)		**(1.88[c])**	(-0.95)		(0.36)	(-1.34)	(0.69)	(0.86)	(-0.17)	(0.90)
Cross-Border Transactions	426	-2.96%	-0.85%	553	6.19%	-0.94%	289	7.18%	0.05%	-0.99%	-0.99%	-10.14%	-0.90%
		(-0.91)	**(-1.85[b])**		**(2.28[b])**	**(2.59[b])**		**(2.09[b])**	(0.08)	(-0.22)	(-1.43)	**(-2.14[b])**	(-1.20)
Mean Difference Primary - Secondary		3.72%	0.64%		0.36%	0.56%		-5.18%	-1.30%				
		(0.67)	(0.84)		(0.08)	(1.04)		(-0.79)	(-1.18)				
D. Relative Size of Target[3]													
Larger Transactions (>5% of Acquirer Value)	333	-2.18%	-0.91%	490	5.66%	-1.10%	223	1.18%	-0.96%	4.48%	-0.14%	-3.36%	0.05%
		(-0.54)	**(-1.77[c])**		**(1.81[c])**	**(-2.94[a])**		(0.29)	(-1.33)	(0.87)	(-0.18)	(-0.58)	(0.20)
Smaller Transactions (<5% of Acquirer Value)	327	-1.11%	-0.33%	429	7.11%	-0.27%	200	10.39%	0.30%	-3.29%	-0.57%	-11.50%	-0.62%
		(0.33)	(-0.63)		**(2.45[b])**	(-0.70)		**(2.49[b])**	(0.43)	(-0.65)	(-0.72)	**(-2.15[b])**	(-0.72)
Mean Difference Larger - Smaller	512	-1.07%	-0.58%		-1.45%	-0.83%		-9.21%	-1.26%				
		(0.20)	(-0.80)		(0.34)	(1.54)		**(-2.03[b])**	(-1.65)				

Continued on next page

	1. High Markets			2. Neutral Markets			3. Low Markets			4. Mean Differences Neutral - Low		5. Mean Differences High - Low	
	N	BHAR	AROA	N	BHAR	AROA	N	BHAR	AROA	BHAR	AROA	BHAR	AROA
E. Target Public Status[4]													
Private Target	223	-0.68%	0.24%	265	6.06%	0.00%	121	3.87%	1.60%	2.19%	-1.60%	-4.55%	-1.37%
		(-0.15)	(0.37)		(1.49)	(0.00)		(0.69)	**(1.77^{a})**	(0.32)	(-1.50)	(-0.63)	(-1.20)
Public Target	136	0.02%	-2.61%	226	1.46%	-1.37%	92	5.83%	-2.24%	-4.37%	0.87%	-5.82%	-0.37%
		(0.00)	**(-3.56^{a})**		(0.34)	**(-2.31^{b})**		(0.88)	**(-1.96^{c})**	(-0.55)	(0.67)	(-0.67)	(-0.27)
Subsidiary/Divestment	275	-3.60%	-0.42%	401	9.25%	-0.92%	192	7.77%	-0.50%	1.48%	-0.42%	**-11.37%**	0.08%
		(-0.87)	(0.71)		**(2.85^{a})**	**(-2.36^{b})**		**(1.78^{c})**	(-0.68)	(0.27)	(-0.51)	**(-1.90^{c})**	(0.09)
Mean Difference Private - Public		-0.70%	2.85%		4.59%	1.38%		-1.96%	3.85%				
		(0.71)	**(2.94^{a})**		(0.77)	**(1.78^{c})**		(-0.23)	**(2.59^{b})**				
Mean Difference Divestment - Public		-3.61%	2.20%		7.79%	0.45%		1.94%	1.74%				
		(0.52)	**(-2.34^{b})**		(1.44)	(0.64)		(0.24)	(-1.29)				
Mean Difference Private - Divestment		-2.92%	-0.65%		3.19%	-0.92%		3.90%	-2.10%				
		(-0.47)	(-0.76)		(0.61)	(-1.46)		(0.55)	**(-1.77^{c})**				
F. Distress Related Transactions[5]													
Distressed Target	43	7.14%	-1.89%	43	9.78%	-4.89%	32	-19.24%	0.03%	29.02%	-0.57%	26.38%	-1.92%
		(0.70)	(-1.27)		(1.09)	**(-2.93^{a})**		**(-2.17^{b})**	(0.02)	**(2.30^{b})**	(-0.16)	**(1.96^{c})**	(1.07)
Non-Distressed Target	437	-2.27%	-0.53%	849	6.17%	-0.63%	282	7.57%	1.74%	-1.40%	-2.37%	-5.30%	-2.27%
		(-0.83)	(-0.70)		**(2.79^{a})**	(-0.64)		**(2.46^{b})**	**(2.62^{a})**	(-0.71)	**(-1.81^{c})**	**(1.67^{c})**	**(-1.66^{c})**
Mean Difference Distress - Non-Distress		9.40%	-1.36%		3.61%	-4.26%		-26.81%	0.41%				
		(0.89)	(-0.89)		(0.39)	**(-2.69^{a})**		**(-2.86^{a})**	(0.33)				

The table shows 24-month long-term buy-and-hold returns (BHAR), 2-year operative improvements (AROA), and mean differences of BHAR and AROA for different sub-groups of M&A transactions in high, neutral, and low valuation markets. Statistic significance of BHAR and AROA is tested with a t-statistic. Corresponding t-values are provided in brackets. Significance of the mean differences is tested with a t-statistic for mean difference tests. Significant values are in bold and marked with "a" if significance is in 1% area, with "b" in 5% area, and with "c" in 10% area. 1) Diversifying transactions show a difference in primary 4-digit Standard Industrial Classification (SIC) code between acquirer and target. 2) Cross-border transactions involve acquirers and targets with different countries of residence. 3) Relative sizes is measured based on transaction value in relation to market value of the acquiring company on announcement day. 4) All target companies classified as privately owned entities (private), public, or divestment based on the SDC database. 5) A transaction is classified as distressed when either marked as bankruptcy and restructuring related in the SDC database or when it had a negative operative cash flow in the quarter (respectively year if quarterly data is not available) preceding the announcement.

4.4.4 Regression analysis

To examine the descriptive observations in more detail, a multivariate regression is applied to determine the combined effects of different transaction characteristics. Short-term announcement effects (CAR) in a 3- and 21-day window, 24-month long-term buy-and-hold abnormal returns (BHAR), and 24-month operational improvements (AROA) are regressed following the model illustrated in Equation (4.7).

$$\begin{aligned} AR = {} & a_0 + a_1 HighValDummy + a_2 LowValDummy + a_3 ShareDummy + \\ & a_4 LogRelativeSize + a_5 CrossBorderDummy + a_6 DiversificationDummy + \\ & a_7 PublicDummy + a_8 DivestmentDummy + a_9 DistressedDummy + \\ & a_{10} HostileDummy + a_{11} RelPreAnnReturn + a_{12} RelMtoBBuyer + \\ & a_{13...20} YearDummy + a_{20...28} IndustryDummy \end{aligned} \tag{4.7}$$

The *HighValDummy* assumes the value 1 for transactions that have been announced in high valuation months. For all other months it is 0. High valuation is determined by classifying the months between January 1st, 1989 and December 31st, 2006 in high, neutral, and low valuation months based on the de-trended industry specific P/E multiple. The *LowValDummy* is 1 or 0 respectively. The *ShareDummy* takes the value 1 for all transactions that are fully paid for by common or preferred stock as well as by share options of the acquiring company. For all other considerations the dummy value is 0. *LogRelativeSize* is the common logarithm of the ratio between transaction value and market value of the acquiring company. The bidder's market value is taken from the day of announcement or the last trading day before announcement. The *CrossBorderDummy* is 1 if the country of residence according to the country code on announcement date in the SDC database differs between target and acquirer. If it is equal the dummy takes the value 0. *DiversificationDummy* is 1 for all transactions in which the acquirer's 4-digit SIC codes in the SDC database differs from the 4-digit code of the target at announcement day. If the SIC codes are equal the value is 0. The *PublicDummy* is 1 for all publicly listed targets on announcement day. *DivestmentDummy* assumes the value 1 if the target status as indicated by the SDC database is subsidiary. It remains 0 for public or private targets. The *DistressedDummy* takes the value 1 when the transaction is labeled bankruptcy or restructuring related in the SDC database. Acquisitions are also considered distress related when the target company has had negative operating income (EBIT) in the last financial quarter (or the last full fiscal year depending on data availability) before the transactions. The classification of distress is imperfect as data availability is limited especially for private and divestment transactions. Therefore, the results have to be interpreted with caution.

In addition to the factors tested above some additional aspects are examined and controlled for in the regression analysis. First, a *HostileDummy* variable as an additional transaction characteristic is included. It assumes the value 1 when the transaction is labeled hostile in the SDC database. Because only 20 (1%) transactions show this attribute in the overall data sample, its predictive power is limited and it is only included in the regression of all transactions. Previous research has yield contradictory results with regard to value creation. One line of argumentation assigns positive long-term effects to completed hostile transactions because they are hypothesized to have superior synergies that lead managers to go hostile despite higher transaction costs (Martynova et al. 2006).

The multiple regression model also controls for the effect of pre-announcement capital market performance to test the hypothesis that relative strong acquirers benefit most from M&A in down-markets (part of 4.H1). *RelPreAnnReturn* is the relative return of the acquirer in the 12 months preceding the month of announcement. To determine the relative return, industry specific benchmark portfolios are constructed. The industry reference portfolios are created by ranking all companies of the respective ICB industry group by previous year-end market-to-book ratios (M/B) and market capitalization on the last trading day of June in every year. Companies are then divided into three M/B groups and three size groups. The resulting nine M/B-size portfolios are created in every of the nine ICB industry groups. For the 81 reference portfolios, average monthly returns are calculated as a benchmark to determine the relative performance of bidding companies prior to a transaction announcement. *RelMtoB* is calculated for every transaction year by subtracting the median industry M/B ratios of the respective 2-digit SIC industry from the M/B ratio of the acquirer. The difference proxies for the relative over- or under-valuation of the divesting company in the year of the announcement. The M/B variable controls for effects from relative individual firm valuation (Ming et al. 2006). Previous results with regard to the effects of relative company valuation have been mixed. Both variables, relative M/B and previous performance, also serve as a control for effects that pertain to the behavioral view on M&A value creation (Harford 2005). Finally, two control variables for the transaction year and acquirer industry are introduced to control for year- and industry-specific effects. *YearDummy* assumes the value 1 when the transaction is announced in the respective year of the 18 year sample period. The year 1989 is excluded to avoid over-specification of the model. *IndustryDummy* is 1 when the acquirer belongs to one of nine included ICB industries. For year and industry dummy only "yes" or "no" is reported when the results are robust or not robust to the respective variable.

A multiple regression is estimated for all transactions to test the effect of market valuation level on overall results. In addition, high and low market transactions are regressed separately to analyze the role of the tested independent variables on abnormal performance in the respective market environment. The regression findings are summarized in Table 4.7.

The regression results mostly confirm the previous findings. The intercept of Panel A. can be interpreted as neutral market abnormal returns and operational improvements for domestic, private acquisitions in the same industry that have been financed with cash or a mix of cash and shares. The CAR intercepts show positive announcement returns. Transactions in low valuation markets have a significantly negative effect on announcement returns of -2.15% in the 21-day window. This finding confirms the negative reaction of investors to transaction announcements in depressed market environments.

The payment method does not have a significant short-term effect. Increasing relative size has a positive effect on CAR and BHAR indicating higher synergies from larger transactions. A significantly negative coefficient (3-day window) for public announcements is consistent with findings from Fuller et al. (2002) and Cooney et al. (2009) proposing that private transactions create more shareholder value at announcement. Cross-border and conglomerate announcements do not significantly influence CAR. The announcement effect of transactions involving a distressed target is also insignificant. The announcement of successful hostile takeovers has a positive value effect. This result in combination with positive long-term returns supports the view that hostile transactions show higher potential synergies (Martynova et al. 2006).

Table 4.7: Multiple regression results for 3- and 21-day CAR, 24-month BHAR, and 2-year AROA – M&A

	A. All Transactions				B. High Market Transaction				C. Low Market Transactions			
	$CAR_{[-1/+1]}$	$CAR_{[+10/-10]}$	BHAR	AROA	$CAR_{[-1/+1]}$	$CAR_{[+10/-10]}$	BHAR	AROA	$CAR_{[-1/+1]}$	$CAR_{[+10/-10]}$	BHAR	AROA
Intercept	0.95%	0.41%	-2.52%	1.90%	0.49%	0.34%	-13.28%	0.38%	0.84%	-3.13%	4.35%	0.11%
	(2.02[b])	(0.43)	(-0.38)	**(1.78[b])**	(0.73)	(0.26)	(-1.34)	(0.28)	(0.91)	**(-2.24[b])**	(0.52)	(0.59)
HighValuationDummy	0.36%	-0.12%	-7.89%	0.06%								
	(1.34)	(-0.23)	**(-2.08[b])**	(0.10)								
LowValuationDummy	-0.28%	-2.15%	4.38%	0.54%								
	(-0.85)	**(3.22[a])**	(0.93)	(0.75)								
ShareDummy	0.37%	-0.51%	-27.26%	-0.48%	-1.33%	-5.02%	-27.32%	-3.05%	1.72%	1.06%	-43.51%	-1.76%
	(0.79)	(-0.54)	**(-4.11[a])**	(0.21)	**(-1.70[c])**	**(-3.24[a])**	**(-2.38[b])**	**(-1.98[b])**	**(1.82[c])**	(0.38)	**(-3.70[a]**	(-0.87)
LogRelativeSize	0.71%	1.37%	12.03%	0.51%	0.50%	3.19%	11.65%	-0.09%	0.05%	0.65%	-5.40%	0.76%
	(1.96[b])	**(1.91[c])**	**(2.37[b])**	(0.96)	(0.70)	**(2.23[b])**	(1.10)	(-0.12)	(0.11)	(0.29)	(-1.01)	(0.44)
CrossBorderDummy	0.05%	0.01%	-1.08%	-1.34%	-0.41%	-0.85%	-5.66%	-0.65%	0.74%	4.29%	3.10%	0.54%
	(0.25)	(0.01)	(-0.35)	**(-2.35[b])**	(-1.05)	(-1.08)	(-0.97)	(-0.84)	(1.41)	**(2.76[c])**	(0.48)	(0.56)
DiversificationDummy	0.07%	0.64%	0.92%	-0.23%	0.33%	1.26%	2.93%	0.51%	0.09%	1.41%	-1.91%	-0.88%
	(0.32)	(1.20)	(0.29)	(-0.38)	(0.84)	(1.61)	(0.51)	(0.67)	(0.19)	(0.95)	(-0.30)	(-0.83)
PublicDummy	-0.82%	-0.91%	-2.72%	-1.89%	-1.04%	-1.74%	-3.88%	-2.72%	-0.49%	2.49%	18.46%	-3.38%
	(-2.70[a])	(-1.51)	(-0.64)	**(-2.36[b])**	**(-1.92[c])**	**(-1.65[c])**	(-0.66)	**(-2.50[b])**	(-0.71)	(1.51)	**(2.14[b])**	**(-2.31[b])**
DivestmentDummy	0.33%	0.89%	0.61%	-0.61%	0.30%	0.11%	-3.88%	-0.78%	0.16%	2.90%	4.16%	-1.59%
	(1.40)	**(1.87[c])**	(0.18)	(-1.52)	(0.78)	(0.13)	(-0.63)	(-0.93)	(0.31)	**(1.83[c])**	(0.92)	(-1.38)
DistressDummy	-0.51%	-1.20%	1.86%	-1.99%	0.91%	-0.98%	15.07%	-0.05%	-0.68%	-1.17%	-30.62%	1.92%
	(-1.11)	(-1.32)	(0.29)	**(-1.68[c])**	(1.14)	(-0.64)	(1.28)	(-0.33)	(-0.73)	(-0.43)	**(-2.63[a])**	(0.94)
HostileDummy	2.72%	1.22%	35.01%	-0.21%								
	(2.10[b])	(0.47)	**(1.92[c])**	(-0.42)								
RelM/B	-0.01%	-0.02%	0.03%	-0.02%	0.00%	-0.01%	0.04%	0.41%	-0.07%	-0.74%	-1.88%	-0.42%
	(-0.83)	**(-1.73[c])**	(0.32)	(-0.85)	(0.47)	(-1.03)	(0.42)	(0.61)	(-1.48)	(-1.19)	(-0.97)	(-0.54)
RelPreAnnReturn	0.87%	0.14%	3.46%	-1.33%	0.97%	0.67%	2.92%	0.57%	0.27%	-0.01%	-2.88%	0.81%
	(4.15[a])	(0.34)	(1.17)	**(-2.47[b])**	**(2.79[a])**	(0.96)	(0.57)	(0.81)	(0.65)	(-0.22)	(-0.65)	(0.86)
IndustryDummies	Yes	Yes	Yes	Yes	Yes	Yes	Yes	Yes	Yes	Yes	Yes	Yes
YearDummies	Yes	Yes	Yes	Yes	Yes	No	Yes	No	Yes	Yes	Yes	No
F-Statistic	**2.276[a]**	**1.687[b]**	**2.180[a]**	**2.612[a]**	**1.826[a]**	**2.547[a]**	**1.737[c]**	**1.745[c]**	0.757	**1.411[b]**	**1.972[a]**	1.312
Adjusted R^2	0.024	0.011	0.021	0.019	0.042	0.025	0.012	0.014	-0.008	0.030	0.057	0.011

The table shows results from a linear OLS regression analysis of short-term cumulative abnormal returns (CAR) in a 3- and 21-day window, 24-month long-term buy-and-hold returns (BHAR), and 2-year operational improvements (AROA). A t-statistic is conducted to test significance of the coefficients. The statistical fit of the model is indicated by the adjusted determination coefficient $R^2_{adjusted}$ and F-statistic. The t- and F-values are bold when significant and marked with "a" if significance is in 1% area, with "b" in 5% area, and with "c" in 10% area.

A relative over-performance of acquirers prior to the announcement increases returns in the 3-day window around announcement day. High relative M/B valuations of the acquirer have a negative effect. The result proposes that strongly performing acquirers benefit from transactions while investors do not reward potentially overvalued acquirers. Panel A. also shows a significantly negative impact from high market takeovers and share payments on long-term results (BHAR). Low market transactions have an insignificant positive coefficient. AROA is positive for the estimated model with significantly negative effects of cross-border, public, and distress related transactions. The acquirer stock market performance has a negative effect on operative improvements.

Panel B. shows regression results for high market transactions. The CAR results largely correspond with regression results of the entire data sample. Share transactions, however, have a significantly negative effect on announcement returns in high markets. This underlines the finding that markets anticipate agency costs of share transactions when market-induced overvaluation may affect management behavior. The BHAR regression only shows a significant negative coefficient for share transactions. AROA in strong markets are negatively influenced by share payments and public transactions.

Panel C. shows the results for low markets. The regression of 3-day CAR does not yield a significant outcome. The 21-day event window, however, shows a significantly negative intercept at -3.13%. Cross-border transactions and acquisitions of subsidiaries positively influence the announcement return. The BHAR intercept for private and domestic transactions in existing industries is insignificant. The highly negative effect of share payment on long-term performance of -43.51% supports the descriptive findings. The effect of transactions size is insignificant. In order to further examine target size effects, some robustness checks are conducted in Table 4.10 (Appendix). The results confirm the descriptive observation that smaller transactions outperform in weak markets. The analysis of quintiles suggests that this relation is not fully linear. Public transactions exhibit a significant positive effect on M&A success in weak markets. This finding suggests that higher transparency with regard to the effects of declining markets on target performance increases the value creation potential of acquisitions in uncertain market environments. The impact of subsidiary acquisitions is insignificantly positive at 4.16%. Transactions involving distressed targets are highly value destroying in weak markets as indicated by the univariate findings. The prediction that transactions of relatively strong performing acquirers increase the value creation potential in weak markets is rejected by the insignificant coefficient. The operational regression results for low market transactions remain inconclusive.

4.5 Conclusion

The presented analysis shows that European market valuation levels have had a significant influence on M&A success over the last 20 years. From an overall perspective the results indicate that low market acquisitions outperform M&A transactions in boom-markets in the long-run while the short-term abnormal returns are higher for takeovers in strong market environments. Investors appear to react reluctant to the announcement of takeovers when market prospects are uncertain. The long-run underperformance of takeovers in high valuation markets is consistent with the behavioral perspective on M&A. Strong markets and subsequent high valuation levels can create agency costs that lead to reduced value creation of M&A (Gorton et al. 2009, Bouwman et al. 2009, Goel and Thakor 2010). In the absence of market-induced overvaluation, low market acquirers appear to apply superior target selection and make sounder investment decisions.

The long-term success of down market M&A depends on a number of transactions characteristics. Takeovers paid for with undervalued shares destroy value for shareholders in weak markets. Distressed targets also have a clearly negative effect on value creation. In down markets, turnarounds seem to be more difficult to achieve than in stronger market environments. The results also indicate that the purchase of divested business units can create more value for shareholders in weak markets compared to boom markets. This finding underlines the hypothesis that corporate sellers are more likely to sell attractive subsidiaries in difficult market environments than in strong markets. Small acquisition targets relative to the buyer's size show the largest positive long-term value creation in weak markets. Cautiously selected smaller sized transactions with limited capital requirements for buyers appear especially value creating in lean times. Surprisingly, higher transaction complexity, assumed for cross-border transactions and diversifying M&A investments, does not appear to negatively influence acquisition performance in weak markets. The hypothesis that additional integration and value capturing complexity could overburden buyers in times when the market environment is challenging cannot be supported.

Overall, the conclusion is that difficult times do indeed present M&A opportunities for willing buyers despite the internal challenges that often arise in weak markets.

4.6 Appendix

4.6.1 Summary Statistics

Table 4.8: Summary statistics M&A transactions

	Number of transactions	Average transaction value (EUR mn)	Median trans-action value (EUR mn)	Total trans-action value (EUR mn)	Share of total transactions	Share of total transaction value	Average market value of acquirers (EUR mn)	Median market value of acquirers (EUR mn)
				A. All market valuations				
All transactions	2'002	644	108	1'288'383	100.00%	100.00%	5'584	1'735
Cash transactions[1]	1'539	359	99	552'723	76.87%	42.90%	5'333	1'789
Share transactions[2]	111	2'089	330	231'492	5.54%	17.97%	6'746	1'898
Hybrid transactions[3]	347	1'452	125	503'992	17.33%	39.12%	6'399	1'582
Divestments[4]	868	386	109	334'710	43.36%	25.98%	5'291	1'791
Private targets[5]	609	150	48	91'243	30.42%	7.08%	3'258	1'299
Public targets[6]	454	1'751	327	794'943	22.68%	61.70%	8'105	2'601
Rel. small targets < 5%[7]	956	169	55	161'690	47.75%	12.55%	7'290	2'467
Rel. Large targets> 5%[8]	1'046	1'077	206	1'126'693	52.25%	87.45%	4'024	1'136
Cross border[9]	1'268	749	123	950'183	63.34%	73.75%	6'510	2'119
Domestic[10]	734	461	73	338'200	36.66%	26.25%	3'984	1'145
Diversifying[11]	1'402	538	104	753'647	70.03%	58.50%	5'143	1'737
Non-diversifying[12]	600	891	111	534'736	29.97%	41.50%	6'634	1'729
				B. High market valuations				
All transactions	660	738	91	486'964	100.00%	100.00%	5'755	1'789
Cash transactions[1]	512	340	87	174'036	77.58%	35.74%	5'734	1'903
Share transactions[2]	42	791	93	33'220	6.36%	6.82%	4'402	1'263
Hybrid transactions[3]	104	2'689	132	279'654	15.76%	57.43%	6'508	1'536
Divestments[4]	275	336	117	92'492	41.67%	18.99%	5'697	1'953
Private targets[5]	223	151	46	33'673	33.79%	6.91%	3'090	1'373
Public targets[6]	136	2'529	319	343'903	20.61%	70.62%	8'987	2'313
Rel. small targets < 5%[7]	327	186	49	60'702	49.55%	12.47%	7'718	2'320
Rel. Large targets > 5%[8]	333	1'280	200	426'262	50.45%	87.53%	3'827	1'160
Cross border[9]	426	965	100	411'035	64.55%	84.41%	6'701	1'947
Domestic[10]	234	324	67	75'930	35.45%	15.59%	4'032	1'466
Diversifying[11]	437	433	97	189'121	66.21%	38.84%	5'029	1'878
Non-diversifying[12]	223	1'336	83	297'844	33.79%	61.16%	7'176	1'639

Continued on next page

Continued from previous page

	Number of transac-tions	Average transac-tion value (EUR mn)	Median trans-ac-tion value (EUR mn)	Total trans-ac-tion value (EUR mn)	Share of total transac-tions	Share of total transac-tion value	Average market value of acquirers (EUR mn)	Median market value of acquirers (EUR mn)
C. Neutral market valuations								
All transactions	919	560	111	514'945	100.00%	100.00%	4'887	1'723
Cash transactions[1]	729	377	105	274'631	79.33%	53.33.%	4'779	1'752
Share transactions[2]	38	2'643	828	100'443	4.13%	19.51%	6'602	2'410
Hybrid transactions[3]	150	932	112	139'759	16.32%	27.14%	5'034	1'426
Divestments[4]	401	423	105	169'494	43.63%	32.91%	4'367	1'716
Private targets[5]	265	136	49	35'934	28.84%	6.98%	3'485	1'271
Public targets[6]	226	1'260	346	284'814	24.59%	55.31%	6'761	3'071
Rel. small targets < 5%[7]	429	136	55	58'492	46.68%	11.36%	5'953	2'476
Rel. Large targets > 5%[8]	490	932	227	456'453	53.32%	88.64%	3'968	1'220
Cross border[9]	553	700	131	387'007	60.17%	75.16%	5'964	2'290
Domestic[10]	366	350	70	127'938	39.83%	24.84%	3'259	1'046
Diversifying[11]	683	542	108	369'950	74.84%	71.84%	5'165	1'685
Non-diversifying[12]	236	615	113	144'995	25.68%	28.16%	4'082	1'886
D. Low market valuations								
All transactions	423	677	116	286'474	100.00%	100.00%	6'832	1'628
Cash transactions[1]	298	349	106	104'056	70.45%	36.32%	5'999	1'544
Share transactions[2]	31	3'156	378	97'829	7.33%	34.15%	10'099	1'837
Hybrid transactions[3]	93	909	140	84'578	21.99%	29.52%	8'480	1'780
Divestments[4]	192	379	120	72'724	45.39%	25.39%	6'640	1'764
Private targets[5]	121	179	47	21'636	28.61%	7.55%	3'067	1'286
Public targets[6]	92	1'807	285	166'226	21.75%	58.02%	10'102	2'406
Rel. small targets < 5%[7]	200	212	64	42'496	47.28%	14.83%	9'495	2'974
Rel. Large targets > 5%[8]	223	1'094	169	243'978	52.72%	85.17%	4'443	1'044
Cross border[9]	289	526	125	152'142	68.32%	53.11%	7'273	2'087
Domestic[10]	134	1'002	97	134'333	31.68%	46.89%	5'880	1'092
Diversifying[11]	282	690	103	194'576	66.67%	67.92%	5'223	1'619
Non-diversifying[12]	141	652	138	91'898	33.33%	32.08%	10'050	1'918

The table shows the mean and median values as well as the distribution of targets and buyers in different market valuation phases and for different transactions types. 1) Cash transactions are takeovers paid for with cash or cash like means. 2) Share transactions are takeovers paid with common or preferred stock of the acquiring company. 3) Hybrid transactions are acquisitions in which the payment method is a mix of stock and cash or also of other alternative payment methods. 4, 5 & 6) All target companies classified in the public status field of the SDC data as private, public, or divestment respectively. Public companies are listed at the time of acquisition, while private companies are privately held, and divestments are purchases of company parts. 7 & 8) Relative sizes are measured based on transaction value in relation to market capitalization of the acquiring company on announcement day. 9 & 10) Cross-border takeovers opposed to domestic transactions are takeovers in which the country code of acquirer differs from that of the target. 11&12) Diversifying transactions show a difference in primary 4-digit Standard Industrial Classification (SIC) code between acquirer and target.

4.6.2 Robustness to value weighting of long-term results

The long-term BHAR results presented in the main body refer to equally weighted BHAR. For this study, the equally weighted perspective is chosen as it best reflects the actual return of an investor who allocates funds equally to investments. It also compares best to the equally weighted CAR and AROA results. However, value weighted BHAR are also commonly used in studies of long-term M&A success. Differences in equal- and value-weights indicate performance differences between smaller and larger firms by assigning more weight to acquirers with a relatively large market capitalization.

The value weighting approach follows the methodology applied by Mitchell and Stafford (2000). Value weights are determined based on acquirer market value at announcement. A stock market deflator then adjusts the weights. The adjustment is made to avoid the problem of increasing stock market valuations over the 18-year sample period that would assign more weight to more recent transactions. The deflator is calculated based on the value weighted European DS-Total Market index from Thomson Reuter's Datastream. Table 4.9 provides the results for equally weighted (EW) and value weighted (VW) 24-month BHAR. The table shows overall results and corresponding results for different transactions characteristics.

The overall results show that value-weighted BHAR are lower than equal-weighted returns for all valuation phases. The positive value creation of acquiring companies found for neutral and low valuation markets turns into negative results when adjusting for market capitalization of the acquirer (-5.45% and -7.67%). Value-weighted high valuation BHAR are highly significant at -15.94%. The negative effect of value weighting indicates a negative influence of acquirer size on M&A success. Results for short-term value effects from Moeller et al. (2004) indicate that increasing firm size negatively effects the choice of M&A transactions and, hence, leads to lower value creation for acquirers' shareholders. The mean difference between high and low market transactions increases in the value weighted view to -8.28% compared to -7.13% equally weighted.

The payment method effect in Panel A. shows a further increase in share transaction underperformance for low valuation markets. The mean difference between cash and share transactions is 62.93% (46.63% equally weighted). The mean difference to high and neutral valuation markets becomes significant at 48.31% (14.50%) for high valuations and increases to 42.33% (29.99%) for neutral valuations emphasizing the negative effect of share payment when valuation levels are low.

Table 4.9: Results for equally (EW) and value weighted (VW) 24-month BHAR – M&A

	1. High Markets			2. Neutral Markets			3. Low Markets			4. Mean Differences Neutral - Low		5. Mean Differences High - Low	
	N	EW BHAR	VW BHAR	N	EW BHAR	VW BHAR	N	EW BHAR	VW BHAR	EW BHAR	VW BHAR	EW BHAR	VW BHAR
All Transactions	512	-1.34% (-0.71)	-15.94% **(6.06[a])**	729	6.34% **(2.95[a])**	-5.45% **(-2.64[b])**	298	5.54% **(1.81[b])**	-7.67% **(3.55[a])**	0.80% (0.26)	2.22% (0.74)	-7.13% **(-2.09[b])**	-8.28% **(-2.43[b])**
A. Payment Method													
Cash Transactions	512	0.61% (0.21)	-15.81% **(-5.33[a])**	729	6.66% **(2.81[a])**	-2.24% (0.89)	298	10.03% **(2.87[a])**	0.89% (0.53)	-3.37% (-0.80)	-3.13% (-0.75)	-9.42% **(-2.05[b])**	-16.70% **(-3.64[a])**
Share Transactions	42	-22.10% (-1.67)	-13.74% (-1.04)	38	-6.61% (-0.67)	-19.71% **(2.01[b])**	31	-36.60% **(-4.00[a])**	-62.04% **(-6.78[a])**	29.99% **(2.23[b])**	42.33% **(3.15[a])**	14.50% (0.90)	48.31% **(3.00[a])**
Mean Difference Cash - Shares		-22.71% (-1.67)	2.93% (-1.26)		-13.27% (1.31)	17.47% **(1.73[c])**		-46.63% **(-4.76[a])**	-62.93% **(-6.42[a])**				
B. Industry Focus of Transaction[1]													
Same Industry Transactions	223	-2.51% (-0.53)	-15.65% **(3.32[a])**	236	5.92% (1.44)	0.09% (0.02)	141	3.84% (0.73)	-12.45% **(-2.38[b])**	2.08% (0.31)	12.55% **(1.91[c])**	-6.35% (-0.90)	-3.20% (-0.45)
Diversifying Transactions	437	-1.20% (-0.38)	-16.16% **(5.10[a])**	683	6.48% **(2.57[b])**	-6.97% **(-2.89[a])**	282	6.39% **(1.80[c])**	-3.62% (-1.02)	0.09% (0.02)	-3.35% (-0.78)	-7.59% (-1.60)	-0.38% (-0.52)
Mean Difference Same - Diversifying		-1.30% (-0.23)	-0.51% (-0.09)		-0.56% (-0.12)	7.07% (1.52)		-2.54% (-0.40)	-8.83% (-1.40)				
C. Geographic Focus of Transaction[2]													
Domestic Transactions	234	0.76% (0.17)	-0.21% (-0.34)	366	6.56% **(1.88[c])**	-0.38% (-0.95)	134	2.00% (0.36)	-1.25% (-1.34)	4.55% (0.69)	0.87% (0.86)	-1.24% (-0.17)	1.34% (0.90)
Cross-Border Transactions	426	-2.96% (-0.91)	-0.85% **(-1.85[b])**	553	6.19% **(2.28[b])**	-0.94% **(2.59[b])**	289	7.18% **(2.09[b])**	0.05% (0.08)	-0.99% (-0.22)	-0.99% (-1.43)	-10.14% **(-2.14[b])**	-12.54% **(-2.63[b])**
Mean Difference Primary - Secondary		3.72% (0.67)	0.64% (0.84)		0.36% (0.08)	0.56% (1.04)		-5.18% (-0.79)	-1.30% (-1.18)				
D. Relative Size of Target[3]													
Larger Transactions (>5% of Acquirer Value)	333	-2.18% (-0.54)	-6.96% (1.72)	490	5.66% **(1.81[c])**	-6.45% **(-2.07[b])**	223	1.18% (0.29)	-13.59% **(-3.31[a])**	4.48% (0.87)	7.14% (1.40)	-3.36% (-0.58)	6.63% (1.15)
Smaller Transactions (<5% of Acquirer Value)	327	-1.11% (0.33)	-20.22% **(6.04[a])**	429	7.11% **(2.45[b])**	-4.31% (-1.42)	200	10.39% **(2.49[b])**	-4.53% (1.09)	-3.29% (-0.65)	0.22% (0.04)	-11.50% **(-2.15[b])**	-15.68% **(-2.93[a])**
Mean Difference Larger - Smaller	512	-1.07% (0.20)	-13.26% **(-2.52[b])**		-1.45% (0.34)	-2.14% (0.52)		-9.21% **(-2.03[b])**	-9.05% **(-1.99[b])**				

Continued on next page

Continued from previous page

	1. High Markets			2. Neutral Markets			3. Low Markets			4. Mean Differences Neutral - Low		5. Mean Differences High - Low	
	N	BHAR	AROA	N	BHAR	AROA	N	BHAR	AROA	BHAR	AROA	BHAR	AROA
E. Target Public Status[4]													
Private Target	223	-0.68%	1.90%	265	6.06%	0.48%	121	3.87%	-3.14%	2.19%	3.62%	-4.55%	5.04%
		(-0.15)	(0.41)		(1.49)	(0.12)		(0.69)	(-0.56)	(0.32)	(0.53)	(-0.63)	(0.69)
Public Target	136	0.02%	-5.06%	226	1.46%	-6.52%	92	5.83%	-12.69%	-4.37%	6.17%	-5.82%	7.63%
		(0.00)	(-0.90)		(0.34)	(-1.52)		(0.88)	**(-1.91[c])**	(-0.55)	(0.78)	(-0.67)	(0.88)
Subsidiary/Divestment	275	-3.60%	-29.17%	401	9.25%	-7.98%	192	7.77%	-4.24%	1.48%	-3.73%	**-11.37%**	-24.93%
		(-0.87)	**(-7.08[a])**		**(2.85[a])**	**(-2.60[b])**		**(1.78[c])**	(-0.93)	(0.27)	(-0.70)	**(-1.90[c])**	**(-4.16[a])**
Mean Difference Private - Public		-0.70%	6.96%		4.59%	7.00%		-1.96%	9.56%				
		(0.71)	(0.96)		(0.77)	(1.21)		(-0.23)	(1.10)				
Mean Difference Divestment - Public		-3.61%	-24.11%		7.79%	-1.49%		1.94%	8.45%				
		(0.52)	**(-3.46[a])**		(1.44)	(-1.21)		(0.24)	(1.09)				
Mean Difference Private - Divestment		-2.92%	31.07%		3.19%	8.47%		3.90%	1.10%				
		(-0.47)	**(5.02[a])**		(0.61)	**(1.70[c])**		(0.55)	(0.16)				
F. Distress Related Transactions[5]													
Distressed Target	43	7.14%	0.33%	43	9.78%	-5.35%	32	-19.24%	-29.79%	29.02%	24.41%	26.38%	30.09%
		(0.70)	(0.03)		(1.09)	(-0.60)		**(-2.17[b])**	**(3.39[a])**	**(2.30[b])**	**(1.91[c])**	**(1.96[c])**	**(2.23[b])**
Non-Distressed Target	437	-2.27%	-18.05%	849	6.17%	-5.56%	282	7.57%	-5.38%	-1.40%	-0.18%	-5.30%	-12.67%
		(-0.83)	**(-6.62[a])**		**(2.79[a])**	**(-2.58[b])**		**(2.46[b])**	**(1.75[c])**	(-0.71)	(-0.24)	**(1.67[c])**	**(-2.61[b])**
Mean Difference Distress - Non-Distress		9.40%	18.38%		3.61%	0.21%		-26.81%	-24.38%				
		(0.89)	**(1.75[c])**		(0.39)	(0.01)		**(-2.86[a])**	**(-2.60[b])**				

The table shows 24-month equally weighted (EW) and value weighted (VW) long-term buy-and-hold returns (BHAR) and mean differences of BHAR for different sub-groups of M&A transactions in high, neutral, and low valuation markets. Statistic significance of BHAR is tested with a t-statistic. Corresponding t-values are provided in brackets. Significance of the mean differences is tested with a t-statistic for mean difference tests. Significant values are bold and marked with "a" if significance is in 1% area, with "b" in 5% area, and with "c" in 10% area. 1) Diversifying transactions show a difference in primary 4-digit Standard Industrial Classification (SIC) code between acquirer and target. 2) Cross-border transactions involve acquirers and targets with different countries of residence. 3) Relative sizes is measured based on transaction value in relation to market value of the acquiring company on announcement day. 4) All target companies classified as privately owned entities (private), public, or divestment based on the SDC database. 5) A transaction is classified as distressed when either marked as bankruptcy and restructuring related in the SDC database or when it had a negative operative cash flow in the quarter (respectively year if quarterly data is not available) preceding the announcement.

The relative effects from different target characteristics remain largely robust to the value weighting of abnormal returns. The value weighted difference between domestic and cross-border acquisitions is, however, significantly positive for neutral market transactions with 8.74% (0.36%) and negative for high market transactions with -15.03% (3.72%). Larger size transaction also outperform relative to small takeovers under high valuations by 13.26% (-1.07%) in the value weighted perspective. Acquisitions of subsidiaries show a strong underperformance compared to public and private transactions in high valuation markets of 24.11% (3.61%) and 31.07% (-2.92%) respectively. This finding suggests that larger acquirers fail to capture value from takeovers of divested assets. The positive mean difference between distressed and non-distressed target of 18.38% (9.40%) in high valuation markets indicates, on the other hand, that strong markets are better suited to capture value from turning around targets in difficulties.

4.6.3 Analysis of transactions size

Relative transaction size has a significant effect on long-term value creation especially for low market transactions. The results of Chapter 4.4 show that transaction with below median relative transaction size (below 5% of acquirer market capitalization at announcement) outperform above median transactions by 9.13% (9.05% value weighted) in low valuation markets. The mean difference of below median relative size transactions between high and low valuation markets amounts to 11.50% (15.68%) in favor of small low market transactions. The regression of low market transaction, however, did not yield significantly high t-values for the discrete relative size variable. In order to further examine the size effect the transaction sample is divided in five equal quintiles based on relative and absolute transaction values. Table 4.10 shows the equal- and value-weighted BHAR results for different market valuation levels and the mean differences between first and fifth quintile as well as between high and low valuation quintiles.

The results confirm the previous finding that smaller transaction relative to acquirer size outperform in weak market environments (Panel A.). Abnormal returns steadily decline from 12.48% (-1.27%) in the first quintile to -0.50% (-32.07%) in the fifth quintile with a mean difference of 12.98% (30.80%) significant for the value weighted result. In high valuation markets a clear pattern cannot be observed with insignificant negative mean difference. The values, however, indicate a slightly positive value effect of increasing size. The mean differences between high and low market quintiles underline a significant outperformance of relatively smaller transaction under low valuation levels.

The absolute transaction size perspective in Panel B. further supports this intuition with high mean differences for smaller transactions between market phases. The sign of mean differences turns in the third and fourth quintiles indicating higher value creation potential of larger transactions in strong markets. The results for the fifth quintile, however, show a significant mean difference in favor of low market transactions for very large transactions of 15.28% (15.27%). The weaker performance of very large transactions in boom markets is consistent with behavioral arguments (e.g., Gorton et al. 2009, Bouwman et al. 2009, Goel and Thakor 2010) that managers engage in ever-larger transactions in booming M&A markets to copy their peers and secure their personal positions on the expense of shareholder value. Despite higher complexity of large transaction that has an adverse effect on takeover returns in weak markets, agency costs appear significantly lower than in strong markets.

Table 4.10: Size quintile analysis of BHAR results – M&A

Quintiles	All Valuations		High Valuations		Low Valuations		Mean Difference High - Low	
	EW BHAR	VW BHAR	EW BHAR	VW BHAR	EW BHAR	VW BHAR	EW BHAR	VW BHAR
(%)			**A. Relative Transaction Size**					
1 (<2)	4.92%	-5.86%	-3.59%	-11.53%	12.48%	-1.27%	-16.07%	-10.27%
	(1.55)	**(-1.85^{c})**	(-0.70)	**(-2.25^{b})**	**(2.07^{b})**	(-0.21)	**(-2.03^{b})**	(-1.30)
2 (<4)	5.16%	-14.59%	2.12%	-29.92%	12.65%	-10.38%	-10.53%	-19.54%
	(1.74^{c})	**(-4.94^{a})**	(0.40)	**(-5.58^{a})**	**(1.75^{c})**	(-1.41))	(-1.43)	**(-2.17^{b})**
3 (<8)	5.92%	2.59%	-0.50%	-8.27%	4.40%	0.40%	-4.90%	-8.67%
	(1.95^{b})	(0.85)	(0.63)	(-1.43)	(0.72)	(0.06)	(-0.58)	(-1.03)
4 (<20)	-1.51%	-6.08%	-3.92%	-13.76%	-1.38%	-3.51%	-2.54%	-10.25%
	(-0.43)	**(-1.71^{c})**	(-0.58)	**(-2.02^{b})**	(-0.19)	(-0.48)	(-0.25)	(-1.03)
5 (>20)	3.28%	-21.95%	-1.71%	-4.53%	-0.50%	-32.07%	-1.21%	27.54%
	(0.92)	**(-6.21^{a})**	(-0.27)	(-0.71)	(-0.08)	**(-5.18^{a})**	(-0.13)	**(3.09^{a})**
1 – 5	1.64%	16.09%	-1.89%	-7.00%	12.98%	30.80%		
	(0.35)	**(3.39^{a})**	(-0.23)	(-0.85)	(1.60)	**(3.57^{a})**		
(EUR mn)			**B. Absolute Transaction Size**					
1 (<27)	4.16%	5.89%	-9.09%	-4.02%	11.56%	14.12%	-20.65%	-18.14%
	(1.09)	(1.55)	(-1.36)	(-0.60)	(1.33)	(1.62)	**(-1.88^{c})**	(-1.65)
2 (<63)	1.19%	1.73%	-9.71%	-9.63%	17.55%	30.26%	-27.25%	-39.89%
	(0.35)	(0.51)	**(-1.73^{c})**	**(-1.72^{c})**	**(2.36^{b})**	**(4.07^{a})**	**(-2.94^{a})**	**(-4.28^{a})**
3 (<170)	5.56%	5.47%	5.78%	5.69%	-1.16%	2.32%	6.93%	3.36%
	(1.91^{c})	**(1.87^{c})**	(1.02)	(1.01)	(-0.18)	(0.37)	(0.82)	(0.40)
4 (<512)	10.53%	7.22%	12.25%	8.04%	-5.82%	-3.43%	18.07%	11.47%
	(3.39^{a})	**(2.32^{b})**	**(2.35^{b})**	(1.54)	(-1.31)	(-0.72)	**(2.56^{b})**	(1.62)
5 (>512)	-3.66%	-19.00%	-7.20%	-28.75%	8.08%	-13.48%	-15.28%	-15.27%
	(-1.24)	**(-6.46^{a})**	(-1.25)	**(-4.98^{a})**	(1.36)	**(-2.43^{b})**	**(-1.91^{c})**	**(-1.91^{c})**
1 – 5	7.82%	24.89%	-1.89%	24.73%	3.48%	27.60%		
	(1.63)	**(-5.19^{a})**	(-0.21)	**(2.80^{a})**	(0.33)	**(2.67^{a})**		

The table shows equally and value-weighted 24-month BHAR results for different size quintiles. Panel A. contains relative target size quintiles measured as deal value relative to acquirer market capitalization at announcement. Panel B. shows quintile results for absolute transaction values. Statistic significance of BHAR is tested with a t-statistic. Corresponding t-values are provided in brackets. Significance of the mean differences is tested with a t-statistic for mean difference tests. Significant values are in bold and marked with "a" if significance is in 1% area, with "b" in 5% area, and with "c" in 10% area.

5. Wealth Creation of Corporate Divestitures: A Market Cycle Perspective

5.1 Introduction

Corporate restructuring through mergers and acquisitions (M&A) is a two-fold process. Firms can decide to acquire new assets or sell business segments. The value implications accompanying these decisions have seen large interest from researchers and practitioners alike. The current consensus is, despite variations in empirical results, that acquisitions on average destroy shareholder value for acquirers' shareholders[12] while divestments create value[13] for sellers' shareholders. The negative results for M&A are often explained by selfish behavior of management that leads to agency costs (Roll 1986, Gorton et al. 2009, Goel and Thakor 2010). Positive effects on sellers' shareholder wealth are explained by increased operational efficiency through refocusing of operations (Berger and Ofek 1995, John and Ofek 1995, Desai and Jain 1999).

Recent findings for M&A shed light on the correlation between market valuation, merger activity, and wealth creation for shareholders (Harford 2005, Bouwman et al. 2009, Chidambaran et al. 2010). A number of studies show that acquisitions in booming markets create less value for shareholders of the acquiring firm than transactions in weak markets due to increased agency costs of overvalued equity (Jensen 2005, Goel and Thakor 2010).

Based on results for M&A, the question emerges whether divestment success also shows variations across market phases. Following the intuition that asset sales are less exposed to agency costs in boom markets than acquisitions while increased asset valuation levels result in higher proceeds for sellers, contrary results are expected for divestments.

The experience of the last 20 years shows that divestment activity strongly depends on the prevailing market environment. European divestment data documents that divestments clustered during the new economy boom at the end of the 1990s and 2000. The second accumulation occurred in 2006 and 2007 at the heights of the credit boom. With the subsequent downfall of stock markets after

12 See Bruner (2002) for a still valid overview and summary of studies that analyze M&A value creation.

13 See e.g., Bates (2005) and Schlingemann et al. (2002) for US results and Veld and Veld-Merkoulova (2004) and Hillier et al. (2009) for European findings.

boom times divestment activity also decreased by 23.25% in number of transactions and 44.24% in value terms from 2000 to 2001 as well as by 26.20% (55.32%) from 2007 to 2008. [14]

Higher valuation levels and increased asset liquidity in strong market environments potentially increases proceeds from divestments and benefits shareholder wealth (Yang 2008 and Schlingemann et al. 2002). Growing markets may also present better opportunities to re-invest proceeds and increase shareholder wealth (Bates 2005). In week markets companies are more likely to be under pressure to increase liquidity and accept high discounts for their assets when selling (Shleifer and Vishny 1992)

This study is motivated by these predictions to empirically examine the role of market cycles on shareholder wealth creation of corporate divestitures. Market cycle effects on divestment value creation have not been studied so far. The presented examination wants to close this gap and introduce market valuation levels as an additional explanation for shareholder wealth creation from divestments. The approach also differs from other studies by applying a short- and long-term view on divestment success to a broad European transaction sample adding to the US-focused research in this field.

The examination of announcement effects and long-term stock market returns of 2'835 European divestments between 1989 and 2007 provide evidence for the starting intuition. The findings show that both announcement returns and abnormal long-term capital market returns are significantly lower for asset sales in depressed markets than in boom markets. Further results propose that shareholder wealth can be increased when managers choose to refocus operations to increase efficiency when the need to restructure and increase liquidity is limited during booming markets.

The remainder of this paper is structured as follows. Chapter 5.2 gives an overview of the theoretical background and develops the underlying hypotheses for the study. Chapter 5.3 describes the data sample and introduces the applied methodology. In Chapter 5.4 the results are discussed in detail and finally a summarizing conclusion is drawn in Chapter 5.5.

14 Based on data from Thomson Reuters' SDC Platinum database.

5.2 Related research and hypotheses

5.2.1 Literature overview

Prior research identifies two general motivations for corporate divestitures. Firms can divest to become more efficient or sell assets to raise additional funds (Schlingeman et al. 2002).

Hite et al. (1987) first lay out that asset sales lead to efficiency gains by allocating assets to the most productive owners. John and Ofek (1995) argue in support of the efficiency explanation that asset sales are motivated by the attempt to remove negative operational synergies and, thus, increase firm efficiency. Desai and Jain (1999) propose that divestments are used to refocus operations to concentrate on core businesses and, hence, increase management focus and reduce complexity costs.

Shleifer and Vishny (1992) and Lang et al. (1995) provide an alternative explanation arguing that asset sales serve as a source of liquidity especially when other sources of finance are unavailable or expensive. Lang et al. (1995) and Lee and Lin (2008) propose that managers are generally reluctant to sell assets and reduce their firm size unless there is a pressing need for additional funds to, e.g., pay down debt.

Related to the discussion of motives for corporate divestiture are questions regarding the benefits for shareholders of sellers. In general, reduction of complexity and allocation of assets to the most efficient owner is expected to increase value. Part of the gains should be captured by the seller and increase shareholder wealth (John and Ofek 1995, Hite et al. 1987). Warusawitharana (2008) adds that shareholder wealth should increase due to fewer agency problems related to divestments in contrast to mergers which are exposed to numerous corporate governance conflicts (as described, e.g., by Jensen 2005, Gorton et. al. 2009, and Goel and Thakor 2010). Desai and Jain (1999) explicitly contrast shareholder wealth creation potential of divestments that target either efficiency gains or additional liquidity. They come to the conclusion that refocusing transactions should generally result in higher efficiency gains and shareholder wealth increases than divestments that are merely targeted on raising liquidity regardless if those are refocusing or within core industries.

Empirical studies of shareholder wealth creation from divestments underpin these predictions. Numerous studies find positive announcement effects for sellers (e.g., Schlingemann et al. 2002 and Bates 2005 for US transactions, Lee and Lin 2008 for a UK sample, Nicolai and Thomas 2006 and Bartsch and Börner 2007 for German divestments).

In the absence of financing constraints in strong market environments refocusing transactions should be mainly targeted on efficiency gains resulting in higher returns to shareholders than core-industry divestments (Berger and Ofek 1995, Desai and Jain 1999). Following the intuition that divestments in strong markets realize higher prices due to a larger number of potential buyers that are more affluent, management is expected to prefer divestments in stronger markets (Shleifer and Vishny 1992). This applies when asset sales are purely motivated by efficiency goals.

It is likely that down-market divestments are more frequently motivated by financing constraints than divestments in strong markets (Shleifer and Vishny 1992, Lang et al. 1995). This applies equally for refocusing and core-industry divestments. Asset sales in non-core industries might even be better suited to ease financing constraints when the market for corporate assets is more liquid than the seller's core industry during a weak market cycle (Schlingemann et al. 2002).

As a result, differences in shareholder wealth creation between refocusing and core-industry divestments should be less strong in week markets or even non-existent. In strong markets, refocusing divestments are expected to be mainly targeted on efficiency gains and, therefore, increase shareholder wealth relative to core-industry divestments.

5.H2: Concentration on core-business segments has higher value creation potential in strong markets than in weak markets.

5.3 Data and methodology

5.3.1 Applied data

Divestment data is obtained from Thomson Reuters' SDC Platinum database. All transactions that meet the following conditions are selected:

- Announcement date between January 1st, 1989 and December 31st, 2007.
- Seller is headquartered in Europe and listed on an European stock exchange including Eastern European countries and Russia.
- Value of divested business exceeds EUR 10 million and constitutes at least 1% of the sellers' market capitalization one month prior to the announcement.
- More than 50% of the asset's equity is transferred to a new unrelated owner.

- Sellers that are financial institutions incl. real estate and private equity companies (ICB sector Financial Institution) are excluded from the analysis.[15]

All financial information including capital market data as well as seller and benchmark company financial information are obtained from Datastream, Thomson Financials, and Worldscope databases. 2'835 transactions are included in the analysis. Following Ince and Porter (2006) special attention is given to return data from Datastream. Adjustment for outliers and potentially flawed data entries that are an often reported challenge of European datasets (Ince and Porter 2006, Espenlaub et al. 2008) is conducted by winsorizing the highest and lowest percentile of CAR and BHAR results.[16]

5.3.2 Classification of market valuation levels

To examine wealth effects of divestments in different market phases the European stock market is classified into different valuation periods. The approach applied builds on the methodology developed by Bouwman et al. (2009). Months of high, neutral, and low market valuation are determined using trailing price-to-earnings (P/E) ratios. The P/E value is de-trended by removing the best straight line fit of the classified month and the preceding five years. The de-trended P/E multiples are then divided in above- and below-average groups based on rolling means of the five preceding years. The top half of the above-average months are classified as high valuation markets, the lower half of the below-average months as low markets, and the rest as neutral markets.[17]

15 The Industry Classification Benchmark (ICB) is published and maintained by Dow Jones und Financial Times Stock Exchange (FTSE). It classifies companies based on their main sources of revenue in 10 industries with 114 sub-sectors. The considered industries are (i) Oil and Gas (0001), (ii) Basic Materials (1000), (iii) Industrials (2000), (iv) Consumer Goods (3000), (v) Health Care (4000), (vi) Consumer Services (5000), (vii) Telecommunication (6000), (viii) Utilities (7000), and (ix) Technology (9000). Financial Institutions (8000) incl. real estate and private equity companies are not considered due to often unclear differentiation between strategic acquisitions and trade sales as well as for the special properties of the applied financial ratios (see Martynova 2006).

16 Results of unadjusted data are comparable but show lower significance levels driven by a number of extreme outliers.

17 Bouwman et al. (2009) discuss and contrast in depth different methodologies of classifiying market valuation levels. Besides P/E ratios they examine market-to-book (M/B) and overall index levels of the S&P 500. They also test the robustness of their approach to changes in de-trended periods and changes in the classification window from month to quarters.

In addition to Bouwman et al. (2009) the presented analysis is performed based on index P/E ratios for the nine ICB industries (excluding financial institutions). The adjustment to Bouwman et al. (2009) was made because valuation phases were found to differ significantly between industries over the 19 year time series. An overall market perspective would falsly classifiy industries with less volatile or unaffected P/E levels. 823 divestments were identified in high, 1'529 in neutral and 483 in low valuation markets. Table 5.5 in Appendix 5.6.1 provides the summary statistics.

5.3.3 Approach to determine shareholder wealth creation

Value creation of divestment decisions is assessed from a capital market perspective. The study applies abnormal announcement returns (CAR) to examine short-term value effects and long-term buy-and-hold abnormal returns (BHAR). In addition to the event-time view a calendar-time perspective to determine long-term returns using the three Fama-French factors and Carhart's (1997) momentum factor (FF4F) is included. Approach and results of the calendar-time analysis is provided in Appendix 5.6.2.

Value creation is analyzed in different time horizons to account for potential deviation in results caused by limited transparency with regard to the future use of proceeds at announcement that may lead to re-assessment by investors over time (Bates 2005).

In a second step, based on the descriptive results, a multivariate regression model is estimated. CAR and BHAR outcomes are regressed with market, transaction, and seller characteristics to control for such variables.

To determine the short-term value effect of acquisitions for shareholders of the acquiring company the cumulative abnormal returns around announcement date (CAR) are calculated. The examined event window consists of 41 days reaching from 20 days before to 20 days after the announcement day of the analyzed transactions. To determine the short-term abnormal return the market model as proposed by Brown and Warner (1980 and 1985) is applied (Equation 5.1).

(5.1) $$AR_{it} = R_{it} - \left(\alpha_i + \beta_i \cdot R_{mt}\right)$$

R_{it} represents the stock return of company i in period t while R_{mt} describes the return of the specific European industry index of the acquiring company's industry as classified by ICB. The market model parameters are estimated with an Ordinary Least Squares (OLS) regression over a period of 180 trading days prior to the analyzed event window. CAR are then calculated by summing the abnormal returns over different event windows (Equation 5.2).

(5.2) $$CAR_{EventWindow(m1,m2)} = \sum_{m1}^{m2} AR_{it}$$

To test the statistical significance the parametric cross-sectional z-Test proposed by Boehmer et al. (1991) (BMP) is applied. In addition, the non-parametric Generalized Sign Test (GST) introduced by Cowan et al. (1990) is calculated.

The strategy to assess long term capital market gains from divestments applies buy-and-hold abnormal returns in event-time (BHAR) as proposed by Barber and Lyon (1997) and Lyon et al. (1999).

BHAR is measured following a control firm approach. Non-selling control firms with comparable characteristics are selected as benchmark following a character based matching approach. As proposed by Lyon et al. (1999) market-to-book ratios (M/B) and firm market value are used to select control firms. In addition to the common approach, special attention is put on finding control companies with matching industry characteristics. The following steps are applied: First, end of June market values and previous fiscal year's M/B ratios are determined for all active European companies in the data sample in every year. For every divestment, non-divesting firms within the same ICB sub-sector (114 sub-sectors) and with market values between 70% and 130% of the bidder's market value at announcement day are identified. If less than three matching firms could be found, companies within the same ICB industry are considered. From all similar sized firms the ones with the smallest absolute difference in M/B value are selected as control firm. The identified control firm for each transaction is then used as a benchmark to calculate the abnormal buy-and-hold returns of divesting companies. Equation (5.3) describes the computation of buy-and-hold abnormal returns.

(5.3) $$BHAR_{iT} = \prod_{t=s}^{s+T}(1+R_{it}) - \prod_{t=s}^{s+T}(1+R_{controlfirm,t})$$

R_{it} and $R_{controlfirm,t}$ describe the monthly returns of the bidder and the control firm respectively. The BHAR are calculated for a 12- and 24-month period as equally and value weighted means. Differences in equal- and value-weights indicate performance differences between smaller and larger firms by assigning more weight to acquirers with a relatively large market capitalization. The value weighting approach follows the methodology applied by Mitchell and Stafford (2000). Value weights are determined based on acquirer market value before announcement. The weights are then adjusted by a stock market deflator. The adjustment is made to avoid the problem of increasing stock market valuations over the 19 year sample period that would assign more weight to more recent transactions. The deflator is calculated based on the value weighted European DS-Total Market index from Datastream.

investors anticipate lower value creation potential from divestments in weak market environments.

Table 5.2: Long-term BHAR - Divestment

			A. All Market Valuation Levels			N = 1'736
Period	$BHAR_{EW}$	t-value	p-value	$BHAR_{VW}$	t-value	p-value
12 months	-0.59%	-0.51	0.62	-6.83%	-13.03	<0.01[a]
24 months	-3.52%	-1.93	0.57[c]	-17.61%	-24.12	<0.01[a]
			B. High Market Valuations			N = 542
12 months	1.96%	0.92	0.36	-3.71%	-3.99	<0.01[a]
24 months	0.00%	0.00	1.00	-8.56%	-5.69	<0.01[a]
			C. Neutral Market Valuations			N = 908
12 months	-0.75%	-0.47	0.65	-7.31%	-9.27	<0.01[a]
24 months	-2.93%	-1.17	0.24	-19.19%	-19.55	<0.01[a]
			D. Low Market Valuations			N = 286
12 months	-4.92%	-1.97	0.05[b]	-11.50%	-11.21	<0.01[a]
24 months	-11.96%	-2.56	0.01[b]	-23.64%	-14.46	<0.01[a]
			E. Mean Difference Neutral - Low			
12 months	4.17%	1.25	0.21	4.55%	3.06	<0.01[a]
24 months	8.98%	1.74	0.08[c]	3.37%	1.75	0.08[c]
			F. Mean Difference High - Low			
12 months	6.88%	2.00	0.04[b]	7.79%	5.49	<0.01[a]
24 months	11.97%	2.06	0.04[b]	15.08%	6.59	<0.01[a]

This table shows results from an analysis of long-term buy-and-hold abnormal capital market returns in event-time (BHAR). Results are provided as equally (EW) and value weighted (VW) averages for 12 and 24 months after the announcement month. All transactions between January 1st 1989 and December 31st 2007 are included for which all required seller information is available until December 31st 2009 (Panel A.). The transaction sample is then divided in months with high valuation levels (Panel B.), neutral valuations (Panel C.), and low valuations (Panel D.). Months are classified based on the de-trended industry P/E ratio of the transaction announcement month. The top half of the above average months are classified as high valuation markets, the lower half of the below average months as low markets, and the rest as neutral markets. Significance is tested with a t-test. To test the difference in means between sub-samples a t-test for mean differences is applied (Panel E. and F.). The p-values resulting from t-statistics are marked with "a" if significance is in 1% area, with "b" in 5% area, and with "c" in 10% area.

The long-term perspective provides further supporting evidence for an underperformance of divestments in low valuation markets. Table 5.2 summarizes the results. The overall sample exhibits negative long-term returns in the 24-month horizon for equally weighted BHAR of -3.52% significant in the 10% confidence interval and of -17.61% for value weighted BHAR significant in the 1% interval. The result is in line with long-term findings from Lee and Lin (2008) for UK selloffs. Lee and Lin (2008) and Bates (2005) argue that investors fail to incorporate all relevant information at the announcement of asset sales mainly because of uncertainty with regard to the use of proceeds from divestments leading to deviations in results between short- and long-term returns.

The result proposes that on average companies cannot realize value from corporate restructuring through asset sales over time. Negative effects on shareholder wealth creation can be explained by agency costs of management discretion with regard to the use of free funds from divestments. Lang et al. (1995) argue that managers tend to re-invest proceed in net present value (NPV) negative projects rather than returning them to their shareholders or use them for debt reduction (Lee and Lin 2008).

The analysis of returns in different market environments shows that negative effects are largely driven by a significant underperformance of transactions in low valuation markets. The results for low valuation markets in Panel D. are significantly negative in all time horizons ranging from -4.92% (12-month) to -11.96% (24-month) equally weighted and from -11.50% (12-month) to -23.64% (24-month) value weighted. Results for high and neutral valuation markets in Panels B. and C. are insignificantly different from zero in the equally weighted view while value weighted results are consistently negative and significant. The finding that value weighted returns are lower than equally weighted returns shows that larger firms fail to extract value from divestments.

The mean differences analysis shows that weak market transactions significantly underperform transactions in high valuation markets. The results in Panel F. are significant in all time horizons with BHAR differentials between 6.88% (12-month) and 11.97% (24-month) for equally weighted results and between 7.79% (12-month) and 15.08% (24-month) value weighted.

The short-and long-term results support Hypothesis 5.H1 showing that divestment in strong markets create more shareholder value than sell-offs in weak markets. The underperformance of divestments in weak markets proposes that companies in depressed market environments fail to realize long-term efficiency gains and increase firm value. In addition, lower prices are likely to be realized when valuation levels are low, the number of potential buyers is reduced, and pressure to sell is higher. High valuation markets in contrast provide a favorable investment environment for proceeds and higher asset valuations increase the available funds for re-investment.

5.4.2 Value creation of different divestment strategies

In a next step value creation effects across market cycles for transaction sub-samples of refocusing and core-industry divestments are tested. The decision to divest company assets in non-core industry has been found to influence divestment success when asset sales are targeted at reducing complexity costs and increasing efficiency of remaining operations (e.g., Desai and Jain 1999, Veld and Veld-Merkoulova 2004). Divestments that are targeted on easing external funding constraints are expected to have lower wealth creation potential form a seller's shareholders perspective (Desai and Jain 1999).

Table 5.3: CAR and BHAR of refocusing and core-industry divestments under different market valuations

	1. All Valuations		2. High Valuations		3. Low Valuations		4. Mean Difference High-Low	
A. CAR								
	CAR$_{[-1/+1]}$	CAR$_{[+10/-10]}$	CAR$_{[-1/+1]}$	CAR$_{[+10/-10]}$	CAR$_{[-1/+1]}$	CAR$_{[+10/-10]}$	CAR$_{[-1/+1]}$	CAR$_{[+10/-10]}$
Core-Industry	0.82% **(5.39^{a})** (N=1'034)	0.64% **(1.86^{b})** (N=1'034	1.00% **(3.66^{a})** (N=331)	1.00% **(1.77^{b})** (N=331)	0.40% (1.14) (N=187)	-0.53% (-0.61) (N=187)	0.60% (1.34)	1.53% (1.47)
Refocusing	0.97% **(8.26^{a})** (N=1'801)	1.11% **(4.27^{a})** (N=1'801)	1.01% **(4.83^{a})** (N=492)	1.74% **(3.86^{a})** (N=492)	0.37% (1.32) (N=296)	-0.07% (-0.12) (N=296)	0.64% **(1.84^{c})**	1.82% **(2.43^{b})**
Mean Difference Core - refocusing	-0.15% (-0.76)	-0.47% (-1.09)	-0.01% (-0.03)	-0.75% (-1.03)	0.03% (0.07)	-0.46% (-0.43)		
B. BHAR								
	BHAR$_{EW}$	BHAR$_{VW}$	BHAR$_{EW}$	BHAR$_{VW}$	BHAR$_{EW}$	BHAR$_{VW}$	BHAR$_{EW}$	BHAR$_{VW}$
Core-Industry	-7.04% **(-2.34^{b})** (N=596)	-15.43% **(-7.27^{a})** (N=596)	-7.64% (-1.56) (N=207)	-17.40% **(-4.31^{a})** (N=207)	-8.27% (1.21) (N=110)	-14.93% **(-4.35^{a})** (N=110)	0.63% (1.04)	-2.37% (1.56)
Refocusing	-1.69% (-0.72) (N=1'140)	-19.00% **(-9.12^{a})** (N=1'140)	4.74% (1.12) (N=335)	-2.38% (-1.25) (N=335)	-14.26% **(-2.35^{b})** (N=176)	-31.67% **(-3.31^{a})** (N=176)	19.00% **(2.06^{b})**	29.29% **(6.73^{a})**
Mean Difference Core - refocusing	-5.35% (-1.41)	3.57% (1.39)	-12.38% **(-1.85^{c})**	-14.37% **(-4.68^{a})**	5.99% (0.63)	16.74% **(5.17^{a})**		

The table shows short-term abnormal announcement returns (CAR) in Panel A. and long-term buy-and-hold abnormal returns (BHAR) in Panel B. for core-business as well as refocusing divestments in high, neutral, and low valuation markets. Industry refocusing transactions show a difference in primary two-digit Standard Industrial Classification (SIC) code between divested asset and divesting parent company. Divestitures in core-segments show the same two-digit SIC code. Results are provided for three- [-1/+1] and 21-day [-10/+10] event windows around the announcement day for CAR and for 24 months following announcement for BHAR. Divestments between January 1st 1989 and December 31st 2007 are included in the analysis (1.). The transaction sample is then divided in months with high valuation levels (2.) and low valuations (3.). Months are classified based on the de-trended industry P/E ratio of the transaction announcement month. Statistical significance of CAR results is tested with the standardized-cross-sectional-test as proposed by Boehmer et al. (1991). Significance of BHAR results is tested with a t-test. Corresponding z- and t-values are provided in brackets. Significance of the mean differences is tested with a t-statistic for mean difference tests. Significant values are bold and marked with "a" if significance is in 1% area, with "b" in 5% area, and with "c" in 10% area.

Refocusing divestments are determined by a difference in 2-digit primary SIC code between parent company and divested entity. Core-industry divestments show equal 2-digit SIC codes. Panel A. in Table 5.3 presents short-term returns (CAR) for 3-day and 21-day event windows. Panel B. provides long-term BHAR results over 24 months in an equally and value weighted view.

Results for the overall sample are provided in column 1. The results indicate higher abnormal returns for refocusing transactions but the mean difference test remains insignificant for both CAR and BHAR results. Columns 2 and 3 show results for high and low valuation markets respectively. For CAR results in Panel A., mean differences between refocusing and core-industry divestments are not significantly different from zero in high or low valuation months. In the mean difference view across market valuation phases in column 4 results show that only refocusing transaction are significantly different across valuation phases. The average outperformance of refocusing transactions in high valuation markets reaches from 0.64% in a 3-day window to 1.82% over 21 days. The finding suggests that differences in announcement returns are driven by positive investor reactions to the announcement of refocusing transactions in high valuation markets.

Panel B. in Table 5.3 provides the corresponding long-term effects. The differential between refocusing and non-core industry transactions is significantly positive for equally and value weighted BHAR in high valuation months by 12.38% and 14.37%. For low valuation markets results show a reverse picture with better performance of core-industry divestments. This leads to a strong outperformance of refocusing transaction across market phases for high valuation market transactions of 19.00% equally and 29.29% value weighted over 24 months.

The long term results support the short-term findings illustrating that refocusing transactions can create relatively more value for shareholders when announced in strong stock market environments. This findings proposes that companies that decide to focus operations when asset prices are high and pressure to sell for liquidity reasons is low are more likely to realize efficiency gains than companies in weak markets. This outcome supports Hypothesis 5.H2.

5.4.3 Multiple regression

In addition to the descriptive findings a multiple regression is estimated to determine the combined effects of different transaction characteristics. 3-day CAR and 24-month BHAR are regressed following the model illustrated in Equation 5.4.

$$
\begin{aligned}
(5.4) \quad & AR = a_0 + a_1 HighValDummy + a_2 LowValDummy + \\
& a_3 RefocusDummy + a_5 RelM/BInd + a_6 RelEBITInd + \\
& a_7 CrossBorderDummy + a_8 LogRelValue + a_9 LogSizeSeller + \\
& a_{10} RelM/BSeller + a_{11} RelEBITSeller + a_{12} RelLeverageSeller + \\
& a_{13} HHISeller
\end{aligned}
$$

The independent variable *AR* represents CAR and BHAR respectively for the overall sample in Table 5.4 (Panel A.) as well as for high (Panel B.) and low (Panel C.) market valuation sub-samples. Panels D. and E. provide regression results for refocusing and core-industry sub-samples. The analyzed dependent variables include indicators of market valuation levels (a), determinants of industry and geographic diversification (b), seller and target characteristics (c), and industry structure (d).

a) In order to examine the effect of different valuation levels on shareholder wealth creation from divestments, dummy variables for industry valuation levels during the announcement month are included in the model. *HighValDummy* assumes the value 1 for divestments that have been announced in high valuation months. For all other transactions it is 0. The *LowValDummy* is 1 or 0 respectively.
b) *RefocusDummy* is 1 for all transactions in which the seller's 2-digit SIC code in the SDC database differs from the SIC code of the divested asset. Colak (2009) proposes that companies tend to move away from relatively weak performing business segments to improve performance. To further examine the focusing decision, relative median market-to-book valuation (*RelM/BInd*) of the divested industry compared to the core industry is included to proxy for relative growth prospects of the two industries. Relative median EBIT margins (*RelEBITInd*) proxy for industry profitability. M/B and EBIT margins are aggregated from individual companies in the respective two-digit SIC industries. Relative industry performance measures are then calculated as the difference between the core industry of the seller and the divested asset's industry. The variables only apply for refocusing sub-samples.

   Denis et al. (2002) include geographic diversification in their examination of value implications from refocusing transactions. They come to the conclusion that geographic refocusing on core markets can increase a firms' efficiency and increase firm value. Geographic diversification of the divestments is addressed by the *CrossBorderDummy* variables. This dummy variables assumes the value 1 if the SDC country code of the divested entity at announcement differs between divested asset and seller.

c) To control for the relative size of the divestment, *LogRelValue* is included calculated as the common logarithm of the ratio between transaction value and market value of the selling company.

   In order to separate idiosyncratic company characteristics from overall market induced determinants the regression analysis controls for a number of firm specific factors. The descriptive results propose that larger firms underperform compared to smaller firms when divesting as shown by lower abnormal returns for value weighted BHAR. To control for seller's size the common logarithm of the seller's market capitalization at end of month in the month preceding transactions announcement (*LogSizeSeller*) is included.

   Bates (2005) and Lee and Lin (2008) propose that growth prospects of the divesting company affects long-run returns when proceeds from asset sales can be invested in NPV positive projects. To control for growth opportunities that are company specific rather than driven by the overall market environment industry adjusted M/B ratios of sellers (*RelM/BSeller*) in the regression are included. Warusawitharana (2008) proposes that relative profitability of companies in an industry determines divestment decisions and affects resulting firm value. Lang et al. (1995), Bartsch and Börner (2007), and Lee and Lin (2008) argue that financial health of sellers can influence returns from asset sales. To control for individual firms' operational performance relative to industry peers, industry median adjusted EBIT margins are included in the regression analysis (*RelEBITSeller*).

   RelEBITSeller and *RelM/BSeller* are calculated by subtracting the median industry EBIT margin and M/B ratios of the respective 2-digit SIC industry from the individual firm figures as in Lee and Lin (2008).

d) Industry concentration has been frequently reported to affect corporate restructuring decisions and success. Potential implications of industry collusion include reduced resalabilty of company assets (Balasubramanian and Sivadasan 2009) and limited future growth and profitability prospects (Ali et al. 2009). To test for the effect of industry concentration the Herfindahl-Index (*HHISeller*) based on the 2-digit SIC industry of the seller is calculated. To calculate the HHI, sales data from public and private companies is considered (Andrade and Stafford 2004).

Table 5.4 provides the results of the multiple regression analysis. Panel A. shows regression results for the overall sample. Panels B. and C. provide the outcome for high and low valuation market transactions. Panels D. and E. exhibit outcome for refocusing and core-industry sub-samples.

Panel A. supports the descriptive findings with regard to market valuation effects on short- and long-term value creation. Coefficients of dummy variables for transactions in low valuation months (*LowValDummy*) are significantly negative for both CAR (regression 1) and BHAR (regression 2). The CAR coefficient remains significantly negative when including control variables for target size (*LogRelValue*), seller size (LogSizeSeller), seller firms relative growth prospects (*RelM/BSeller*) and profitability (*RelEBITSeller*), as well as industry concentration (*HHISeller*). The BHAR coefficients for low valuations is negative but falls out of the 10% confidence interval relative to neutral valuation markets with a t-value of 1.57.

The finding illustrated that the market environment in which divestment transactions are announced influences shareholder wealth creation. Hypothesis 5.H1 is supported by the results. The outcome suggests that lower proceeds from asset sales due to low market-wide valuation levels and a smaller group of potential buyers lead to less shareholder wealth creation in weak markets. Long-term results suggest that strong markets also provide a better environment to re-invest proceeds. The finding supports predictions from Yang (2008) and relates findings from Bates (2005) to market cycles.

The results for refocusing and core-industry divestments in Panels D. and E. show a significantly negative coefficient for refocusing transactions. Market valuation variables remain insignificant for core-industry transactions. Panel B. provides results for the high valuation market sub-sample. The refocusing dummy (*RefocusDummy*) is significantly positive for BHAR results (regression 6). These results supports the descriptive finding that the outperformance of high market transactions compared to low market transactions is driven by refocusing divestments. In the long-term, refocusing increases shareholder wealth when market valuations are high at announcement. A positive effect of refocusing on shareholder wealth can does not appear for low market transactions and the overall sample.

The results support Hypothesis 5.H2. The outcome underlines the predictions and findings of Berger and Ofek (1995), John and Ofek (1995) and Desai and Jain (1999) with regard to efficiency gains from refocusing transactions for high-valuation markets. Desai and Jain (1999) show that refocusing transactions that target efficiency increases create more value than transactions that are supposed to provide additional liquidity. The market cycle view proposes that divestments in strong markets are more likely to focus on efficiency increases than on raising funds and improving liquidity and, thus, are more likely to increase shareholder wealth. The results in low valuation months, in contrast, indicate that these transactions are more likely to target liquidity rather than efficiency leading to relatively lower shareholder wealth creation.

The regression analysis provides a number of additional insights from included control variables. Regression 10 in Panel D. shows a significantly positive coefficient for sales of assets in industry that have lower growth prospects (*RelM/BInd*) than the core industry of the seller. The coefficient suggests that long-term shareholder wealth creation is highest when firms reallocate assets to industries with high growth prospects.

The positive effect of relative size of the divested assets (*LogSizeSeller*) is widely reported in previous studies (e.g., Boone and Mulherin 2000). The variable shows consistently significant coefficients. The finding is intuitive as larger divestments have a higher potential to reduce complexity and focus management. An interesting finding is the significantly negative coefficient of seller size (*LogSizeSeller*). All BHAR regressions show a negative result for the size control variable with the exception of low market transactions (regression 8). The outcome corresponds with the descriptive value weighted BHAR results. Regressions 3 and 9 also show negative CAR results for the total and refocusing sub-sample. A possible implication of this finding is that larger firms are more exposed to agency costs of management discretion with regard to the use of divestment proceeds than smaller firms. Another explanation could be that larger firms are likely to have higher complexity costs through diversification in multiple segments and geographies leading to reduced marginal benefits of individual divestments (Schlingemann et al. 2002).

Coefficients of the *RelM/BSeller* variable are significantly positive in all BHAR regressions. The variable shows that long-term shareholder wealth effects are higher for low M/B sellers than for growth companies. The result is interesting in two ways. First, it supports the efficiency explanation advanced by Hite et al. (1987) who argue that divestments that allocate assets to owners who can extract most value benefit both seller's and buyer's shareholder wealth. Second, positive effects from favorable investment opportunities for proceeds in high M/B companies cannot be observed (Bates 2005). This provides some indication that positive investment opportunities depend more on the overall market environment than on individual firm prospects. The relative profitability of a Seller (*RelEBITSeller*) has a significant effect on value creation of refocusing transaction (Panel D.). The negative coefficients for CAR (regression 9) and BHAR (regression 10) shows that companies with weak profitability compared to peers have higher potential to increase shareholder wealth by refocusing. This finding is consistent with predictions from Berger and Ofek (1995), Desai and Jain (1999), and Colak (2008) for refocusing activity.

Table 5.4: Multiple regression results - Divestments

	A. All transactions				B. High Valuations		C. Low Valuations		D. Refocusing		E. Core-Industry	
	(1)	(2)	(3)	(4)	(5)	(6)	(7)	(8)	(9)	(10)	(11)	(12)
	CAR	BHAR]	CAR	BHAR	CAR	BHAR]	CAR	BHAR]	CAR	BHAR]	CAR	BHAR]
Intercept	1.03%	-3.68%	0.90%	4.16%	1.79%	12.08%	0.01%	9.01%	1.19%	11.21%	0.30%	-4.74%
	(8.00^{a})	(-1.43)	**(3.14^{a})**	(0.73)	**(1.81^{c})**	**(2.16^{b})**	(0.02)		**(3.43^{a})**	**(1.78^{c})**	(0.69)	(-0.56)
HighValDummy	0.01%	3.06%	0.11%	2.67%					0.23%	1.15%	-0.05%	-8.80%
	(0.02)	(0.73)	(0.44)	(0.58)					(0.72)	(0.20)	(-0.12)	(-1.13)
LowValDummy	-0.62%	-8.27%	-0.60%	-9.14%					-0.63%	-12.82%	-0.13%	-5.97%
	(-2.41^{b})	**(-1.66^{c})**	(-1.57)	**(-1.70^{c})**					**(-1.69^{c})**	**(-1.78^{c})**	(-0.27)	(-0.64)
RefocusDummy			0.12%	-0.81%	0.55%	9.87%	0.35%	9.82%				
			(0.49)	(-0.18)	(0.62)	**(2.48^{b})**	(0.59)	(0.97)				
CrossBorder-Dummy			-0.29%	3.27%	0.04%	-5.74%	0.10%	7.42%	0.10%	3.35%	-0.84%	3.71%
			(1.12)	(-0.72)	(-0.04)	(-1.17)	(-0.16)	(-0.72)	(-0.33)	(-0.61)	**(2.23^{b})**	(-0.51)
RelM/BInd									-0.05%	7.29%		
									(-0.13)	**(2.23^{b})**		
RelEBITInd									-1.39%	24.51%		
									(-1.24)	(1.16)		
LogRelValue			0.33%	6.05%	-0.14%	5.01%	1.04%	25.98%	0.29%	4.54%	0.39%	7.37%
			(3.03^{a})	**(3.26^{a})**	(-0.40)	**(2.85^{a})**	**(2.05^{b})**	**(3.35^{a})**	**(2.28^{b})**	**(1.85^{c})**	**(2.17^{b})**	**(2.59^{b})**
LogSizeSeller			-0.02%	-0.59%	-0.02%	-0.41%	0.00%	-0.32%	-0.02%	-0.63%	-0.01%	-0.48%
			(-2.14^{b})	**(-3.02^{a})**	(-0.82)	**(-1.95^{c})**	(0.17)	(-0.72)	**(-1.93^{c})**	**(-2.38^{b})**	(-0.92)	**(-1.67^{c})**
RelM/BSeller			0.01%	-7.57%	0.05%	-3.26%	0.06%	-6.89%	-0.06%	-10.55%	-0.01%	-5.14%
			(0.14)	**(-2.89^{a}**	(0.28)	**(-1.80^{c})**	(0.47)	**(-3.08^{a})**	(-0.91)	**(-3.28^{a})**	(-0.92)	**(-2.55^{b})**
RelEBITSeller			-1.74%	-14.94%	-1.93%	-8.74%	-1.59%	8.33%	-1.88%	-35.42%	0.08%	17.81%
			(-2.24^{a})	(-1.10)	**(-2.56^{b})**	(-1.20)	(-0.74)	(0.22)	**(-1.90^{c})**	**(-2.03^{b})**	(1.16)	(0.79)
HHISeller			0.47%	21.80%	-2.12%	32.84%	0.72%	21.27%	-0.18%	-5.61%	2.07%	94.61%
			(0.35)	(0.95)	(-0.46)	(1.42)	(0.18)	(0.32)	(-0.17)	(-0.21)	(0.73)	**(2.54^{b})**
N=	2'635	1'740	1'927	1'422	617	458	349	258	1'247	960	680	471
$R^2_{adjusted}$	0.006	0.017	0.017	0.071	0.004	0.060	0.000	0.087	0.012	0.084	0.010	0.071
F-Statistic	3.17^{a}	2.07^{b}	3.29^{a}	11.88^{a}	1.31	4.65^{a}	0.78	4.08^{a}	2.66^{a}	10.83^{a}	2.33^{b}	5.02^{a}

The table shows results from an OLS regression analysis of three- and 21-day short-term cumulative abnormal returns (CAR) and 24-month buy-and-hold returns (BHAR). In Panel A. all European transactions between January 1st 1989 and December 31st 2007 in data sample are included. Panels B. and C. contain regression results for high valuation and low valuation months transaction sub-samples. Months are classified based on the de-trended industry P/E ratio of the transaction announcement month. The top half of the above average months are classified as high valuation markets, the lower half of the below average months as low valuation markets. Panels D. and E. include refocusing and core-industry transactions. Refocusing transactions show different 2-digit SIC codes. Core-industry transactions (Panel E.) have equal 2-digit SIC codes. A t-statistic is conducted to test significance of the coefficients. The statistical fit of the model is indicated by the adjusted determination coefficient R^2 adjusted and F-statistic. The t- and F-values are marked with "a" if significance is in 1% area, with "b" in 5% area, and with "c" in 10% area. Coefficients are in bold font when significance is at least in 10% confidence interval.

Lastly, the control variable for industry concentration (*HHISeller*) shows a significantly positive coefficient for BHAR of core-industry divestments. This finding points to the interesting implication that companies in colluded industries benefit their shareholders most when they sell assets in their core market. This finding is supporting the view that highly concentrated industries face declining firm valuations in the long term (Ali et al. 2009).

5.5 Conclusion

The presented study examines short- and long-term shareholder wealth creation of divestments from European sellers in dependence of the prevailing market valuation in the months between 1989 and 2007. The analysis contributes to the discussion of corporate restructuring success by introducing market valuation levels as a determinant of shareholder wealth creation from divestments. It also provides insights based on a broad European sample of divestitures complementing the US-focused research in this field.

The results show that European divestments during the analyzed period had positive announcement returns while the long-term capital market returns over 12 and 24 months were insignificantly different from zero or negative. The widely reported positive announcement returns of divestments for European transactions are confirmed. The difference in shareholder wealth creation across time horizons supports predictions from Bates (2005) that investors have difficulties to assess the effects of divestments on firm value at announcement due to intransparency with regard to the future use of proceeds. Negative effects on wealth creation following divestments indicate agency costs of management discretion when proceeds are re-invested in value decreasing projects which are not anticipated by investors at announcement (Lang et al. 1995, Lee and Lin 2008).

Focus of the examination are potential differences of shareholder wealth creation from divestments in months with high and low market valuations. The results provide strong evidence for a relation between market valuation phase and shareholder wealth creation. The main finding shows that divestments in weak markets significantly underperform asset sales in stronger markets in a short- and long-term view (Hypothesis 5.H1). This finding can be explained with higher asset prices and value increasing investment opportunities for proceeds in booming markets. Weak markets suffer from depressed asset prices, limited number of potential buyers, and a weak investment environment reducing the potential to increase shareholder wealth.

In a second step differences between refocusing and core-industry divestments are examined. Evidence is found that refocusing drives outperformance of

5.6.2 4-factor calendar-time results

To test for robustness of the long-term results a calendar time perspective is added to the event-time view of the BHAR analysis. The calendar-time methodology introduced by Fama and French (1993) is applied. The selected 4-factor model (FF4F) addresses some of the shortcomings of the BHAR methodology, e. g., the cross-sectional correlation of firms in event-time (Mitchell and Stafford 2000). It, however, is potentially exposed to other pitfalls, e.g., heteroscedasticity. The four-factor model determines excess returns of a portfolio of sample firms by regressing the time series of (i) the market excess return, (ii) the differences in return between small and big firms, (iii) the excess returns of high vs. low book-to-market (B/M) companies, and (iv) the Carhart momentum factor. The model takes the form of Equation 5.5

$$R_{pt} - R_{ft} = a_p + b_p\left(R_{mt} - R_{ft}\right) + s_p SMB + h_p HML + m_p PR1YR + e_{pt} \quad (5.5)$$

R_{pt} is the return of a continuously changing portfolio of companies or subgroups of these companies that conducted asset sales within the preceding 24 months. The acquirer portfolio is re-constructed on a monthly basis when new bidders are included and inactive companies leave after the 24-month period. R_{mt} - R_{ft} represents the market factor, calculated by subtracting the risk free rate (three months Euribor after 1999, Libor until 1999) from the value weighted market portfolio (Europe DS-Total Market index). SMB is the size factor. The companies of the Europe DS-Total Market index are ranked based on their market value on the last trading day of June each year. The median is used to split the companies into big (B) and small (S) portfolios. HML is the book-to-market factor which is formed by subtracting high B/M value stocks and low B/M growth stocks. The portfolios are formed by ranking the companies according to their B/M level and distributing the top and bottom 30% to the respective portfolios (H and L) and the remaining 40% in a medium portfolio (M). Six portfolios are created each year (S/L, S/M, S/H, B/L, B/M, and B/H). The SMB portfolio is supposed to replicate the risk factor in returns related to size. It is calculated using the average of the monthly returns on the three small (S) portfolios minus the three big (B) portfolios. The HML portfolio mimics the risk factor related to book-to-market valuation and is calculated in the same way using the two high (H) and the two low (L) portfolios. Due to simple averaging of the portfolios the factors should be largely free of the other factor's effect.

Table 5.6: Monthly calendar-time return regression (FF4F) - Divestments

	a	b	s	h	m	F-statistic	$R^2_{adjusted}$
1. All Valuations	0.12%	**0.913**	**-1.24**	-0.09	**-0.17**	385.34[a]	0.86
	(0.62)	(31.80[a])	(-17.88[a])	(-1.30)	(-4.15[a])		
2. High Valuations	0.66%	**0.97**	**-1.17**	-0.25	**-0.16**	83.67[a]	0.58
	(1.48)	(14.80[a])	(-7.35[a])	(-1.56)	(-1.68[c])		
3. Neutral Valuations	0.12%	**0.91**	**-1.27**	-0.09	**-0.14**	297.87[a]	0.84
	(0.57)	(29.23[a])	(-16.88[a])	(-1.12)	(-3.10[b])		
4. Low Valuations	-0.11%	**0.90**	**-1.23**	0.12	-0.11	80.97[a]	0.62
	(-0.26)	(15.07[a])	(-8.38[a])	(0.81)	(-1.31)		

This table presents results from 4-factor calendar-time (FF4F) portfolio regressions. The intercept "a" represents the monthly abnormal return of a continuously adapted portfolio of divesting companies that sold within the 36 months preceding the respective month. The analysis is conducted for portfolios of All (1.), High (2.), Neutral (3.), and Low (4.) market sellers between January 1st 1989 and December 31st 2007. Results shown are based on equally weighted returns. The coefficients "b", "s", "h", and "m" represent the loadings of the regressed market factors. b is the classical beta coefficient of the market excess return. s expresses the composition of the acquirer's portfolio in terms of size distribution while h indicates the same for value vs. growth distribution (Fama and French 1993). m indicates the effects of momentum within the market portfolio (Carhart 1997). The classic t-statistic is conducted to test significance. The statistical fit of the model is indicated by the adjusted determination coefficient $R^2_{adjusted}$ and F-statistic. The test values are marked with "a" if significance is in 1% area, with "b" in 5% area, and with "c" in 10% area.

In addition, a momentum factor is included to account for portfolio momentum effects as proposed by Carhart (1997). PR1YR is the return differentials of two equally weighted portfolios constructed out of firms with the highest and lowest 30% of eleven months returns prior to the announcement month. The coefficients b_p, s_p, h_p, and m_p determine the loading of the respective factor indicating the composition of the sample portfolio and the factor's effect on returns. The a_p coefficient finally represents the monthly return of the sample portfolio over a 24-month period that cannot be explained by the four factors. The sum of the error terms e_{pt} is assumed to be zero. Table 5.6 shows the results.

The alphas of the FF4F regression are not significantly different from zero. The results, however, provide some indication that low market transactions show lower abnormal monthly returns than neutral and high market asset sales. Loughran and Ritter (2000) argue that the Fama-French calendar-time approach potentially underestimates abnormal returns because it averages months of "hot" and "cold" merger markets. The market valuation phase perspective applied is particularly exposed to this effect due to high correlation of divestment activity with valuation levels.

The results directionally support the overall result of the BHAR analysis. The total sample of divesting companies shows a monthly alpha of 0.12% amounting to 2.88% over 24 months. High valuation alphas indicate a higher monthly abnormal return of 0.66%. This alpha remains insignificant with a t-value of 1.48. The low valuation alpha is with -0.11% the lowest among market phases.

Although the calendar-time findings are less strong than the event-time BHAR results, some indication is found that asset sales in weak market environments underperform from a capital market perspective in the long run.

5.6.3 Operative performance effects (AROA)

In addition to the capital market perspective an analysis of abnormal operative performance development following divestments is conducted. The methodology applied follows Bouwman et al. (2009). In order to measure abnormal return on assets (AROA), earnings before interest, tax, depreciation, and amortization (EBITDA) are analyzed over a three year period after the transaction excluding the year of announcement. EBITDA is normalized by average total assets. To assess abnormal performance, control firms are determined following the approach applied for the BHAR analysis. The control firm matching, however, is conducted using the smallest absolute difference in pre-divestment EBITDA over average total assets instead of market-to-book ratios to select companies with comparable operative performance as benchmarks. AROA is then calculated as the difference in normalized operative result between acquirer and non-merging control firm. Significance is tested using a t-test.

Table 5.7 exhibits mean and median abnormal operative returns (AROA) from divestments. The AROA are significantly negative for the overall sample (Panel A.) with means between -1.59% (-1.32% median) one year after the announcement year to -1.05% (-0.62%) three years after announcement. The long-term return findings are, thus, also reflected in weaker operative performance of sellers. The negative results for the European samples are not consistent with positive effects from asset sales in the UK reported by Hillier et al. (2009). The results for different market valuation levels in Panels B., C., and D. also show negative operational effects from divestments independent of prevailing market cycle. The mean difference view does not indicate a significant underperformance of weak market transactions as found for long-term stock market returns. The results give a weak indication that median operative improvements in low markets are higher than in other market phases. These findings suggest that companies focus on operative improvements when restructuring in weak markets on the expense of future growth opportunities driving stock market underperformance. The results, remain however inconclusive.

Table 5.7: Long-term abnormal operational improvements (AROA) - Divestments

			A. All Market Valuation Levels			N = 1'251
Period	$AROA_{AV}$	t-value	p-value	$AROA_{MD}$	Z-value	p-value
t + 1 year	-1,59%	-7,80	<0,01[a]	-1.32%	7.90	<0.01[a]
t + 2 years	-1,05%	-4,81	<0,01[a]	-0.72%	5.05	<0.01[a]
t + 3 years	-1,05%	-4,87	<0,01[a]	-0.62%	4.98	<0.01[a]
			B. High Market Valuations			N = 431
t + 1 year	-1.37%	-4.03	<0.01[a]	-1.22%	3.39	<0.01[a]
t + 2 years	-0.81%	-2.00	0.05[b]	-0.72%	2.43	0.01[b]
t + 3 years	-0.74%	-1.91	0.57[c]	-0.50%	1.69	0.09[c]
			C. Neutral Market Valuations			N = 556
t + 1 year	-1.56%	-5.20	<0.01[a]	-1.45%	4.85	<0.01[a]
t + 2 years	-1.24%	-3.97	<0.01[a]	-0.79%	2.89	<0.01[a]
t + 3 years	-1.36%	-4.46	<0.01[a]	-0.95%	3.16	<0.01[a]
			D. Low Market Valuations			N = 264
t + 1 year	-2.01%	-4.23	<0.01[a]	-1.51%	4.16	<0.01[a]
t + 2 years	-1.07%	-2.32	0.02[b]	-0.66%	2.35	0.02[b]
t + 3 years	-0.89%	-1.88	0.06[c]	-0.18%	2.04	0.04[b]
			E. Mean and Median Difference Neutral - Low			
t + 1 year	0.46%	0.81	0.41	0.06%	0.53	0.60
t + 2 years	-0.16%	-0.29	0.77	-0.13%	0.56	0.58
t + 3 years	-0.47%	-0.84	0.40	-0.78%	1.27	0.20
			F. Mean and Median Difference High - Low			
t + 1 year	0.64%	1.10	0.27	0.29%	1.06	0.29
t + 2 years	0.27%	0.44	0.66	-0.05%	0.19	0.85
t + 3 years	0.14%	0.23	0.81	-0.33%	0.19	0.85

This table shows results from an analysis of long-term abnormal returns on operative income (AROA). Results are provided as mean ($AROA_{AV}$) and median ($AROA_{MD}$) abnormal EBITDA normalized by the average book value of assets. Abnormal returns are calculated in comparison to a control firm within the same industry, with comparable market value, and with the closest match of operative performance. AROA is provided for one, two, and three fiscal years after the announcement year. All transactions between January 1st, 1989 and December 31st, 2006 are included for which all required seller information is available until December 31st, 2009 (Panel A.). The transaction sample is then divided in months with high valuation levels (Panel B.), neutral valuations (Panel C.), and low valuations (Panel D.). Months are classified based on the de-trended industry P/E ratio of the transaction announcement month. The top half of the above median months are classified as high valuation markets, the lower half of the below median months as low markets, and the rest as neutral markets. Significance is indicated by t-statistics for means and Z-statistics for medians. To test the difference in means and medians between sub-samples a t-test for mean differences is applied and the Wilcoxon-Mann-Whitney Test for median differences. The p-values resulting from t- and Z-statistics are marked with "a" if significance is in 1% area, with "b" in 5% area, and with "c" in 10% area.

Section B

Wealth Creation of Corporate Restructuring across Industries

6. Industry Characteristics and M&A Value Creation

6.1 Introduction

Motivation for merger and acquisitions (M&A) is frequently discussed in corporate finance research. Companies acquire to realize operational synergies, gain market power, replace ineffective management, reduce market capacity, or seek financial synergies (Jensen and Ruback 1983, Morck at al. 1990). Behavioral explanations of activity add empire building, envy, and herding of managers to this list of possible reasons for M&A (Roll 1986, Goel and Thakor 2010, Bouwman et al. 2009). Motivations can depend on idiosyncratic company factors such as strategy, technology, asset productivity, and management. They are, however, also influenced by market and industry factors that determine growth and productivity prospects of the firm. Previous studies propose an important role of industry and market factors on M&A activity. Empirical evidence shows that M&A clusters in time and across industries. Numerous studies have examined the determinants of these differences in takeover activity from a market and industry perspective. The results propose that changes in industry fundamentals best explain increases in M&A activity (Mitchell and Mulherin 1996, Andrade et al. 2001, Harford 2005). Significant effects have been found, e.g., from changes in demand, variations in R&D investment requirements, new production technologies, and changes in factor costs. Companies react to these industry specific shocks with expansionary or contractory corporate restructuring. The motivation to engage in M&A can, thus, be induced by industry determinants and structural changes in these charcateristics.

In addition to research on drivers of M&A activity, a continuously growing body of studies examines the success of M&A transactions from a shareholder perspective. Studies focused on M&A success from an individual industry perspective show large variations in shareholder wealth effects across industries and sectors. These differences are frequently related to specific industry characteristics. Possible effects proposed in recent studies are, e.g., reduced value capturing in R&D intensive industries (Wang and Chung 2009), larger synergies in industries with high capital investment requirements (Devos et al. 2009), and reduced value creation from M&A in industries with high concentration levels (Shahrur 2005).

While the effect of industry characteristics on M&A activity across industries is well documented, little empirical evidence exists with regard to the implications of general industry structure and dynamics on the success of M&A transactions.

Based on the intuition that M&A value creation differs significantly across industries, this study wants to shed light on the determinants of these variations. In addition to existing research that focuses on individual firm characteristics to explain M&A success, the analysis examines M&A from a cross-industry perspective in order to provide evidence on M&A value drivers that pertain to the general industry structure and changes within this structure.

The analyses show that significant differences in corporate restructuring activity and value creation exist across European industries. These variations can be partially predicted based on generalized industry characteristics. The results show that expanding industries are more active and generate higher value creation potential from M&A than stagnant industries. Positive value effects from M&A are also observed for industries with increased capital investment needs. Further results show that takeovers in already highly concentrated industries and in industries with high debt levels are likely to reduce shareholder value.

The remainder of this paper is structured as follows: Chapter 6.2 gives an overview of related literature; Chapter 6.3 describes the applied dataset and the analytical approach; Chapter 6.4 presents and discusses the results; Chapter 6.5 draws a conclusion.

6.2 Literature review and hypotheses

6.2.1 Literature review

Numerous studies examine the causes of corporate restructuring activity. The neoclassical perspective identifies M&A as a rational investment decision by managers to increase the value of their firms. Value enhancing effects of acquisitions can be, e.g., efficiency increases through operative synergies, financial synergies due to tax reasons, the replacement of uneffective management, or increased market power (Jensen and Ruback 1983, Morck at al. 1990, Shahrur 2005, Devos et al. 2009). A group of studies takes a distinct industry perpective to explain clustering of M&A activity over time and within sectors. A number of industry specific drivers have been proposed in this research. Gort (1969) identifies economic disturbances in industries as a possible reason for firms to seek economies of scale and to establish monopolies. Dutz (1989) suggests that a sudden decline in industry demand can cause M&A activity to reduce capacity. Jensen (1993) proposes in support of this view that a majority of M&A transactions reduce capacity in reaction to technological or supply shocks.

Mitchell and Mulherin (1996) build on this idea and find empirical evidence that changes in industry fundamentals correlate with increased M&A activity. To test the effect of changes in industry structure, Mitchell and Mulherin (1996) analyze US takeover activity between 1982 and 1989. They measure industry shocks as deviations in sales and employment growth within 51 industries compared to the sample average. Possible reasons for deviations are, e.g., deregulation, changes in input factor prices or broader effects such as changes in demographics or technological innovations. They find that large changes in growth correlate with M&A activity while the level of growth does not provide a sufficient explanation of variations in takeover frequency. In addition, results show that changes in R&D spending and deregulation events have significant influence on M&A activity. Andrade and Stafford (2004) separate expansionary and contractionary M&A transactions to analyze the efffect of industry dynamics on activity. They argue that activity can be explained by industry factors that motivate firms to expand their size and scale in oder to afford large capital investments or to reduce the asset base by removing over-capacity. They test the effects of industry market-to-book valuations, cash flow levels, growth, demand shocks, concentration, and capacity utilization. The presented evidence indicates that on industry level low capacity utilization drives M&A within the same industry, supporting the role of contractionary M&A.

Harford (2005) further expands the analysis of industry specific factors that determine M&A activity. He first tests the effect of neo-classical predictors of economic shocks measured by cash flow, asset turnover, research and development (R&D), capital expenditure (CAPEX), sales and employee growth as well as return on assets. He then examines behavioral drivers using the cross-sectional standard deviation of market-to-book ratios and the 1- and 3-year stock returns to control for valuation induced M&A activity. In addition, he analyzes the effect of capital liquidity measured by the spread of commercial loans. Based on US transactions between 1981 and 2001, he finds that neo-classical factors best explain M&A activity when sufficient liquidity is present.

Shleifer and Vishny (2003) and Rhodes-Kropf and Viswanathan (2004) provide an explanation of merger activity based on the exploitation of relative overvaluation and market timing of managers. They argue that differences in valuation levels are often industry specific and lead to acquisitions of companies in relatively lower valued industries. The behavioral view on M&A frequently associates relative over-valuation with agency conflicts that can lead to value destroying M&A transactions (Jensen 2005, Gorton et al. 2009). Cremers et al. (2009) argue that aggregated cash flow shocks foster agency problems when acquirers engage in empire building with excess cash.

A large body of studies scrutinizes value creation of M&A transactions for buyers, targets, and combined entities. Despite significant variations in results, in general, a positive value effect for targets' shareholders can be observed while buyers' shareholders usually do not profit from M&A (see, e.g., Bruner 2002 or Jensen and Ruback 1983 for an overview).

This study takes special interest in value creation of acquiring firms from an inter-industry perspective. Numerous studies have examined M&A success within a specific industry or sector. The resulting industry insights provide strong evidence for large variations in value creation across industries. Examples include evidence from the automotive supply sector by Laabs and Schiereck (2010), who find significantly positive announcement returns and significantly negative long-term buy-and-hold returns; from the media and technology sector by Jope et al. (2009), who report significantly negative announcement returns; or from the banking industry by Beitel et al. (2004), who report insignificant negative announcement results. Reasons for these deviations are often found in specific industry characteristics. Wang and Chung (2009) argue that high tech acquisitions realize lower synergies, because substantial value is attached to human capital in R&D heavy industries, which is hard to retain in a merger. Chari et al. (2010) argue that industries with large intangible asset bases (e.g., patents) as in R&D intensive industries profit especially from acquisition in foreign emerging markets.

Devos et al. (2009) show that large M&A synergies stem from reductions in CAPEX investments through takeovers. Takeovers can, thus, lead to a more efficient utilization of capital. A higher level of synergies is, therefore, found for industries with large capital investment needs.

Another frequently discussed factor is industry concentration. Prior studies suggest that horizontal mergers can aim at increasing buying power and raising price levels when competition is reduced in an industry. Empirical evidence on whether M&A that increases industry collusion creates value for shareholders of the acquirer is, however, inconclusive (Eckbo 1992, Shahrur 2005, Devos et al. 2009). Hou and Robinson (2006) argue that more concentrated industries earn lower returns while more fragmented industries invest more in growth and create higher returns to shareholders. Ali et al. (2009), however, find some contradictory evidence when including private companies in the analysis.

The presented study is motivated by the insight gained from Mitchell and Mulherin (1996) and related papers that M&A activity is driven by changes in industry fundamentals. In particular, the approach of Harford (2005) to include a wide range of industry fundamentals to identify drivers of corporate restructuring activity is adapted. The focus of this study is, however, not on activity level but to identify determinants of variation in value creation of corporate restructuring across industries.

6.2.2 Specific predictions

Starting point of the presented study is the intuition that corporate restructuring activity and value creation differ significantly across industries. In addition to the evidence on industry variations in M&A activity (e.g., Mitchell and Mulherin 1996, Boone and Mulherin 2000, Andrade et al. 2001, Harford 2005, Komlenovic et al. 2011), numerous studies of M&A in specific industries show differences in M&A value creation. Therefore, a significant variation in value creation is expected across European industries.

6.H1: M&A activity and value creation differ significantly across industries.

Previous research proposes a number of industry specific factors that can influence the value creation potential of M&A. These factors include, e.g., growth prospects, R&D intensity, CAPEX requirements, asset productivity, and industry concentration (Celikyurt et al. 2010, Brown and Fung 2009, Shahrur 2005). Other industry factors, which potentially affect M&A success, refer to behavioral arguments suggesting negative effects from industry market-to-book valuations and cash flow increases (Shleifer and Vishny 2003, Cremers et al. 2009).

Industries that experience structural change are expected to benefit from M&A. This prediction is based on findings from, e.g., Mitchell and Mulherin (1996), Harford (2005), and Jovanovic and Rousseau (2008) who argue that M&A activity is influenced by industry shocks that motivate M&A decisions. Corporate restructuring is thought to be an efficient, i.e. least costly, way to adjust to fundamental change in an industry. Industry dynamic can be reflected in changes in demand and profitability, in new production technologies that change the productivity of assets, or in large variations in industry wide capital investment and R&D requirements (Maksimovic and Phillips 2001, Warusawitharana 2008, Devos et al. 2009). These industry are expected to not only determine the decision to purchase additional asset on the market for corporate control, they are also thought to increase or decrease the value creation potential of M&A.

6.H2: Industry characteristics explain deviations in M&A activity and value creation across industries.

Based on prior research, prediction regarding the effect of specific industry characteristics can be made. Recent studies propose, e.g., a relation between the investment requirement within industries and the value creation potential of M&A transactions. Devos et al. (2009) show that a significant source of M&A synergies stems from reductions in CAPEX investments through takeovers. Companies can, thus, substitute internal investments through acquisition. Wang and Chung (2009) argue, on the other hand, that industries with high R&D investment requirements realize lower synergies from M&A because substantial value is attached to human capital, which is hard to retain in a merger.

6.H2a: Industry investment requirements affect M&A value creation.

Some studies propose that industry productivity and industry asset structure may influence the success of M&A. Chari et al. (2010) argue, e.g., that industries with large intangible asset bases can profit from acquisitions, because intellectual property can be easily transferred and deployed by existing productive assets of the acquirer. Further effects are expected from the share of tangible assets (Maksimovic and Phillips 2001) and labor intensity (Wang and Chung 2009) of an industry. Besides overall asset structure of an industry, changes in asset productivity may affect M&A activity and value creation potential. Warusawitharana (2009) sets-forth that asset purchases are often a reaction to asset productivity changes that may be caused by overall industry trends.

6.H2b: Industry productivity and asset structure influence M&A value creation potential.

Shahrur (2005) examines the value implications of industry structure by analyzing horizontal mergers within an industry that increase concentration and thus market power of the acquirer. He concludes that further increases in industry collusion through M&A in already highly concentrated industries has a negative effect on wealth creation for shareholders. This finding is supported by lower shareholder returns in highly concentrated industries found by Hou and Robinson (2006). Therefore, lower value creation potential is expected for industries with high concentration levels.

6.H2c: M&A in highly concentrated industries has lower value creation potential.

6.2 Data and Methodology

6.2.1 Industry M&A Data

Companies for analysis were obtained from the Factset database. Considered for analysis were all companies with headquarters in Europe according to their regional code. The overall data sample includes active and inactive companies that could be allocated to one of 114 Industry Classification Benchmark (ICB) sub-sectors as provided by the Thomson Financial database.[18] A total of 9'168 companies with available financial information were active between January 1st, 1998 and December 31st, 2007 constituting the company data sample.

Based on the classification of active and inactive companies in industry groups, M&A activity levels and value creation of the respective industries are computed in a next step. The applied M&A data was downloaded from Thomson Reuter's SDC Platinum database and includes completed transactions announced between January 1st, 1998 and December 31st, 2007. The relatively short time frame of ten years is owed to two considerations. First reason is a decline of data availability on a detailed income statement and balance sheet level for European companies in the Thomson Financial database before 1998. To avoid any selection bias, the 10-year time frame appears most robust measured by percentage of companies with fully available datasets. The second reason considers the integration of European markets. In contrast to most previous studies that focus on the single, highly transparent US market, the decision to take a European perspective relies on aggregating industry specific factors across many local markets. The harmonization of regulations and accounting standards is therefore critical to generate viable test results. The 1998 starting point appears to secure sufficient market integration. The specific M&A transactions considered for analysis have the following further characteristics:

- Acquirer is based in Europe with headquarters in one of the European countries including Eastern Europe and Russia.
- Transaction value equals or exceeds EUR 10 million and constitutes at least 1% of the acquirers' market capitalization in the month before announcement.
- The bidder can be allocated to one of 114 ICB industries.
- More than 50% of the target's equity is transferred to a non-related acquirer.

A total of 8'181 acquisitions with matching criteria were obtained.

In a next step, ICB sub-sectors are selected for analysis. In order to ensure a sufficient number of observations to calculate abnormal returns per industry and to aggregate industry fundamentals from individual firm financials, the industry sample is reduced. The applied regime considers only industries with a minimum of ten transactions during the sample period for which short- and long-term abnormal returns can be calculated. Furthermore, only industries with at least ten

18 The ICB classification chosen for industry categorization is generated and maintained jointly by Dow Jones and FTSE. The classification of companies is conducted based on the main source of revenues of the evaluated company. The ICB system has a 4-tier structure with 10 industries, 19 supersectors, 41 sectors, and 114 sub-sectors. For further description of the Industry Classification Benchmark (ICB) see www.icbbenchmark.com.

European constituents in each year of the observation period for which the examined financial information is available are included. After applying these restrictions, 52 out of 114 ICB sub-sectors are included in the sample. 6'322 transactions remain for analysis. The applied selection regime is, however, somewhat arbitrary. I test for sensitivity to these restrictions by reducing the minimum observations to five and increasing them to 20. The results arc comparable. Another possible approach to ensure a sufficient number of observations would be to look at industries on a higher aggregation level, e.g., by applying 3- or 2-digit ICB codes. I shy away from this approach, because I see value in looking at industries on a high level of granularity. 4-digit ICB codes assure sufficient similarity in business model and asset structure, which is the prerequisite for the following analyses.

6.2.2 Industry fundamental data

In order to examine causes for variation in M&A value creation across sectors, industry characteristics are calculated based on individual firm financial information. These industry determinants are aggregated for the 520 industry years included in the sample. Two sets of industry data are computed. The first set includes annual median financials of all publicly listed companies that were active in the respective industry year. The second set of industry data comprises changes in these determinants over time. These structural change measures are defined as annual change in industry medians. The specific change value that pertains to an industry year is calculated as the 3-year average including the year considered and the two preceding years. The level of this measure indicates whether the industry has experienced fundamental changes prior and during the analyzed transaction year.

The industry determinants that are calculated in this way can be allocated to five categories of measures. The groups are: a) industry performance which includes growth and profitability measures of an industry; b) investment requirements including investments in capital and research and development; c) industry productivity referring to asset and labor productivity; d) asset/liability structure controlling for the nature of assets a firm operates and leverage; and e) industry structure referring to concentration levels. Structural change measures are considered for variations in industry performance, investment requirements, productivity measures, and changes in leverage. Median level variables are aggregated for measures in all five categories. The applied variables are described below:

a) Industry performance pertains to profitability and growth prospects of an industry.

Market-to-book (M/B): Year-end M/B variables are calculated as the ratio of companies' market price to the book value of its assets. The measure indicates the value creation potential of company assets as attributed by the capital market. Availability is limited to companies that were listed on a European stock exchange in the analyzed year. The M/B variable serves neo-classical as well as behavioral theories to explain value implications of M&A transactions. Findings from Shleifer and Vishny (2003) propose an important role of market induced over- and under-valuation on transaction activity and value creation. The behavioral view finds overvaluation as a cause of agency costs that reduce shareholder value when managers make selfish decisions (Jensen 2005). The neo-classical view identifies changes in valuation levels as an indicator of, e.g., changes in industry prospects or differences in management performance that can be exploited through M&A (Wang and Chung 2009).

Sales Growth: Sales growth is measured as annual percentage change of total year-end sales of individual companies within an industry. It determines, e.g., changes in demand within an industry. Demand reduction may lead to over-capacity that can be addressed by M&A (Andrade and Stafford 2004). A positive demand shock can in turn require additional assets or technologies that can be acquired through M&A (Mitchell and Mulherin 1996, Harford 2005).

EBITDA: Operative income measured as earnings before interests, taxes, depreciation, and amortization (EBITDA), normalized by year-end sales. The aggregated measure indicates industry profitability and proxies cash flow generated within an industry. Deviations in the profitability measure can be caused, e.g., by changes in factor costs. Warusawitharana (2008) shows in his model that firms augment their size when industry profitability increases. Cremers et al. (2009) find that aggregated cash flow shocks are, however, related to agency problems when acquirers engage in empire building with excess cash.

b) Industry Investments variables describe the investment requirements within an industry.

R&D: Research and development (R&D) spending is normalized by year-end sales and indicates the role of technology within an industry. In industries with high technology levels, R&D investment is an important driver of growth (Miyazaki 2009). Technological shock in an industry is indicated by increased R&D investment requirements (Harford 2005). Miyazaki (2009) proposes that M&A can be a less risky method to build technological know-how. Wang and Chung (2009), on the other hand, argue that R&D intensive industries fail to create sufficient synergies from M&A because they often fail to retain knowledge after a takeover.

determine the short-term abnormal return, the market model as introduced by Brown and Warner (1980) and Brown and Warner (1985) is applied. Following the market model approach, abnormal returns are determined using Equation (6.1).

$$(6.1) \qquad AR_{it} = R_{it} - \left(\alpha_i + \beta_i \cdot R_{mt}\right)$$

R_{it} represents the stock return of company i in period t, while R_{mt} describes the return of the specific 4-digit European ICB industry index of the acquiring company's industry. The market model parameters are calculated using Ordinary Least Squares (OLS) regression over a period of 180 trading days prior to the largest event window that is set at 20 days before the announcement. Cumulative abnormal returns (CAR) are then calculated by summing the abnormal returns over different event windows (Equation (6.2)).

$$(6.2) \qquad CAR_{EventWindow(m1,m2)} = \sum_{m1}^{m2} AR_{it}$$

Statistical significance is tested with the standardized cross-sectional-test proposed by Boehmer et al. (1991). The parametric Generalized-Sign-Test (Cowan et al. 1990) is conducted as additional robustness check (not reported).

The approach to determine long-term transaction success applies buy-and-hold abnormal returns (BHAR) in event-time proposed by Barber and Lyon (1997) and Lyon et al. (1999). The BHAR of acquiring companies are determined by constructing monthly reference portfolios of non-merging firms. As proposed by Fama and French (1993), year-end market-to-book ratios (M/B) of year t-1 and the market value on the last trading day of June are used to construct the reference portfolios in order to account for differences in return between small and large as well as between value and growth companies. All listed companies included in the data sample are divided at their median in two equally sized M/B- and two equal size-groups within each of the 52 ICB sub-sectors. Companies with zero or negative M/B figures and companies with a market value of below EUR 10 mn are removed from the sample. 208 size- and M/B-portfolios result from the classification for which equally weighted average returns are calculated. The resulting portfolio returns are free of the rebalancing bias and the new listing bias found by Lyon et al. (1999). Included in the monthly changing reference portfolios are all companies that did not acquire or divest in the 36 months prior to the respective month. Reference portfolio returns are calculated by first compounding returns of the portfolio constituents and then summing across securities (Bouwman et al. 2009). Equation (6.3) illustrates the computation.

(6.3) $$R_{referenceportfolio,T} = \sum_{j=1}^{n_s} \frac{\left[\prod_{t=s}^{s+T}\left(1+R_{jt}\right)\right]-1}{n_s}$$

$R_{referenceportfolio,T}$ describes the monthly returns of the reference portfolio, R_{jt} is the simple return of portfolio company *j* in month *t*, and n_s is the number of portfolio firms in the respective industry size-M/B portfolio. *T* represents the investment horizon. The abnormal returns of the event firms are calculated following Equation (6.4).

(6.4) $$BHAR_{iT} = \prod_{t=s}^{s+T}(1+R_{it}) - \prod_{t=s}^{s+T}(1+R_t)$$

R_{it} describes the monthly returns of the bidder. The BHAR are calculated for a 24-month period.

In addition, to the event-time analysis of abnormal long-term returns, a calendar-time approach is applied. The 4-factor model (FF4F) addresses some of the shortcomings of the BHAR methodology, e.g., the cross-sectional correlation of firms in event-time (Mitchell and Stafford 2000). It is however potentially exposed to other pitfalls, e.g., heteroscedasticity. The 4-factor model determines excess returns of a portfolio of sample firms by regressing the time series of (i) the markets excess return, (ii) the differences in return between small and large firms, (iii) the excess returns of high vs. low book-to-market (B/M) companies, and (iv) the Carhart (1997) momentum factor. The model takes the form of Equation (6.5).

(6.5) $$R_{pt} - R_{ft} = a_p + b_p\left(R_{mt} - R_{ft}\right) + s_p SMB + h_p HML + m_p PR1YR + e_{pt}$$

R_{pt} is the return of a continuously changing portfolio of companies or subgroups of these companies that conducted acquisitions within the preceding 24 months. The acquirer portfolio is reconstructed on a monthly basis when new bidders are included and inactive companies leave after the 24-month period. R_{mt} - R_{ft} represents the market factor, calculated by subtracting the risk free rate (three months Euribor after 1999, Libor until 1999) from the value weighted market portfolio (Europe DS-Total Market index). SMB is the size factor that is determined by the return of a portfolio of big company stocks minus the return of a portfolio of small company stocks. All European companies included in the data sample are ranked based on their market value on the last trading day of June each year. The median is used to split the companies into big (B) and small (S) portfolios. HML is the book-to-market factor that is formed by subtracting high B/M value stocks and low B/M growth stocks. The portfolios are formed by ranking the companies according to their B/M level and distributing the top and bottom

30% to the respective portfolios (H and L) and the remaining 40% in a medium portfolio (M). Six portfolios are created each year (S/L, S/M, S/H, B/L, B/M, and B/H). The SMB portfolio is supposed to replicate the risk factor in returns related to size. It is calculated using the average of the monthly returns on the three small (S) portfolios minus the three big (B) portfolios. The HML portfolio mimics the risk factor related to book-to-market valuation and is calculated in the same way using the two high (H) and the two low (L) portfolios. Due to simple averaging of the portfolios the factors should be largely free of the other factor's effect. In addition, a momentum factor is included to account for portfolio momentum effects as proposed by Carhart (1997). PR1YR is the return differentials of two equally weighted portfolios constructed out of firms with the highest and lowest 30% of eleven months returns prior to the announcement month. The coefficients b_p, s_p, h_p, and m_p determine the loading of the respective factor indicating the composition of the sample portfolio and the factor's effect on returns. The a_p coefficient is the intercept of the model and represents the monthly return of the sample portfolio over a 24-month period that cannot be explained by the four factors. The sum of the error terms e_{pt} is assumed to be zero.

All applied data is downloaded from Datastream. Ince and Porter (2006) hint to a number of potential flaws when using individual company share data from Datastream. The adjustments proposed by Ince and Porter (2006) (e.g., removing American Depository Receipts (ADR), illogical data entries, and extreme returns) have been applied to all data. The inclusion of unadjusted returns leads to comparable analysis results.

After data cleaning, a total of 3'562 CAR and 1'805 BHAR remain for analysis. Table 6.1 provides an overview of the applied data sample.

Table 6.1: Descriptive overview of the applied industry data sample - M&A

ICB sector	Number of Companies	Total Market Cap. in EUR	Number of Acquisitions	Average Transaction Value in EUR mn	Total Transactions Value in EUR mn	Activity Index	3-day CAR in %	N	24-month BHAR in %	N
Exploration & Production (533)	104	78'839	63	142	17'433	32.67	1.22	45	-4.39	37
Integrated Oil & Gas (537)	36	2'370'059	94	3'090	197'751	23.44	0.30	36	32.20**	21
Oil Equipment & Services (573)	68	104'637	78	152	13'396	32.18	-0.66	49	14.17	30
Specialty Chemicals (1357)	103	287'368	131	577	92'378	26.11	1.20**	79	-21.98***	86
Paper (1737)	19	58'483	40	639	26'838	23.81	-0.75	28	-0.60	26
Iron & Steel (1757)	49	280'915	64	1'046	85'788	26.83	0.54	31	-30.18**	20
General Mining (1775)	58	433'134	74	916	72'384	35.56	0.06	52	-19.30**	14
Building Materials (1775)	146	277'144	233	276	64'057	19.13	0.78***	118	-7.68*	48
Heavy Construction (2357)	87	216'490	187	263	43'849	26.95	1.76***	140	4.04	97
Aerospace (2713)	20	81'598	99	136	3'808	35.71	0.96**	76	-3.62	23
Containers & Packaging (2723)	43	27'281	55	185	10'159	27.27	1.02***	48	-19.24***	19
Diversified Industrials (2727)	40	61'395	92	136	8'155	33.33	1.92***	59	-7.47	47
Electrical Components (2733)	87	66'871	91	261	32'832	19.51	1.25	74	29.98***	37
Electronic Equipment (2737)	133	294'984	126	390	68'328	22.99	0.62	69	-12.21	46
Commercial Vehicles (2753)	54	109'161	40	184	16'049	19.54	1.76	28	9.46	12
Industrial Machinery 2757)	205	247'228	202	108	36'576	23.58	1.61***	144	-15.81***	84
Transportation Services (2777)	51	104'103	94	134	12'499	32.97	0.59	48	-36.26***	16
Business Support Services	174	96'517	376	79	22'371	37.99	1.09***	267	6.26*	83
Busi Train. & Eplmt. Ag. (2793)	59	38'512	89	138	11'882	37.21	-0.04	47	-11.77	14
Industrial Suppliers (2797)	30	48'053	111	130	6'352	36.73	1.45***	72	4.28	24
Automobiles (3353)	31	319'549	36	1'545	60'269	30.77	1.28**	21	-15.46	34
Auto Parts (3355)	60	32'006	29	150	12'614	12.05	0.88	20	-14.82	16
Brewers (3533)	36	154'461	43	598	31'674	15.09	1.29	21	12.24	17
Food Products (3577)	166	618'416	256	445	109'452	25.82	1.00***	176	-1.61	88

Continued on next page

Continued from previous page

Home Construction (3728)	17	26'294	40	354	12'025	44.12	2.50**	22	-14.93	11
Clothing & Accessories (3763)	154	203'897	63	172	38'329	13.00	3.25***	39	-13.76	10
Medical Equipment (4535)	65	58'561	58	135	11'045	25.61	2.35**	26	15.09	19
Biotechnology (4573)	109	43'995	76	83	11'683	25.93	0.36	46	-5.74	14
Pharmaceuticals (4577)	114	1'077'524	147	1'071	159'636	34.69	0.56	91	6.79	40
Food Retailers (5337)	32	262'893	86	608	40'135	36.36	-0.16	49	3.45	38
Broadline Retailers (5373)	28	103'648	48	253	13'176	32.00	0.26	40	-16.25*	29
Specialty Retailers (5379)	66	41'051	83	84	10'205	24.37	0.45**	60	8.96	23
Broadc.. & Entertain. (5553)	124	175'979	155	722	118'464	27.95	0.08	86	-4.07	24
Publishing (5557)	123	190'225	259	246	43'264	34.13	0.66	125	-9.04**	40
Airlines (5751)	18	88'330	15	246	7'637	25.81	1.67	12	-8.90	20
Hotels (5751)	38	44'513	64	124	8'465	27.27	0.71**	17	-8.02	22
Restaurants & Bars (5757)	46	74'344	73	291	20'669	32.86	1.35***	60	18.75**	37
Travel & Tourism (5759)	40	33'533	104	187	13'838	20.55	-0.39	66	-11.08	27
Fixed Line Telco. (6535)	75	777'887	201	1'325	147'031	25.45	0.93**	87	-10.89	41
Conventional Electr. (7535)	138	646'393	98	774	171'093	8.45	0.38	40	15.23**	13
Alternative Electricity (7537)	37	55'257	23	311	14'935	17.39	2.8	17	-17.19	13
Multiutilities (7575)	11	442'367	91	1'387	24'958	27.78	0.27	36	-53.42**	41
Water (7577)	18	90'960	50	157	4'721	27.59	-0.47	29	11.02	19
Banks (8355)	222	3'133'367	793	833	290'879	20.92	-0.25**	272	-9.85***	155
Full Line Insurance (8532)	21	470'873	152	838	44'401	26.42	-0.28	45	4.91	45
Life Insurance (8575)	23	433'679	209	597	24'472	46.34	0.23	83	17.36**	61
Asset Managers (8771)	33	49'660	74	143	8'270	20.69	1.16**	58	-18.26**	17

Continued on next page

Continued from previous page

Computer Services (9533)	210	47'245	233	161	49'908	29.97	2.02***	148	-1.97	27
Internet (9535)	84	23'922	74	227	24'982	27.78	0.71	37	-17.44*	14
Software (9537)	250	148'092	235	85	31'379	24.03	1.13***	144	-5.34	24
Computer Hardware (9572)	52	9'107	15	75	5'356	11.27	3.29**	11	13.60	11
Telco. Equipment (9578)	82	327'388	110	518	56'474	27.78	2.68***	68	-12.5	31
Sum	4'089	15'488'1	6'332		2'464'323			3'562		1'805
Average	79	297'850	122	456	47'391	27.00	0.89***		-2.94**	
Median	59	104'370	90	250	24'970	26.89	0.44		-7.54	
Minimum	11	9'107	15	75	3'808	8.45	-0.75		-53.42**	
Maximum	4089	15'488'1	6'332	3'090	2'464'323	46.34	3.29**		32.20**	

The table provides the summary statistics of the applied M&A data sample split into 52 ICB sub-sectors. Out of the total of 114 sub-sectors, those were selected with at least ten active listed companies and at least ten transactions for which CAR and 24-month BHAR could be calculated. Further industries that include mainly investment vehicles were removed (e.g., REITs, Private Equity companies, etc.). Company data was obtained from Factset. Companies were included in the observation when they are based in Europe according to the Factset region code (Western and Eastern Europe including Russia), when they could be allocated to an ICB sub-sectors based on data from Thomson Financial, and when they were active in the ten years between January 1st, 1998 and December 31st, 2007. Activity is measured by availability of sales data in the Thomson Financial database for all companies and by availability of market value in the Datastream database for listed companies. Companies are counted as active when at least one year with available data exists over the ten years included in the sample. Transaction data was obtained from the SDC Platinum database. Transactions were included in the analysis when they were announced between January 1st, 1998 and December 31st, 2007 and could be allocated to one of the companies of the European set of industry sorted companies obtained from Factset. Transactions were selected only when more then 50% of equity changed hands to an unrelated acquirer, the transaction value was available, and the transaction value exceeded EUR 10 mn. The activity index is calculated by share of companies within an industry that were involved in M&A transactions during the 10-year period analyzed. The equity index is composed as share of industry market capitalization involved in M&A compared to overall industry market capitalization as of December 31st, 2007. This measure is, however, not fully precise because companies that are not active at the end of the sample period are not included. CAR values report the cumulated abnormal announcement returns three days around the transactions announcement for the 52 ICB sub-sectors. BHAR are reported for 24 months after announcement. Statistically significant values are marked with "***" in the 1% confidence interval; with "**" in the 5% interval; and with "*" in the 10% interval.

Table 6.2: Test of differences in industry means for activity and value creation – M&A

	All	**Inter-Industry**	**Intra-Industry**
		A. Transaction Activity	
Number of industries	52	52	52
Mean Deal Activity Companies %	27.00	30.32	17.90
Min %	8.45	7.51	4.48
Max %	46.32	40.93	34.32
Pearson Chi-square-Test p-value	<0.01***	<0.01***	<0.01***
		B. Transaction value creation at announcement (3-day CAR)	
Number of Transactions	3'561	1'951	1'472
Mean CAR %	0.88***	0.87***	0.91***
Median CAR %	0.44	0.44	0.45
Min %	-0.75	-1.50	-1.22
Max %	3.29**	5.82	4.97***
ANOVA F-test p-value	<0.01***	0.03**	0.31
		C. Transaction value creation 24-month post-transacation (BHAR)	
Number of Transactions	2'668	1'519	1'048
Mean BHAR %	-2.94**	-3.55***	-2.03
Median BHAR %	-7.54	-8.19	-7.29
Min %	-53.42**	-41.97**	-46.77***
Max %	32.20**	29.93*	40.71**
ANOVA F-test p-value	<0.01***	<0.01***	<0.01***

The table shows results from tests of mean differences in M&A activity and value creation across 52 ICB sub-sectors. The activity level is determined by (i) share of companies within an industry that are involved in M&A activity as a buyer in the ten-year period between 1998 and 2007 and (ii) the share of acquirers equity in relation to industry equity in this period. The difference in means across industries is tested with two chi-square tests: the Pearson Chi-square-Test and the Likelihood Chi-square-Test. Reported are p-values of the respective tests. Value creation is measured as 3-day abnormal announcement return (CAR) and 24-month buy-and-hold return to acquirers' shareholders. The mean in differences is tested with an ANOVA test of mean differences. The transaction sample is split in inter-industry and intra-industry M&A. Inter-industry activity is defined as takeovers in which the acquired asset has a different 3-digit SIC code from the acquiring company. Intra-industry transactions show a corresponding SIC code. The independent variables are industry median levels and median change (Panel B.).The p-values of the F-statistic are reported. Significance levels resulting from t-, z-, and F-statistics are marked with *** in 1%, with ** in 5%, and with * in 10% confidence interval.

To test the predicted difference in value creation, a one-way ANOVA test[21] of mean differences in 3-day CAR and 24-month BHAR across industries is calculated. Panel B. in Table 6.2 shows significantly positive CAR of 0.88% for the overall sample, 0.87% for inter-industry transactions, and 0.91% for intra-indus-

21 The F-test of one-way ANOVA assesses if the industry CAR and BHAR are significantly different from each other based on the industry means and the variances of results. The results do not indicate which industry means significantly differ. The equation of the one-way Anova test is:

$$F = \frac{Explained\ s^2}{Unexplained\ s^2} \quad with\ Explained\ s^2 = \sum_i n_i \left(\bar{Y}_i - \bar{Y}\right)^2 / (K-1) \quad and\ Unexplained\ s^2 = \sum_{ij} \left(Y_{ij} - \bar{Y}_i\right)^2 / (N-K)$$

Y_i is the sample mean in the ith industry, n_i is the number of observations ,Y represents the overall mean of the data. Y_{ij} is the jth observation in the ith industry out of K industry groups. N is the overall sample size.

try transactions. The industry results show a large variation in announcement returns from insignificant -0.75% (Paper) to significant 3.29% (Computer Hardware) for the overall sample. Inter- and intra-industry transactions exhibit even larger ranges of CAR. The results indicate on average a positive short-term value effect of M&A transactions for the European data sample over the ten analyzed years. Bruner (2002) finds in his summary of M&A studies that takeovers on average destroy value or are at least value neutral for acquirers' shareholders. However, he also reports large variations in results. The differences in results to the majority of studies analyzed by Bruner (2002) may be caused by a focus on US-transactions of the included studies and potentially an improvement in announcement returns within the last decade. The results of the ANOVA F-statistic show that industry CAR are significantly different for the overall sample and for inter-industry transactions. The intra-industry results do not show significant differences in announcement returns.

Panel C. provides results for industry BHAR. The average of the full sample shows a negative abnormal value effect of -2.94% over 24 months. The industry specific results indicate a large range of BHAR across industries. The overall sample has a minimum of -53.42% (Multi-Utilities) and a maximum industry BHAR of 32.20% (Integrated Oil and Gas). The inter- and intra-industry sample show comparable means and ranges. The p-values of the one-way ANOVA test clearly indicate that BHAR differ across industry groups for all analyzed transactions samples.

All above findings are robust to the use of alternative industry classification schemes. Table 6.8 (Appendix) contains the results of the analysis for different classification schemes. The results support Hypothesis 6.H1.

6.3.2 Industry determinants of M&A activity

In order to test the effect of different industry characteristics on the level of annual industry M&A activity, two groups of independent variables are regressed with the activity level of the 520 industry years included in the sample. Yearly activity is measured as share of acquiring companies within an industry in the respective year (Mitchell and Mulherin 1996). The two groups of independent variables are the industry median levels (Panel A.) and median changes over time (Panel B.). Table 6.3 presents the regression results.

Panel A. in Table 6.3 shows the effects of industry level variables on transaction activity. The coefficients indicate a positive influence of high industry market valuation, growth levels, and, to a smaller extend, profitability on transaction activity. These results suggest that higher growth and higher margins increase M&A activity on an industry level. The effect on activity is stronger for transactions within the same industry sub-sector, proposing that companies seek to profit from good market prospects and expanding demand in their core markets by growing their business through M&A (Maksimovic and Phillips 2001).

Table 6.3: Regression of industry M&A activity levels

	A. Industry Level			**B. Industry Dynamic**		
	(1)	(2)	(3)	(4)	(5)	(6)
Intercept	0.080 (4.74)	0.087 (4.99)	0.087 (4.99)	0.094 (31.33***)	0.095 (31.69***)	0.095 (31.41***)
M/B	0.014 (3.89***)		0.010 (2.63***)	0.004 (1.39)		0.001 (0.27)
SalesGrowth		0.074 (2.48**)	0.051 (1.66*)		-0.001 (-0.44)	0.000 (0.02)
EBITDA		0.098 (1.80*)	0.057 (1.02)	0.164 (2.32**)		0.155 (2.10**)
R&D	-0.018 (-0.66)	0.016 (0.58)	-0.001 (-0.22)	-0.005 (-0.21)	-0.007 (-0.27)	-0.006 (-0.24)
CAPEX	0.341 (2.08**)	0.398 (2.45**)	0.304 (1.83*)	-0.065 (-0.35)	-0.102 (-0.56)	-0.088 (-0.47)
AssetTurnover	-0.023 (-3.59***)	-0.013 (-1.81*)	-0.018 (-2.46**)	-0.080 (-4.77***)	-0.078 (-4.46***)	-0.081 (-4.51***)
LaborProductivity	0.076 (5.63***)	0.076 (5.57***)	0.074 (5.50***)	0.251 (6.96***)	0.246 (6.73***)	0.245 (2.84***)
Leverage	0.046 (1.12)	0.015 (0.35)	0.034 (0.81)	0.148 (2.73**)	0.158 (2.90***)	0.155 (2.84***)
PPE	-0.059 (-3.21***)	-0.060 (-3.26***)	-0.054 (-2.89***)			
Intangibles	0.039 (0.88)	0.067 (1.54)	0.047 (1.07)			
HHI	0.091 (2.40**)	0.091 (2.36**)	0.093 (2.45**)			
YearDummy	Yes	Yes	Yes	Yes	No	Yes
F-Statistic	13.44***	11.91***	11.63***	12.35***	11.31***	9.95***
R^2 adjusted	0.202	0.197	0.207	0.122	0.128	0.128

This table presents OLS regressions of industry M&A activity levels. The dependent variable is the annual transaction activity of companies within 52 ICB industries. A total of 520 industries years are regressed over the ten year period from 1998 to 2007. Activity is measured on a transaction basis as share of companies that have been acquiring in the respective year compared to all active companies in that industry year. The independent variables are measured as: (i.) industry median level in the announcement year (Panel A.) and (ii.) industry dynamic measured as average median change over three years from two years before the transaction to the transaction year (Panel B.). The statistical significance of the coefficiencts is tested with a t-statistic. The statistical fit of the model is indicated by the adjusted determination coefficient R^2 adjusted and F-statistic. The test values are marked with "***" if significance is in 1% area, with "**" in 5% area, and with "*" in 10% area.

CAPEX intensive industries are also more active. Industries that require large recurring capital investments show higher activity when companies substitute internal investments with external acquisitions (Devos et al. 2009).

Another observation is that industries with high asset turnover levels show lower M&A activity while high labor productivity leads to increased M&A activity. This finding suggests that asset intensive industries more frequently engage in M&A, while industries which are more labor intensive are less active. A potential reason for this is the ability of asset intensive companies to employ additional assets with existing labor resources, realizing synergies through more efficient operation of the increased asset stock. The negative coefficient for the PPE variable shows that this effect is not driven by physical assets like production plants, but rather by intangible assets like patents and by financial assets that can be more easily transferred and operated with existing resources of the acquirer.

The industry concentration measured as normalized HHI shows a positive effect. The result suggests that highly concentrated, mature industries seek further growth through acquisitions when the organic growth potential is limited and market position becomes more significant to increase buying power and pursue monopoly rents (Shahrur 2005). This finding is consistent with results from Hou and Robinson (2006) who show that fragmented industry show higher organic investments in R&D and asset stock.

Panel B. shows the effects of changes in industry fundamentals. The results propose that increases in profitability lead to higher M&A activity. The sales growth results are insignificant when included in the multiple regression model for ICB industries. Other industry classifications, however, show significantly positive regression coefficients for increases in industry growth. The positive effect of increasing profitability and thus, cash flows, proposes that companies apply excess cash to grow their business inorganically when industry performance increases.

Increases in industry asset turnover decrease industry transaction activity, while higher labor productivity has a positive effect on activity. The result indicates that a reduction in asset productivity within an industry increases the motivation of industry constituents to engage in M&A to more efficiently operate the asset stock. Higher labor productivity has a reciprocal effect. When companies experience reduction in labor intensity, they are motivated to increase the asset stock operated by its labor force.

Increases in industry wide debt levels (leverage) increases M&A activity. A possible explanation could be the attempt of companies to reduce leverage through the acquisition of firms with lower debt levels with own shares (Harford et al. 2009). Another explanation for increased leverage in highly active industries could be that the increase in debt is caused by additional borrowing to engage in M&A.

The results support the hypotheses under 6.H2 with regard to M&A activity levels.

Table 6.4: 3-day CAR results for industry groups - M&A

Quintiles	Performance			Investment		Productivity		Asset/Liability Structure			Ind. Structure
	M/B	**Sales Growth**	**EBITDA**	**R&D**	**CAPEX**	**Asset Turnover**	**Labor Product.**	**Leverage**	**PPE**	**Intangibles**	**HHI**
					A. Industry Level						
1	0.75% (3.18***)	0.50% (2.23**)	0.53% (3.87***)	1.06% (5.06***)	0.67% (4.10***)	0.13% (0.38)	1.21% (8.44***)	1.22% (6.55***)	1.02% (5.94***)	0.04% (0.39)	0.87% (8.68***)
5	0.99% (6.06***)	0.55% (3.70***)	0.03% (0.12)	1.06% (4.95***)	0.91% (5.86***)	1.22% (7.56***)	0.26% (1.69**)	0.24% (1.80**)	0.52% (4.13***)	0.92% (6.98***)	0.65% (2.37***)
5 - 1	0.24% (0.75)	0.05% (0.17)	-0.50% (-1.60)	0.00% (0.01)	0.24% (0.91)	1.09% (3.13***)	-0.95% (-3.22***)	-0.98% (-3.29***)	-0.50% (-1.74*)	0.87% (3.16***)	-0.22% (-0.54)
					B. Industry Dynamic						
1	0.55% (3.77***)	0.69% (3.67***)	0.58% (3.05***)	1.29% (6.74***)	0.26% (2.13**)	1.17% (7.68***)	0.71% (2.97***)	0.91% (4.42***)			
5	1.28% (7.60***)	0.75% (3.67***)	0.99% (5.67***)	0.76% (4.06***)	1.38% (6.48***)	0.80% (4.93***)	0.21% (1.41*)	0.55% (3.03***)			
5 – 1	0.73% (2.75***)	0.06% (0.22)	0.41% (1.37)	-0.54% (-1.64)	1.12% (3.59***)	-0.37% (-1.45)	-0.50% (-1.34)	-0.36% (-1.12)			

The table shows results from an analysis of short-term abnormal returns (3-day CAR) to acquirers' shareholders from an industry perspective. Each industry transaction year (520 over the ten year period) is ranked based on the absolute level of the tested variable in the transaction year. The ranked industry years are then divided into quintiles to test the effect of the relative size of the variable on the transaction success. The table reports the first and fifth quintile results and the mean differences between the two. Industry level parameters (Panel A.) are calculated as median industry values of the transaction year. Industry dynamic measures (Panel B.) are calculated as the average of the absolute annual change in the three years from two years before transaction year to the transaction year. Statistical significance is tested using the standardized cross-sectional test for the group means. Significance of mean differences is tested with a t-test. T- and z-values are marked with *** in the 1% confidence interval, with ** in the 5% confidence interval, and with * in the 10% confidence interval.

Table 6.5: 24-month BHAR results for industry groups - M&A

	Performance			Investment		Productivity		Asset/Liability Structure			Ind. Structure
Quintiles	**M/B**	**Sales Growth**	**EBITDA**	**R&D**	**CAPEX**	**Asset Turnover**	**Labor Product.**	**Leverage**	**PPE**	**Intangibles**	**HHI**
					A. Industry Level						
1	0.20% (0.06)	-7.34% (-1.99**)	-2.34% (-0.41)	-3.15% (-1.00)	-2.32% (-0.45)	2.89% (0.40)	4.31% (1.66*)	2.72% (0.53)	-5.81% (-1.56)	10.96% (1.05)	-0.93% (-0.49)
5	4.61% (1.29)	2.19% (0.70)	-11.41% (-1.41)	5.01% (0.87)	7.33% (1.55)	7.55% (2.61***)	4.89% (0.57)	-12.34% (2.58***)	-5.55% (-1.31)	-2.02% (-0.69)	-13.02% (-1.88*)
5 - 1	4.40% (0.81)	10.12% (1.89*)	-9.07% (-1.21)	8.16% (1.28)	9.66% (1.35)	4.67% (0.43)	0.57% (0.07)	-15.06% (-2.01**)	0.25% (0.05)	-12.98% (-1.04)	-12.09% (-1.72*)
					B. Industry Dynamic						
1	1.45% (0.48)	-4.20% (-1.33)	-1.80% (-0.41)	0.75% (0.21)	-4.20% (-1.42)	-3.73% (-1.42)	-2.07% (-0.49)	-3.68% (-0.94)			
5	-0.63% (-0.20)	-1.72% (-0.52)	-4.39% (-1.06)	3.27% (0.86)	1.67% (0.43)	-7.80% (-1.89*)	-2.49% (-0.47)	-8.94% (-2.03**)			
5 – 1	-2.08% (-0.47)	2.48% (0.61)	-2.59% (-0.39)	2.52% (0.44)	5.87% (1.01)	-4.06% (-0.78)	-0.41% (-0.06)	-5.26% (-0.83)			

The table shows results from an analysis of long-term abnormal returns (24-month BHAR) to acquirers' shareholders from an industry perspective. Each industry transaction year (520 over the ten year period) is ranked based on the absolute level of the tested variable in the transaction year. The ranked industry years are then divided into quintiles to test the effect of the relative size of the variable on the transaction success. The table reports the first and fifth quintile results and the mean differences between the two. Industry level parameters (Panel A.) are calculated as median industry values of the transaction year. Industry dynamic measures (Panel B.) are calculated as the average of the absolute annual change in the three years from two years before transaction year to the transaction year. t-values are marked with *** in the 1% confidence interval, with ** in the 5% confidence interval, and with * in the 10% confidence interval.

Panel B. shows results for changes in industry dynamics. The mean differences, however, do not show significant effects from changes in industry structure.

Table 6.6 shows the results of an analysis of long-term abnormal returns in calendar-time (FF4F). The methodologies applied to test the effects of the examined industry factors follows the same approach as for the BHAR analysis. In order to test the effect of industry fundamentals on abnormal returns, monthly returns of acquirer portfolios formed with companies from the first and fifths quintile of the tested industry variable are regressed with the Fama-French factors. Abnormal returns are then indicated by the intercept of the model. In addition, returns of a short-long portfolio of fifth and first quintile companies are regressed to determine performance differences between the two groups. Table 6.6 reports the respective intercepts (a_p) and corresponding p-values in brackets.

The results mostly confirm the BHAR results. They are, however, less strong. Loughran and Ritter (2000) argue that the calendar time approach has less power to detect abnormal returns because it averages over time periods and, thus, does not account for managers' timing decision. The FF4F results show a significant outperformance of industries with high CAPEX levels underlining the previous BHAR findings. The results also confirm negative value effects from M&A in highly concentrated industries compared to less fragmented industries. In contrast to the BHAR findings, a significantly positive monthly abnormal return is found for industries in the fifth EBITDA quintile. The long-term results, thus, also provide evidence for Hypothesis 6.H2a by showing that industries with high capital investment requirements can realize higher synergies from more efficient utilization of capital. This finding is in line with results from Devos et al. (2009) on individual firm level. BHAR and FF4F also show that M&A in already highly concentrated industries destroys shareholder value in the long-run, while takeovers in more fragmented industries have a positive value effect (Hypothesis 6.H2c). In general, the descriptive results support Hypothesis 6.H2 with regard to the power of industry determinants and changes in industry structure to predict M&A value creation.

In order to further evaluate the effects of industry determinates on M&A value creation, the examined industry variables are tested in a multiple regression model. Table 6.7 provides the results. Panel A. shows the outcome of the regression of 3-day CAR with annual median industry determinants (Industry Level) and median changes (Industry Dynamics). Panel B. contains the respective results for 24-month BHAR

.

Table 6.6: Long-term value creation in calendar-time (FF4F) for industry groups - M&A

	Performance			Investment		Productivity		Asset/Liability Structure			Ind. Structure
Quintiles	**M/B**	**Sales Growth**	**EBITDA**	**R&D**	**CAPEX**	**Asset Turnover**	**Labor Product.**	**Leverage**	**PPE**	**Intangibles**	**HHI**
					A. Industry Level						
1	0.001 [0.905]	0.001 [0.530]	0.001 [0.502]	0.006 [0.071]	-0.002 [0.484]	-0.000 [0.954]	0.002 [0.512]	0.002 [0.343]	0.001 [0.543]	0.002 [0.543]	0.004 [0.144]
5	-0.001 [0.605]	0.000 [0.846]	0.006 [0.069]	-0.001 [0.666]	0.007 [0.046]	0.001 [0.649]	0.005 [0.081]	-0.002 [0.365]	-0.002 [0.343]	0.002 [0.584]	-0.003 [0.246]
5 - 1	-0.001 [0.726]	-0.002 [0.524]	0.004 [0.107]	-0.004 [0.219]	0.009 [0.031]	0.002 [0.675]	0.003 [0.193]	-0.004 [0.289]	-0.002 [0.313]	-0.001 [0.847]	-0.007 [0.089]
					B. Industry Dynamic						
1	-0.000 [0.885]	-0.001 [0.905]	-0.002 [0.596]	0.002 [0.412]	0.001 [0.728]	0.001 [0.405]	0.001 [0.622]	0.003 [0.113]			
5	0.003 [0.244]	0.001 [0.905]	0.002 [0.512]	0.001 [0.757]	0.007 [0.032]	0.001 [0.805]	0.006 [0.081]	0.001 [0.543]			
5 - 1	0.003 [0.227]	0.003 [0.232]	0.003 [0.296]	-0.001 [0.699]	0.006 [0.105]	0.000 [0.952]	0.004 [0.121]	-0.002 [0.200]			

This table presents alphas from 4-factor (FF4F) portfolio regressions. The reported intercept represents the monthly abnormal return of a continuously adapted portfolio of acquiring companies that bought within the 24 months preceding the respective month. The analysis is conducted for portfolios constructed from companies in an industry that belongs to the lowest (1) and highest 20% (5) of industries ranked by the respective tested variable. In addition, a long-short portfolio of the two groups is regressed. The coefficients "b", "s", "h", and "m" represent the loadings of the regressed market factors (not reported). "b" is the classical beta coefficient of the market excess return. "s" expresses the composition of the acquirers portfolio in terms of size distribution while "h" indicates the same for value vs. growth distribution. "m" indicates the effects of momentum within the market portfolio. The classic t-statistic is conducted to test significance. The statistical fit of the model is indicated by the adjusted determination coefficient R^2 adjusted (not reported). p-values of the coefficients are provided in brackets.

The regression results for transaction CAR in Panel A. support the descriptive findings of the quintile analysis. The *AssetTurnover* coefficient shows a positive effect on M&A value creation of high asset turnover levels while high leverage (*Leverage*) negatively affects shareholder returns at announcement. The results for *PPE* and *Intangibles* are less significant than in the quintile analysis. They, however, provide some indication in support of the previous finding that companies with high shares of intangible assets create more shareholder value through takeovers than in industries with large tangible assets bases. With regard to changes in the examined industry factors, the short-term results in the Industry Dynamic column show significantly positive coefficients for *M/B* levels and the *CAPEX* variable. A significantly negative coefficient is reported for the *LaborProductivity* variable. The results propose in line with the previous findings that industries with increasing investment requirements and positive future growth prospects show higher shareholder returns at announcement. An additional finding of the regression analysis is the significantly negative coefficient for the *R&D* level variable. Wang and Chung (2009) propose that higher R&D intensity can negatively affect value capturing from M&A. They argue that acquirers often fail to retain knowledge when key personnel leave the company after takeovers. The coefficient for the industry *SalesGrowth* variable is only insignificantly positive when included in the multiple regressions. The results for alternative industry classifications in Table 6.9 (Appendix) show, however, a consistently positive coefficient indicating that M&A in expanding industries creates more shareholder value in the long-term.

The BHAR regression in Panel B. shows a significantly positive coefficient for the *CAPEX* and *LaborProductivity* variables in the Industry Level column. Significantly negative coefficients are found for industries with high debt levels (*Leverage*) and high concentration levels (*HHI*). The industry change variables in the Industry Dynamic column are only significant for *LaborProductivity* with a positive coefficient. The results propose that companies acquiring in industries with high investment requirements return more to shareholders than companies in less investment intensive industries. High leverage and industry collusion, on the other hand, reduce the value creation potential of takeovers.

Table 6.7: Regression of 3-day CAR and 24-month BHAR for industry groups - M&A

	A. Short-term abnormal returns (3-day CAR)				B. Long-term abnormal returns (24-month BHAR)			
	Industry Level		Industry Dynamic		Industry Level		Industry Dynamic	
	(1)	(2)	(3)	(4)	(5)	(6)	(7)	(8)
Intercept	-1.88% (-1.49)	-0.73% (-0.59)	1.01% (9.61***)	1.05% (9.89***)	2.78% (0.32)	4.87% (0.52)	-2.50% (-1.83*)	-2.79% (-2.10**)
M/B	0.16% (1.23)		0.16% (1.66*)		-2.31% (-1.23)		-0.81% (-0.56)	
SalesGrowth		-1.51% (-1.35)		0.07% (0.09)		17.02% (1.11)		10.91% (0.91)
EBITDA		2.97% (1.55)	-0.31% (-1.28)			-37.87% (-1.41)	-50.74% (-1.55)	
R&D	-0.22% (-1.77*)	-0.18% (-1.45)	-1.62% (-1.14)	-1.50% (-1.06)	17.20% (0.98)	8.77% (0.53)	19.34% (1.07)	19.22% (1.07)
CAPEX	-0.32% (-0.78)	-0.03% (-1.15)	2.12% (2.93***)	2.57% (3.68***)	71.51% (1.87*)	64.47% (1.71*)	34.43% (0.36)	33.53% (0.36)
AssetTurnover	1.21% (2.88***)	1.64% (3.14***)	-0.39% (-0.68)	-0.21% (-0.36)	7.25% (1.38)	3.15% (0.92)	6.34% (0.83)	5.90% (0.75)
LaborProd.	-0.42% (-0.93)	-0.31% (-0.67)	-2.42% (-1.99*)	-2.41% (-1.95*)	15.91% (2.15**)	12.94% (1.74*)	24.80% (2.04**)	33.59% (1.96**)
Leverage	-0.55% (-1.77*)	-0.69% (-2.25**)	0.21% (0.11)	-0.05% (-0.02)	-40.57% (-2.10**)	-31.24% (-1.55)	-24.85% (-0.93)	-18.78% (-0.71)
Cash	-0.27% (0.20)	0.14% (0.75)			-15.09% (-0.49)	-24.52% (-0.81)		
PPE	-0.31% (-0.84)	-0.42% (-0.86)			-8.94% (-1.44)	-6.57% (-0.66)		
Intangibles	0.33% (1.62)	0.27% (1.31)			-23.53% (-1.39)	-33.31% (-1.92*)		
HHI	-0.18% (-0.52)	-0.21% (-0.63)			-40.17% (-2.21**)	-39.94% (-2.16**)		
YearDummy	Yes	Yes	No	Yes	Yes	Yes	Yes	No
F-Statistic	4.01***	3.81**	3.37***	3.41***	3.25***	3.17***	2.31***	2.47***
R^2 adjusted	0.017	0.016	0.012	0.010	0.023	0.023	0.016	0.014

This table presents OLS estimations of M&A value creation in dependence of industry factors. The short-term value effects (Panel A.) to acquirers' shareholders are determined by abnormal announcement returns (CAR) measured from 1 day before announcement to 1 day after announcment of the transaction (3 days). The long-term value effect (Panel B.) is determined by 24-month buy-and-hold abnormal returns (BHAR) to acquirers' shareholders. Short- and long-term abnormal transaction returns are the dependent variable of the OLS regression respectively. The independent variables are measured as: (i.) industry median level in the announcement year (Industry Levels); (ii.) industry dynamic measured as average median change over three years from two years before the transaction to the transaction year (Industry Dynamic). The statistical significance of the coefficiencts is tested with a t-statistic. The statistical fit of the model is indicated by the adjusted determination coefficient R^2 adjusted and F-statistic. The test values are marked with "***" if significance is in 1% area, with "**" in 5% area, and with "*" in 10% area.

6.4 Conclusions

The presented study examines industry determinants of M&A activity and value creation. Value creation and activity are analyzed based on 52 ICB sub-sectors (4-digit ICB codes). The results strongly support the intuition that activity levels and value creation of takeovers differ across industries. This finding suggests that industry characteristics may determine activity and success of M&A. Further findings provide evidence for this prediction.

First, industry drivers of activity are analyzed. The results show that industries see more M&A activity when they expand and have high profitability levels. The effect is largest for intra-industry transactions when companies seek to increase market share in strong industries. A positive effect on activity is also found for industries that show high levels of intangible assets while industries with large stocks of physical assets are less active. More labor intensive industries are also less active indicating that human capital and fixed assets are less liquid on the market for corporate control.

The second part of the analysis examines effects of industry characteristics on M&A value creation. The results show that transactions in industries with strong growth prospects create more value for shareholders than takeovers in stagnant or declining industries. Positive value effects from M&A are also observed in industries that see increases in capital investment needs (CAPEX). Acquisitions of additional assets instead of internal investments when new capacity or new production technologies are needed within an industry can be a value increasing strategy from a shareholder perspective. Companies realize largest synergies from more efficient utilization of capital.

Announcement effects in asset intensive industries are lower than in industries which rely more on productive labor. The negative effect is driven by lower value creation of industries with physical productive assets that are more difficult to combine. Industries with large intangible asset bases, on the other hand, realize more value from transferring intellectual property on the market for corporate control. Further results show that takeovers in already highly concentrated industries and in industries with high debt levels are likely to reduce shareholder value.

The results illustrate that not only M&A activity levels, but also M&A success can be partially predicted based on general industry characteristics.

6.5 Appendix

6.5.1 Robustness to alternative industry classifications

The industry classification scheme applied for analysis constitutes the basis of the presented analysis. In this appendix chapter the three most common alternative classification schemes, SIC, FF, and GICS, are briefly introduced and then applied to control for the robustness of the ICB results.

SIC codes: The Standard Industrial Classification (SIC) system has been developed by the U.S. Office of Management and Budget and was first introduced in 1939. It is the most widely-used classification system among researchers (Weiner 2005). The system is based on a four digit code. The first digit covers 10 divisions, the first two digits 81 major industries, the first three digits approximately 350 industry groups and, all four codes approximately 1000 specific industries[22]. Each company is linked to one code, typically based on sales information from the largest segment. Out of the 4-tier classification structure, the 3-digit SIC code is the most frequently used (Weiner 2005). SIC codes, in contrast to the GICS and ICB classification, are only a classification methodology and structure that is then applied by third party data providers. Therefore, SIC classification of one company can differ between data providers. The advantage of SIC codes is the broad availability in financial databases such as Datastream and SDC Platinum. It is, however, not centrally managed and therefore relies on the accuracy of database analysts.
FF-industries: Fama and French (1997) propose a classification system that links the existing SIC groups based on 4-digits to 48 industries. Recently, a 49th industry for computer software was added. Goal of the aggregation is to generate a comprehensive yet manageable set of industries. The FF-industry classification has been widely used in research, e.g., by Mitchell and Mulherin (1996) and Harford (2005). The classification, however, is based on the US-American corporate landscape and therefore emphasizes industry with relative importance in the US economy. The European corporate landscape differs in some aspect from this structure. The presented study focuses on a more granular analysis of industry characteristics than the aggregation into 49 industry groups allows. In addition, the same shortcomings as for SIC codes apply.
GICS codes: The Global Industry Classification Standard (GICS) is maintained by Morgan Stanley Capital International (MSCI) and Standard & Poor's (S&P). The GICS system consists of 10 sectors, 23 industry groups, 59 industries, and

22 An overview of major SIC industries is provided by the US Security and Exchange Commission (SEC) under http://www.sec.gov/info/edgar/siccodes.htm. However, this overview does not cover all SIC codes in use within the Worldscope database. A full overview of the SIC structure is provided under http://www.ehso.com/siccodes.php.

122 sub-industries. The scheme classifies industries by an eight-digit code. Data are available from 1994 for S&P 1500 companies and from 1999 for non-S&P companies. The classification of companies is mainly based on revenues but also on earnings and further market indicators.[23]

Hoberg and Philips (2010) criticize the application of commonly applied industry classification schemes. They propose a text-based matching of US companies' 10-k product description to determine similarities in product characteristics. They find, e.g., that 2-digit SIC codes provide an inferior matching of companies with regard to product similarities. To mitigate these concerns and to control for robustness of the ICB-based results discussed above, the analysis of industry determinants of M&A is conducted for industry fundamentals aggregated based on 3-digit SIC, GICS, and FF industries. Table 6.8 provides results for the analysis of differences in activity level and value creation across industries. Table 6.9 shows results from a regression of short- and long-term value creation with industry characteristics and changes in these determinants. Industries are included in the analysis when more than ten companies with all required financial data are available in each of the 10 analyzed industry years and when at least ten M&A transactions with all data required for CAR and BHAR calculation could be identified. The selection yields 68 SIC 3 industries (out of 350), 64 GICS industries (out of 122), and 38 FF industries (out of 49).

The robustness checks widely underline the findings and conclusions from the ICB-based analysis. Table 6.8 shows that activity levels as well as short- and long-term value creation differ significantly across industries for all classification schemes. The Pearson Chi-square-Tests and the Likelihood-Ratio-Test in Panel A. show significant differences of activity levels within the 1% confidence interval for SIC 3 and GICS industries. For FF industries, the difference in activity is significant in the 5% confidence interval for both tests. Differences in CAR and BHAR in Panels B. and C. are significant with ANOVA p-values in the 1% confidence interval for all classification schemes.

23 Further information on Global Industry Classification Standard can be found under http://www.mscibarra .com/products/indices/gics/.

Table 6.8: Differences in M&A activity and value creation under different industry classification schemes

	ICB 4	SIC 3	GICS	FF
		A. Transaction Activity		
Number of industries	52	68	64	38
Mean Deal Activity Companies %	27.00	25.48	26.06	22.83
Min %	46.34	48.00	64.71	32.26
Max %	8.45	11.64	3.16	10.00
Pearson Chi-square-Test p-value	<0.01***	<0.01***	<0.01***	0.02**
		B. Transaction value creation at announcement (3-day CAR)		
Number of Transactions	3'561	3'573	3'635	3'038
Mean CAR %	0.89***	0.85***	0.89***	0.75***
Min %	-1.90	-1.23	-1.20	-1.27
Max %	6.42***	4.85***	4.03***	1.92***
ANOVA F-test p-value	<0.01***	<0.01***	<0.01***	0.01***
		C. Transaction value creation 24-month post-transacation (BHAR)		
Number of Transactions	2'668	2'794	2'936	2'263
Mean BHAR %	-2.94**	-0.92	-1.38	-1.45*
Min %	-53.42**	-47.07***	-55.40***	-35.36***
Max %	32.20**	46.59**	32.20**	14.11***
ANOVA F-test p-value	<0.01***	<0.01***	<0.01***	<0.01***

The table shows results from tests of mean differences in M&A activity and value creation across industries. The results illustrate differences in mean for various industry classification standards. ICB 4 refers to the 4-digit Industry Classification Code; SIC 3 is the Standardized Industry Classification 3-digit codes as provided by Thomson Financials; GICS represents the Global Industry Classification System codes. The activity level is determined by (i) share of companies within an industry that is involved in M&A activity as a buyer in the 10 year period between 1998 and 2007 and (ii) the share of acquirers' equity in relation to industry equity in this period. The number of industries indicates the total of industries from each classification scheme that is included in the analysis. Industries are selected when at least ten buyers with all required data available are present. The difference in means across industries is tested with two chi-square tests: the Pearson Chi-square-Test and the Likelihood Chi-square-Test. Reported are p-values of the respective tests. Value creation is measured as 3 day abnormal announcement returns (CAR) and 24-monthsbuy-and-hold returns to acquirers' shareholders. The mean in differences is tested with an ANOVA test of mean differences. The p-values of the F-statistic are reported. Significance levels resulting from t- and F-statistics are marked with *** in 1%, with ** in 5%, and with * in 10% confidence interval.

Panel A. in Table 6.9 reports regression outcomes for CAR. The level of M/B valuation has a significant, positive effect on short-term value creation under all schemes indicating a positive investor sentiment towards transaction announcements in industries with positive growth and profitability prospects. Asset turnover levels have a generally positive effect on CAR across classifications while labor productivity negatively affects short term returns. The industry dynamic column in Panel A confirms the ICB finding that increases in M/B valuation levels positively influence CAR across all classification schemes.

Table 6.9: Drivers of M&A value creation for alternative industry classification schemes

	SIC 3		GICS		FF		SIC 3		GICS		FF	
	Industry Level	Industry Dynamic	Industry Level	Industry Dynamic	Industry Level	Industry Dynamic	Industry Level	Industry Dynamic	Industry Level	Industry Dynamic	Industry Level	Industry Dynamic
Intercept	0.61% (1.30)	1.05% (6.10***)	0.13% (0.29)	1.02% (6.62***)	-0.32% (-0.63)	0.93% (6.51***)	-4.07% (-0.66)	-19.48% (-8.61***)	-19.51% (-3.43***)	-15.44% (-8.08***)	-9.18% (-1.37)	-26.05% (-9.93***)
M/B	0.26% (1.92*)	0.13% (1.12)	0.10% (0.73)	0.26% (2.21**)	0.33% (2.18**)	0.42% (3.15***)	-9.48% (-5.37***)	-1.03% (-0.69)	-5.13 (-2.90***)	-1.07% (-0.68)	-8.64 (-4.38***)	-5.15% (-2.84***)
SalesGrowth	-0.74% (-0.61)	-0.54% (-0.53)	-0.76% (-0.81)	-0.35% (-0.45)	-0.89% (-0.71)	-2.42% (-2.24**)	36.42% (2.36**)	28.07% (2.17**)	13.49% (1.16)	18.96% (2.02**)	42.82% (2.53**)	45.89% (3.13***)
EBITDA	-0.35% (-0.24)	1.15% (0.42)	-0.90% (-0.62)	-1.40% (-0.65)	0.83% (0.61)	2.36% (0.93)	6.84% (0.39)	-18.24% (-0.56)	0.85% (0.48)	-30.0% (-1.17)	-22.80% (-1.30)	-23.28% (-0.73)
R&D	-0.49 (-0.23)	1.62% (0.69)	-0.25% (-0.11)	-4.18% (-1.04)	-0.22% (-0.58)	-0.33% (-0.14)	58.67% (2.09**)	-27.63% (-0.98)	7.12% (0.21)	-2.61% (-0.05)	-15.64% (-0.70)	-63.73% (-2.59**)
CAPEX	-0.61% (-0.17)	1.37% (2.06**)	-4.38% (-1.12)	-0.59% (-0.06)	-3.47% (-0.85)	-1.45%% (-0.17)	87.06% (1.94*)	43.47% (0.53)	91.67% (2.51**)	80.79% (1.97**)	12.43% (0.23)	81.79% (1.22)
AssetTurnover	0.29% (1.06)	-0.81% (-1.42)	1.08% (3.71***)	0.44% (0.78)	0.92% (3.04***)	-1.41% (-2.15**)	-9.82% (-2.90***)	-0.20% (-0.03)	-4.21% (-1.16)	19.20% (2.67***)	-2.28% (-0.57)	-7.14% (-0.81)
LaborProductivity	-0.76% (-1.50)	-3.24% (-2.58**)	-0.44% (-0.82)	-2.48% (-1.86*)	-0.71% (-1.16)	-0.66% (-0.37)	-1.72% (-0.27)	-3.69% (-0.26)	13.48% (2.04**)	0.35% (0.02)	3.69% (0.50)	-28.17% (-1.33)
HHI	-0.87% (-0.74)	0.09% (0.08)	-0.62% (-0.74)	0.13% (0.16)	-0.81% (-0.64)	-0.85%% (-0.67)	-19.63% (-1.29)	-2.00 (-0.14)	-32.32% (-3.03***)	-30.34% (-3.17***)	-4.41% (-0.25)	-7.15% (-0.44)
YearDummy	No	No	Yes	No	No	No	No	No	No	No	No	No
F-Statistic	2.60***	2.25**	3.90***	1.58*	4.76***	2.52***	9.70***	2.28**	6.31***	5.29***	8.79***	8.08***
R^2 adjusted	0.009	0.007	0.011	0.003	0.013	0.006	0.029	0.004	0.017	0.014	0.018	0.017

This table presents OLS estimations of long-and long-term value effects form M&A in dependence of different industry characteristics. Short-term value effects to acquirers' shareholders are determined by abnormal announcement returns (CAR) measured from 1 day before announcement to 1 day after announcment of the transactions. The long-term value effect is determined by 24-month abnormal buy-and-hold returns (BHAR) to acquirers' shareholders. The independent variables are industry median levels and 3-year median changes. The determinants are calculated for different industry classification schemes. these schemes include 68 3-digit SIC industries, 64 GICS industries, and 38 Fama-French (FF) industries. Industries are selected for analysis when at least ten companies are availbale in each industry year to calculated the industry determinants and when at least ten CAR and BHAR could be calculated. The statistical significance of the coefficiencts is tested with a t-statistic. The statistical fit of the model is indicated by the adjusted determination coefficient R^2 adjusted and F-statistic. The test values are marked with "***" if significance is in 1% area, with "**" in 5% area, and with "*" in 10% area.

The previous result for ICB classifications that increasing CAPEX requirements within industries positively impact announcement returns is in line with SIC results while the coefficient for other industry classifications are insignificantly negative. Increases in revenues per employee (labor productivity) negatively affect CAR.

Panel B. in Table 6.9 shows the long-term value creation (BHAR) results for alternative industry classifications. Acquisitions in industries with high market-to-book valuations underperform lower M/B industries in the long term for all industry classification. The indication that transactions in industries with high growth levels show higher long-term value creation is confirmed by these results. The asset turnover results for ICB industries is in accordance with SIC industry findings. The coefficients for GICS and FF industries are insignificant. The industry dynamic column shows that positive demand shocks indicated by increases in industry growth augment long-term value creation of M&A transactions independent of classification method. The results also show that transactions in industries with high concentration levels (HHI) perform weaker than in more fragmented industries.

6.5.2 Overview of industry characteristics

This Appendix provides an overview of the 52 ICB sub-sectors included in the analyses. Tables 6.10 and 6.11 provide an overview of the industry fundamentals applied for analysis. Table 6.10 shows the median levels of industry factors averaged over the ten-year sample period. Table 6.11 returns the standard deviation of the respective measures over ten years. The measures are aggregate over the ten-year time period analyzed and, hence, do not represent the individual yearly measures used in the preceding analyses. The aggregated measures, however, provide an indication of the level of cross-industry deviation in the applied determinants.

Table 6.10: Overview of industry characteristics - medians

ICB sectors (Codes)	Marhet to Book	Sales Growth	EBIT margin	R&D	CAPEX	Asset Turnover	Labor Prod.	Leverage	PP&E	Intangi-bles	HHI
Exploration & Production (533)	1.57	18.1%	16.0%	0.0%	8.0%	0.28	0.27	7.2%	42.2%	2.2%	0.23
Integrated Oil & Gas (537)	1.91	16.5%	12.5%	0.3%	7.6%	1.11	1.12	16.8%	76.8%	2.3%	0.06
Oil Equipment & Services (573)	1.81	15.9%	9.2%	0.5%	5.9%	0.73	0.18	28.7%	48.3%	5.2%	0.07
Specialty Chemicals (1357)	1.52	5.8%	7.4%	2.8%	5.2%	0.95	0.19	22.1%	63.7%	4.1%	0.05
Paper (1737)	1.06	0.7%	6.0%	0.5%	4.7%	0.87	0.25	31.0%	71.9%	2.9%	0.10
Iron & Steel (1757)	1.20	9.6%	6.8%	0.7%	5.2%	0.98	0.22	23.4%	61.6%	0.5%	0.11
General Mining (1775)	1.76	4.1%	13.8%	0.2%	5.2%	0.57	0.08	14.5%	20.4%	5.2%	0.13
Building Materials (1775)	1.63	7.8%	10.0%	0.9%	5.0%	0.98	0.17	22.5%	67.5%	1.7%	0.05
Heavy Construction (2357)	1.33	11.8%	5.3%	0.4%	3.2%	1.12	0.18	14.3%	28.8%	1.9%	0.04
Aerospace (2713)	1.93	11.4%	9.5%	5.0%	3.1%	0.79	0.18	19.9%	36.3%	9.5%	0.21
Containers & Packaging (2723)	1.38	5.7%	7.0%	0.6%	6.6%	0.96	0.16	24.8%	75.6%	3.0%	0.10
Diversified Industrials (2727)	1.51	7.7%	6.9%	1.4%	4.5%	1.05	0.16	24.6%	50.1%	7.7%	0.15
Electrical Components (2733)	1.79	8.0%	6.8%	3.0%	3.6%	1.28	0.12	16.3%	43.5%	2.8%	0.09
Electronic Equipment (2737)	2.37	10.0%	5.7%	5.8%	2.8%	1.14	0.14	16.2%	33.7%	8.0%	0.22
Commercial Vehicles (2753)	1.74	11.7%	6.3%	2.2%	3.9%	1.21	0.18	21.5%	45.1%	3.2%	0.11
Industrial Machinery 2757)	1.73	6.4%	6.6%	2.3%	3.6%	1.17	0.15	19.8%	48.1%	3.7%	0.03
Transportation Services (2777)	1.76	7.3%	15.2%	0.0%	6.4%	0.48	0.17	26.9%	54.9%	2.0%	0.05
Business Support Services (2791)	2.40	13.8%	5.8%	2.0%	3.3%	1.28	0.12	17.0%	26.3%	11.2%	0.03
Busi Train. & Eplmt. Ag. (2793)	2.77	21.0%	3.9%	0.0%	1.9%	1.98	0.13	10.9%	14.5%	15.5%	0.18
Industrial Suppliers (2797)	1.72	7.6%	6.0%	0.0%	3.3%	1.66	0.27	21.9%	33.7%	6.5%	0.13
Automobiles (3353)	1.25	7.5%	5.2%	3.2%	6.0%	0.90	0.27	32.7%	56.6%	4.7%	0.10
Auto Parts (3355)	1.45	10.8%	5.4%	4.1%	6.6%	1.21	0.13	23.7%	64.0%	6.0%	0.16
Brewers (3533)	2.45	6.1%	9.0%	0.1%	7.5%	0.81	0.20	24.1%	72.2%	4.7%	0.10
Food Products (3577)	1.79	5.6%	5.9%	0.6%	4.7%	1.20	0.20	27.9%	61.0%	3.3%	0.07
Home Construction (3728)	1.19	13.9%	11.8%	0.0%	0.5%	0.97	0.63	18.5%	3.0%	0.7%	0.09
Clothing & Accessories (3763)	1.28	3.7%	5.5%	0.7%	3.0%	0.99	0.12	23.4%	46.6%	1.0%	0.08
Medical Equipment (4535)	2.69	12.6%	9.7%	7.1%	3.7%	0.85	0.16	16.0%	27.2%	13.3%	0.08
Biotechnology (4573)	3.46	19.4%	0.2%	74.2%	2.4%	0.24	0.07	3.8%	19.7%	5.5%	0.14

Continued on next oage

Continued from previous page

Pharmaceuticals (4577)	3.21	10.0%	10.4%	15.7%	3.1%	0.73	0.17	10.9%	30.2%	9.8%	0.07
Food Retailers (5337)	2.77	5.8%	3.8%	0.0%	6.6%	1.92	0.16	20.9%	63.3%	4.2%	0.07
Broadline Retailers (5373)	1.88	5.0%	5.1%	0.0%	5.6%	1.44	0.16	19.6%	53.4%	3.5%	0.12
Specialty Retailers (5379)	1.80	11.1%	4.0%	1.1%	4.1%	1.65	0.21	17.9%	32.7%	3.4%	0.06
Broadcast. & Entertain. (5553)	1.90	11.4%	8.7%	3.5%	2.6%	0.65	0.25	18.0%	17.3%	29.6%	0.16
Publishing (5557)	2.59	6.0%	9.5%	1.6%	2.3%	0.90	0.16	15.5%	22.3%	15.4%	0.06
Airlines (5751)	1.52	10.3%	4.8%	0.0%	7.7%	0.94	0.21	31.3%	65.4%	1.0%	0.11
Hotels (5751)	1.37	5.4%	10.9%	0.0%	5.0%	0.42	0.08	35.5%	81.1%	1.1%	0.14
Restaurants & Bars (5757)	1.78	11.3%	8.6%	0.0%	8.0%	0.90	0.06	31.5%	78.9%	5.5%	0.14
Travel & Tourism (5759)	1.66	5.3%	5.9%	0.0%	6.6%	0.63	0.12	35.3%	57.1%	1.1%	0.13
Fixed Line Telco. (6535)	2.27	12.5%	13.1%	0.7%	8.3%	0.54	0.21	31.0%	63.8%	7.9%	0.06
Conventional Electr. (7535)	1.44	8.0%	10.0%	0.4%	4.5%	0.50	0.31	13.2%	68.4%	0.4%	0.05
Alternative Electricity (7537)	1.90	12.5%	15.9%	0.0%	4.1%	0.28	0.35	21.4%	40.3%	1.1%	0.23
Multiutilities (7575)	2.20	7.9%	12.8%	0.3%	4.6%	0.44	0.40	23.6%	76.6%	10.7%	0.12
Water (7577)	1.71	4.4%	25.2%	0.2%	6.7%	0.31	0.19	29.9%	66.0%	1.1%	0.30
Banks (8355)	1.35	8.5%	25.4%	0.0%	0.2%	0.07	0.29	33.5%	0.0%	0.1%	0.02
Full Line Insurance (8532)	1.59	5.8%	5.1%	0.0%	0.3%	0.24	0.68	2.1%	0.0%	0.7%	0.08
Life Insurance (8575)	2.11	7.2%	6.6%	0.0%	0.1%	0.15	1.36	2.2%	0.0%	0.2%	0.08
Asset Managers (8771)	2.76	19.8%	24.7%	0.0%	0.7%	0.34	0.29	3.8%	4.3%	0.9%	0.18
Computer Services (9533)	2.25	16.0%	4.8%	4.5%	2.2%	1.32	0.11	7.6%	16.3%	13.9%	0.04
Internet (9535)	2.72	29.7%	3.0%	11.9%	3.0%	0.91	0.10	2.0%	16.2%	12.5%	0.11
Software (9537)	2.65	14.6%	5.4%	15.1%	2.1%	0.98	0.12	2.3%	15.7%	13.7%	0.11
Computer Hardware (9572)	1.98	4.6%	2.9%	6.6%	1.8%	1.59	0.29	12.7%	18.3%	2.7%	0.07
Telco. Equipment (9578)	2.45	12.9%	6.4%	8.1%	3.0%	0.99	0.17	9.6%	25.2%	5.5%	0.14
Average	1.93	9.93%	8.70%	3.63%	4.24%	0.90	0.24	19.3%	42.4%	5.5%	0.11
Median	1.79	8.33%	6.91%	0.59%	4.24%	0.87	0.18	19.8%	35.0%	3.2%	0.13
StDev	0.54	5.23%	8.44%	8.98%	2.11%	0.46	0.26	9.9%	26.5%	5.8%	0.10

The table provides an overview of the industry factors applied in the previous analyses. In contrast to the data used for analysis the table returns aggregated values over the ten year sample period. The ten-year median is shown. The annual industry factors are calculated for every year between 1998 and 2007 from all active listed firms with the respective 4-digit ICB code (4'581) that show valid entries for the examined financial data in the Worldscope data base.

7. Wealth Creation of Corporate Divestiture: An Industry Perspective

7.1 Introduction

It is often noted that asset sales cluster in time and across industries. Anecdotal evidence also suggests that the success of asset reallocation from a shareholder wealth perspective differs over the market cycle and between industries. This intuition implies that industry characteristics not only influence the decision to sell assets but also determine the value creation potential of these divestments from a seller's perspective.

Previous research finds empirical evidence for industry specific factors that influence M&A activity. Significant effects have been found, e.g., from changes in demand, variations in investment requirements, and productivity changes (Mitchell and Mulherin 1996, Andrade et al. 2001, and Harford 2005). The results imply that companies in industries that undergo structural change can efficiently address these changes with M&A. Maksimovic and Phillips (2001) include corporate divestitures in the analysis of industry determinants of corporate restructuring. They find based on a simple production model that changes in demand in an industry affect the decision to sell parts of firm operations. Recent studies by Yang (2008) and Warusawitharana (2008) further develop this model by relating asset sales to an optimal asset allocation on firm level. The optimal amount of productive assets a company aims to operate is determined by productivity, demand development, profitablity, and investment needs. Yang (2008) and Warusawitharana (2008) find that these factors are largely determined by specific characteristics and trends of a firm's industry. Their models, thus, imply that managers engage in divestments to adjust to their specific industry context.

While the influence of industry factors on divestment activity is well studied, little research exists with regard to the implications of industry characteristics on shareholder wealth creation following divestment decisions. In general, reallocation of assets to the most productive owner increases firm value. Sellers should capture a significant share of the economic gains from asset reallocations (Lang et al. 1995). In contrast to M&A transactions, divestments are less exposed to agency costs caused, e.g., by empire building of managers (Roll 1986) or envy with regard to higher management compensation of larger firms (Goel and Thakor 2010). On the contrary, managers are rather reluctant to sell assets and reduce their firm's size (Lang et al. 1995 and Bates 2005).

A number of studies provide empirical evidence for value creation of divestitures. Results show that shareholder returns following divestments are significantly positive on average and generally higher than for M&A transactions (Boone and Mulherin 2000, Schlingemann et al. 2002, Bates 2005). Findings from studies of divestitures in specific industry contexts, however, propose that value creation can differ between industries (e.g., Benou et al. 2008).

These results and further anectodel evidence indicate that industry chararcteristics not only foster the decision to reallocate firm assets. They also appear to determine the magnitude of economic gains that can be realized from asset sales. Hence, industry characteristics and trends are expected to influence the level of shareholder returns resulting from divestitures.

Based on this intuition this study wants to empirically test the role of industry characteristics in explaining value creation of corporate divestitures. This paper analyzes industry wide divestment activity and value creation based on 579 major divestitures of European sellers between January 1st, 1998 and December 31st, 2007 in 20 Industry Classification Benchmark (ICB) sectors. The short-term value effect from asset disposals is addressed with an analysis of abnormal stock returns at transaction announcement. Long-term returns are determined using abnormal buy-and-hold returns over a 2-year period.

The results show that industry characteristics help explaining variations in activity levels as well as value creation of corporate divestitures. Managers are more likely to divest assets in stagnant industries with low valuation levels and weak growth rates. Temporary increases in valuation levels, however, drive activity suggesting that managers time their divestments to increase gains from sell-offs. Increasing asset productivity, on the other hand, drives refocusing when managers reallocate firm assets to a more productive use.

Focus of the analysis is, however, to explore industry variations in shareholder wealth creation. Factors driving success differ for the immediate announcement return and long-term success of divestitures. In the short term, investors react positively when divestments are announced during high and increasing industry valuations when asset prices are high. Investors also favor refocusing on core industries when these expand. Long-term abnormal returns on the other hand are mainly driven by industry wide productivity changes and technology shocks. Shareholder profit when firms sell assets in industries that see declining profitability levels or increasing R&D investment requirements. These findings are consistent with theories that relate asset sales to changes in asset productivity and a resulting reallocation of firm resources to the most productive use.

The remainder of this paper is structured as follows: Chapter 2 gives an overview of related literature and introduces the underlying predictions; Chapter 3 describes the applied dataset and the methodology to identify short- and long-term value effects; Chapter 4 presents and discusses the results; Chapter 5 draws a final conclusion.

7.2 Literature review and hypotheses

7.2.1 Literature review

A variety of studies examine drivers of corporate restructuring. John and Ofek (1995) argue, for example, that asset sales are motivated by the attempt to remove value decreasing asset allocations and, thus, increase firm value. Desai and Jain (1999) propose that divestments refocus operations to concentrate on core businesses and, hence, reduce complexity costs. Another possible motivation is the need to generate liquidity from the sale of business units to weather bad market condition or finance new projects. Lang et al. (1995) suggest that managers are generally reluctant to selling parts of their business. However, when additional capital is needed for required investments and external financing is costly, managers sell assets to invest the proceeds in new projects.

A growing body of research examines industry effects that influence corporate restructuring activity. Mitchell and Mulherin (1996) and Harford (2005) link M&A activity to fundamental industry factors. These authors set forth evidence that particularly changes in industry structure due to demand and technological shocks cause M&A activity levels to increase. M&A is viewed as an efficient way for managers of a firm to adapt to a new industry context. Maksimovic and Phillips (2001) also include divestments in their analysis of corporate restructuring. They relate both acquisition and divestment decisions to variations in plant level productivity and industry demand growth, which motivate managers to reallocate assets. Based on a simple production model they argue that increases in industry demand and industry asset price levels lead to reallocation of assets from poorly managed less productive to stronger firms. Applying US manufacturing plant data from 1974 to 1992 they provide empirical evidence for their predictions and show that large differences in asset trade activity exist across industries.

A recent study by Yang (2008) introduces a model that links dynamic in industry structure specifically to divestment activity. She argues that productivity shocks within an industry can increase asset transfers when firms adjust their productive asset base to an optimal level. She also asserts that asset transfers are more frequent when asset prices are high and gains are, thus, larger for sellers. Yang (2008) finds a neo-classical explanation for this effect by demonstrating that higher gains and the ability to trade corporate assets in expanding markets determine divestment activity and success. This approach provides an alternative view to Maksimovic and Phillips' (2001) marginal productivity based model. She finds empirical evidence for her prediction based on US plant level data that expand Maksimovic and Phillips' (2001) sample until 2000. Warusawitharana (2008) introduces a comparable model in which he links the acquisition and divestment decision to achieving an optimal firm size. The optimal size of a firm is thereby determined through profitability levels of assets. He concludes that corporate asset sales are consistent with efficient divestment decisions reallocating assets between less and more profitable companies. Warusawitharana (2008) provides empirical evidence for his predictions based on US acquisition and divestment data from Thomson Reuters' SDC database between 1984 and 2004. Although his model focuses on firm specific characteristics he also includes industry level medians. The industry results show that his main conclusions hold true on an industry level. This finding clearly indicates that aggregated industry characteristics are a main driver of asset reallocation.

Colak (2009) examines a firm's decision to refocus operation on their core industry or to diversify. He argues based on a sample of 6'233 US firms between 1989 and 1998 that individual firm characteristics as well as industry factors affect the decision to increase or decrease the number of business segments. He suggests that industry growth, profitability, and R&D intensity are among the factors that determine the choice to refocus or diversify. Another implication of his analysis is that refocusing or diversification does not per se lead to predictable changes in firm valuation. In response to studies that examine diversification discounts Colak (2009) argues that changes in firm valuation rather depend on the causes that led to refocusing or diversification decisions. He identifies firm, industry and general market factors as potentially drivers of valuation effects.

A lively discussion exists with regard to the value implication of corporate divestitures from a shareholder perspective. Shareholder returns from divestments are widely documented and found to be positive at announcement (e.g., Boone and Mulherin 2000, Schlingemann et al. 2002, and Bates 2005 for US transactions; Lee and Lin 2008 for a UK sample). Warusawitharana (2008) argues that this finding is due to the lack of agency problems in asset sales in contrast to mergers which are exposed to numerous corporate governance conflicts (as described, e.g., by Jensen 2005, Gorton et al. 2005, and Goel and Thakor 2010). Some studies propose that announcement effects from corporate divestitures can differ between industries. Benou et al. (2008) show, for example, that annoucement returns for high technology divestments differ from other industries. They report lower announcement effects for sellers than for buyers and suggest that these are caused by discounts due to higher uncertainty about the value of high tech assets.

Results from studies of long-term returns from divestments are controversial. McConnell et al. (2001) and Bates (2005) find positive abnormal stock market returns for a US sample while Veld and Veld-Merkoulova (2004) report insignificantly negative returns for an European sample of spin-offs. Lee and Lin (2008) show significantly negative long-term returns for a sample of UK corporate sell-offs. Desai and Savickas (2010) propose that productivity and operational efficiency of sellers increase after divestments.

Bates (2005) argues that long-term value effects from divestments can be explained by the use of proceeds from asset sales. He pertains to two opposing theories. In general, proceeds should be invested in un-funded but value generating projects or returned to shareholders. However, managerial incentives to retain proceeds can extend to projects that benefit managers rather than shareholders. He argues that financial benefits from divestments can, thus, easily be off-set by agency costs of retained proceeds that lead to excessive investment. An implication of management discretion with regard to divestment proceeds, which Bates (2005) points out, is the difficulty of investors at announcement to assess the value effects of divestments. He sets forth that long-term returns depend on the attractiveness of the seller's industry. Based on this argumentation, he provides some empirical evidence showing that asset sales may be more value increasing when industries experience high growth and, thus, provide favorable investment opportunities.

The presented study is motivated by the insights gained from Maksimovic and Phillips (2001), Colak (2009), Yang (2008), and Warusawitharana (2008) who link divestment activity to industry structure and changes in industry characteristics. In addition to explaining the management decision to dispose corporate assets, their research implies that divestments in reaction to specific industry characteristics increase firm value and positively affect the returns to shareholders of divesting firms. Based on this implication the role of industry characteristics with regard to the value creation potential of corporate divestitures from a shareholder perspective is empirically tested. Intuition and prior research proposes that shareholder returns from asset reallocation vary significantly across industry contexts. This paper, therefore, wants to contribute to the discussion of divestment success by introducing industry specific factors as determinants of value creation from corporate divestitures.

7.2.2 Predictions

The starting point of this study is the intuition that not only corporate restructuring activity but also value creation from asset sales differ significantly across industries. The analysis starts by testing activity levels and value creation in different industries to identify variations.

7.H1: Divestment activity and value creation differ significantly across industries.

Results from prior research suggest that industry variations in divestment activity can partially be explained by aggregated industry characteristics. Factors that potentially influence divestment decisions include industry demand development (Maksimovic and Phillips 2001, Bates 2005), asset productivity and profitability within an industry (Colak 2009, Warusawitharana 2008, Yang 2008, and Maksimovic and Phillips 2001), industry cycle and asset valuation levels (Yang 2008, Harford 2005), and investment needs (Colak 2009, Mitchell and Mulherin 1996).

Mitchell and Mulherin (1996) argue that changes in industry structure (industry shocks) drive M&A activity within an industry. Yang (2008) relates this finding to her productivity model showing that changes in industry characteristics result in new optimal asset allocations. Divestment activity is, therefore, likely to cluster in industries that experiences shocks.

Further industry factors that may affect divestment decision pertain to asset liquidity within an industry (Yang 2008, Schlingemann et al. 2002), asset structure (Benou et al. 2008), and industry concentration (Balasubramanian and Sivadasan 2009).

7.H2: Industry specific factors such as growth prospects, asset productivity, asset valuations, investment requirements, as well as industry and asset structure determine divestment activity. Especially fundamental changes within these factors affect divestment decisions.

The main research interest of this examination is, however, whether these industry characteristics can also explain industry variations in shareholder wealth creation. Following a neo-classical perspective, managers engage in asset sales to optimize the value of their firms. Empirical findings support this view by showing positive abnormal returns to shareholders of companies that sell assets. Results from studies of divestments in specific industries and anecdotal evidence suggest, however, that abnormal returns for seller's shareholder differ across industry. Average value creation from corporate divestitures within an industry is expected to depend on the underlying industry drivers that lead to the management decision to divest.

7.H3: Industry characteristics determine the value creation potential of corporate divestitures.

7.3 Data and Methodology

7.3.1 Industry M&A Data

In order to construct this divestment data sample, M&A data from Thomson Reuter's SDC database was downloaded. Completed transactions with the following characteristics are included:

- The transaction is a partial firm acquisition or the acquisition of a subsidiary from a seller (ultimate parent company of the target) headquartered in Europe (including Russia and Turkey) and listed on a European stock exchange.
- The transaction was announced between January 1st, 1998 and December 31st, 2007.
- More than 50% of the divested entity's equity is transferred to a non-related acquirer.
- Based on the seller's CUSIP code from SDC financial information for the selling firm is available in the Thomson Financial, Datastream, and Worldscope databases.
- The Transaction value is reported and equals or exceeds EUR 10 mn.
- Transaction value of major divestments account for at least 10% of the seller's market capitalization in the month before announcement.

The transaction search returns data of 945 major European corporate divestitures for this analysis out of 5'039 transactions with reported transaction values of above EUR 10 mn.

In a next step, an industry transaction sample is built. ICB codes to classify sellers in 41 3-digit ICB sectors are applied. In order to ensure a sufficient number of observations for analyzing divestment activity and calculating abnormal returns on an industry level only industries with a minimum of ten major transactions during the sample period are considered.[24] In addition, industries that focus on financial investments (trade sales) rather than strategic divestitures are excluded. The excluded industries comprise real estate investment firms (ICB 863 and 867), financial service firms including private equity companies and hedge funds (877), as well as equity and non-equity investment vehicles (ICB 898 and 899). 20 ICB sectors remain with a total of 579 major transactions out of 2'758

24 The applied regime of excluding industries with less than 10 major divestments from different publically listed sellers is somewhat arbitrary. The analysis is therefore repeated for industry samples applying 5 and 20 transactions as a cut-off point. The results are comparable.

transactions with reported transaction values. Table 7.5 in the Appendix provides an overview of the sample derivation.

7.3.2 Industry Fundamental Data

In order to examine industry effects on divestment activity and value creation, industry characteristics are aggregated based on individual firm financial information for the 200 industry years in this industry sample. For calculating industry factors, first a list of all company identifiers of European firms included in the Thomson Financials database is downloaded. Out of the 14'557 ISIN codes received those that pertain to American Depository Receipts (ADR) and to companies that were not active during at least one year of this sample period are excluded. The remaining firms are classified by assigning 3-digit ICB codes from the Thomson Financials database. 9'459 classified companies result that split into 6’383 listed and 3'076 private firms. In a next step, annual financial information for the 3'102 public companies in the 20 ICB sectors of this industry sample for the 10 years between 1998 and 2007 is downloaded. Data is obtained from Thomson Reuters' Datastream, Thomson Financials, and Worldscope databases. Before aggregating financial data for the 200 industry years, illogical data (e.g., negative sales data and M/B ratios) is removed. Extreme values are trimmed at the 0.1% level to remove outliers and flawed data.

Two distinct sets of industry factors are calculated based on the resulting company data: a) Annual industry median levels (industry levels) and b) changes in industry medians over time (industry dynamics). The following factors are included in the analysis:

a) *Industry levels:* Annual industry medians are calculated for ICB sectors from individual company financial data of the sectors constituents. Based on previous research the following groups of industry medians are calculated: industry valuation levels, demand growth, productivity levels, investment requirements, as well as asset and industry structure.

   Industry valuation levels are determined by industry market-to-book *(MtoB)* ratios. Year-end MtoB multiples are calculated as companies’ equity market value over lagging book value of total assets. Yang (2008) proposes that highly valued industries provide a favorable environment for divestitures enabling managers to realize high prices for disposed assets. Demand growth is measured as annual sales growth *(SalesGrowth)*. Sales growth is calculated as annual percentage change of total year-end sales of individual companies within an industry. It determines annual changes in demand. Maksimovic and Phillips (2001) show that industry demand developments strongly affect asset sale decisions. Bates (2005) argues that high growth rates within an industry can also present value increasing investment opportunities for the proceeds from asset sales. Determinants of productivity level comprise industry EBIT margin *(EBIT)* and asset turnover *(AssetTurn)*. EBIT is defined as year-end operative income measured as earnings before interests and taxes. It is normalized by year-end sales. The aggregated measure indicates industry profitability. Warusawitharana (2008) argues that companies with weak profitability are more likely to sell assets and downsize operations. His results indicate that profitability levels and changes in profitability are industry specific. A second productivity measure is asset turnover calculated as year-end sales over year-end total assets (Harford 2005). This factor indicates asset productivity within an industry. It also provides an indication for asset intensity. The asset turnover value is high in industries that require a relatively small stock of asset and rely more on human labor (e.g., Business Training). It is small in industries that rely on a large asset stock (e.g., Water Utilities). The industry investment requirement is measured based on research and development *(R&D)* spending and capital expenditure *(CAPEX)*. R&D spending is normalized by sales and CAPEX is normalized by total beginning of year assets. R&D levels indicate the dependence on technology of an industry. Colak (2009) finds a positive relation between technology levels and divestment decisions. Lang et al. (1995) propose that high capital investment requirements within an industry can lead managers to reconsider the current capital allocation. Firms may be inclined to sell assets to finance new capital investments.

In addition to the factors outlined above this analysis includes indicators of asset structure and industry concentration. To account for the nature of productive assets within an industry the median share of tangible assets within total assets at year-end is applied. Tangible assets are defined as property, plants, and equipment *(PP&E)*. The nature of productive assets may affect the ability to trade parts of a firm's operations. Balasubramanian and Sivadasan (2009) propose that increasing industry concentration reduces asset resalabilty. To test for the effect of industry concentration the Herfindahl-Index *(HHI)* is calculated for the 200 industry years in this sample. Sales data from public and private companies are considered for calculating the HHI.

b) *Industry dynamics:* Industry dynamics are changes in industry characteristics over time. These structural change measures are defined as annual change in industry medians. The specific change value that pertains to an industry year is calculated as the 3-year average of median changes. The 3-year time span includes the announcement year (t=0) and the two preceding years (t = -1 and t = -2). The level of this measure indicates whether the industry has experienced fundamental changes prior and during the analyzed transaction year (also see Harford 2005). Previous research from Mitchell and Mulherin (1996), Maksimovic and Phillips (2001), Harford (2005) and Yang (2008) point out that especially dynamic within industries characteristics can explain clustering of corporate restructuring activity across industries. Firms' management addresses sudden changes in industry structure induced, e.g., by new technologies, new production methods, or shifts in customer preferences by reallocating assets to refocus on or diversify away from their core industries. Yang (2008) points out that changes in industry valuation can facilitate asset sales when asset prices and asset liquidity increase.

This study includes four groups of industry dynamic determinants in the analysis: Valuation shocks measured as changes in median industry market-to-book ratios $(\Delta_{t-2/0}M/B)$; demand shocks measured as change in sales growth rates $(\Delta_{t-2/0}Growth)$; productivity shocks indicated by changes in operating profitability $(\Delta_{t-2/0}EBIT)$ and asset turnover $(\Delta_{t-2/0}AssetTurn)$; investment and technology shocks measured as changes in industry CAPEX $(\Delta_{t-2/0}CAPEX)$ and R&D $((\Delta_{t-2/0}R\&D)$ respectively.

Table 7.6 in the Appendix provides an overview of aggregated industry factors for the ten-year sample period.

7.3.3 Approach to determine value creation

In a next step, short- and long-term abnormal capital market returns to shareholders of the selling firms are calculated. The motivation for analyzing different time horizons is not based on general doubts regarding the efficient market hypothesis for corporate divestitures. The reasoning follows Bates (2005) who points out that investors do not have full transparency on the use of proceeds from divestments at announcement. Hence, investors are likely to adapt their assessment of corporate control decisions over time.

To determine the short-term value effects of divestments, cumulative abnormal returns (CAR) are calculated. The examined event window consists of three days reaching from one day before to one day after the announcement day. The Market Model as introduced by Brown and Warner (1980) and Brown and Warner (1985) is applied to determine the short-term abnormal return. Following the Market Model approach, abnormal returns are determined using Equation (7.1).

$$AR_{it} = R_{it} - \left(\alpha_i + \beta_i \cdot R_{mt}\right) \quad (7.1)$$

R_{it} represents the stock return of company i in period t, while R_{mt} describes the return of the value weighted 3-digit European ICB industry index of the selling company's industry as provided by Datastream. The market model parameters are calculated using ordinary least squares (OLS) regression over a period of 180 trading days prior to the largest event window that is set at 20 days before the announcement. CAR are then calculated by summing the abnormal returns over different event windows (Equation (7.2)).

$$CAR_{EventWindow(m1,m2)} = \sum_{m1}^{m2} AR_{it} \tag{7.2}$$

Statistical significance is tested with the standardized cross-sectional test proposed by Boehmer et al. (1991). The parametric Generalized-Sign-Test (Cowan et al. 1990) is conducted as additional robustness check (available on request).

The approach to determine long-term transaction success applies buy-and-hold abnormal returns (BHAR) in event-time proposed by Barber and Lyon (1997) and Lyon et al. (1999). BHAR are determined by constructing monthly reference portfolios of non-selling firms. As proposed by Fama and French (1993), year-end market-to-book ratios (M/B) of year t-1 and the market value on the last trading day of June are used to construct annual reference portfolios in order to account for differences in return between small and large as well as between value and growth companies. In addition to the traditional approach,thisresearch set-up requires a clear separation of portfolio firms by industry to capture abnormal returns that are free from industry specific effects. Hence, book-to-market and size portfolios are constructed for all ICB sectors. In order to derive reference portfolios, all listed companies with available financial data included in the data sample are divided at their median in two M/B- and two size-groups based on market capitalization within each ICB sector. Companies with zero or negative M/B figures and companies with a market value of below EUR 10 mn are removed from the sample. 80 size- and M/B-portfolios for every year in the ten-year sample period result from the classification. All companies that did not acquire or divest in the 36 months prior to the respective month are included in the monthly changing reference portfolios. Reference portfolio returns are calculated by compounding the average monthly returns of the portfolio constituents over a 24-month time horizon following the transaction month. Equation (7.3) illustrates the computation following Bouwman et al. (2009).

(7.3) $$R_{referenceportfolio,T} = \prod_{t=s}^{s+T} \left[1 + \frac{\sum_{j}^{n_t} R_{jt}}{n_t} \right] - 1$$

$R_{referenceportfolio,T}$ describes the monthly returns of the reference portfolio, R_{jt} is the simple return of portfolio company j in month t, and n_t is the number of portfolio firms in the respective industry size-M/B portfolio in month t. T represents the investment horizon. The abnormal returns of the event firms are calculated based on Equation (7.4).

(7.4) $$BHAR_{iT} = \prod_{t=s}^{s+T} (1 + R_{it}) - R_{referenceportfolio,T} - 1$$

R_{it} describes the monthly returns of the bidder. In order to account for changes in the risk structure of sellers following a major asset sale, divesting firms are allowed to change their reference portfolio subsequent to the divestment. Since this study focuses on major divestments that account for at least 10% of market capitalization at time of the announcement, the risk profile may change when firms decrease in size leading to an inappropriate benchmarking portfolio if kept unchanged (see Bouwman et al. 2009).

A descriptive overview of industry results is provided in Table 7.1.

Table 7.1: Descriptive overview of the applied industry data sample

ICB sector	Number of Public Companies	Total Market Capitalization in EUR	Number of Divestments	Average Transaction Value in EUR mn	Total Transactions Value in EUR mn	Activity Index	3-day CAR in %	N	24-month BHAR in %	N
Oil Equipment, & Services (57)	78	107'400	45	328	14'775	0.18	3.99***	19	41.88***	14
Chemicals (135)	178	439'350	200	475	95'080	0.45	3.12***	25	-3.06	19
Forestry & Paper (173)	47	59'742	52	392	20'401	0.38	0.42	13	-13.88	10
Construction & Materials (235)	322	493'637	243	222	53'913	0.40	1.63*	58	-7.79*	50
General Industrials (272)	96	88'676	106	210	22'234	0.53	0.65	20	11.08	19
Electronic & Equipment (273)	248	361'857	151	382	57'685	0.47	2.29**	34	9.75	27
Industrial Engineering (275)	359	356'443	163	297	48'479	0.24	2.84*	47	-1.89	35
Industrial Transportation (277)	175	250'097	107	291	31'179	0.21	0.60	17	-14.98***	13
Support Services (279)	368	191'926	175	134	23'407	0.34	5.03***	64	31.03***	51
Automobiles & Parts (335)	116	405'970	83	671	55'652	0.42	0.14	21	11.97	17
Beverages (353)	108	299'404	66	602	39'760	0.29	-1.94*	11	8.35	11
Food Producers (357)	271	639'532	183	497	90'999	0.42	2.48***	43	-1.13	33
Household Goods (372)	180	130'688	67	189	12'681	0.42	0.03	14	6.63	13
Health Care Eqpmt. & Serv. (453)	172	154'793	51	234	11'932	0.09	5.17*	22	21.75	18
Pharmaceuticals & Biotech. (457)	238	1'121'520	157	627	98'511	0.34	3.23**	20	29.52	14
General Retailers (537)	235	275'109	161	359	57'865	0.29	2.12	28	11.40	21
Media (555)	382	432'543	212	687	145'720	0.25	2.07	31	6.50	21
Travel & Leisure (575)	287	303'971	251	299	74'980	0.24	0.31	41	10.49*	41

Continued on next page

Continued from previous page

Nonlife Insurance (853)	78	642'987	167	428	71'559	0.47	-1.33*	13	-5.36	12
Software & Computer Serv. (953)	643	220'438	118	83	9'757	0.10	-0.50*	38	-11.40	15
Sum	4'581	6'976'083	2'758		1'036'568			579		454
Average	229	348'804	138	370	51'828	0.33	2.03***		8.05***	
Median	208	301'687	154	344	51'196	0.34	1.13***		5.54***	
Minimum	47	59'742	45	83	9'757	0.09	-1.94*		-14.98***	
Maximum	643	1'121'520	251	687	145'720	0.53	5.17*		41.88***	
Pearson Chi-Square p-value						<0.01***				
ANOVA F-test p-value							<0.01***		<0.01***	

The table provides summary statistics of the applied divestment data sample split into 20 ICB sectors (3-digit ICB codes). Out of a total of 41 sectors those were selected with at least ten listed constituents with a complete set of financial data available for any of the 10 years in the data sample. In addition, at least ten transactions for which CAR and 24-month BHAR could be calculated are required in order to include industries in the analysis. Financial industries that engage primarily in financial (trade) transactions are excluded. The excluded industries comprise real estate investment firms (ICB 863 and 867), financial service firms incl. private equity companies and hedge funds (877), as well as equity and non-equity investment vehicles (ICB 898 and 899). Firms were included in the sample when based in Europe according to their region code in Thomson Financials (Western and Eastern Europe including Russia and Turkey); when they could be allocated to an ICB sectors based on data from Thomson Financials; when they were active in the analyzed year. Transaction data was obtained from Thomson Reuters' SDC Platinum database. Transactions are included in the analysis when they were announced between January 1st, 1998 and December 31st, 2007. Transactions are selected when more then 50% of equity changed hands to an unrelated acquirer; transaction value is known; the transaction value exceeded EUR 10 mn. The activity index is calculated by share of companies within an industry that were involved in corporate divestitures during the 10 year period analyzed. CAR and BHAR illustrate abnormal returns for shareholders of sellers that completed a major transactions with a transaction value of at least 10% of the seller's market capitalization at announcement. CAR values report the cumulated abnormal announcement returns three days around the transactions announcement for the 20 ICB sub-sectors. BHAR report abnormal buy-and-hold 24 months after announcement. The significance is tested with the standardized cross-sectional t-statistic for CAR and a boot-strapped t-statistic for BHAR. The last rows of the table report results from tests of mean differences in divestment activity and value creation across industries. Differences in divestment activity across industries is tested with the Pearson Chi-square-test. Reported are p-values of the test. The mean in differences of CAR and BHAR are tested with an ANOVA test of mean differences. The p-values of the F-statistic are reported. Significance levels resulting from t- and F-statistics are marked with *** in 1%, with ** in 5%, and with * in 10% confidence interval.

7.3.4 Multiple regression model

The impact of industry determinants on divestment activity and value creation is tested with different regression models. This study applies a linear multiple regression model to test industry effects on short- and long-term abnormal returns (*AbnormalReturn*). Industry effects on divestment activity (*FirmDivestment*) is tested with a logistic regression model.

Equation (7.5) shows the specification of the applied logit model to test determinants of divestment decisions.

$$
\begin{aligned}
z_{FirmDivestment} = {} & \beta_0 + \beta_1 MtoB + \beta_2\, SalesGrowth + \beta_3\, EBIT + \\
& \beta_4\, AssetTurn + \beta_5\, R\&D + \beta_6\, CAPEX + \beta_7\, PP\&E + \\
& \beta_8\, HHI + \beta_9 \Delta_{t-2/0}\, MtoB + \beta_{10}\, \Delta_{t-2/0}\, Growth + \beta_{11}\, \Delta_{t-2/0}\, EBIT + \\
& \beta_{12} \Delta_{t-2/0} AssetTurn + \beta_{13} \Delta_{t-2/0} R\&D + \beta_{14} \Delta_{t-2/0} CAPEX
\end{aligned}
\tag{7.5}
$$

The logit z indicates the likelihood for an individual firm to divest in one of the 10 years in this sample period. The regression bases on 31'104 active company years for the 4'581 companies within the 20 ICB sectors in this industry sample. $Z_{FirmDivestment}$ assumes the value 1 for all company years in which a divestment is announced. The value is 0 for years without divestments. The regressors are two sets of industry variables. The first set tests the effect of annual median industry ratios (*MtoB, SalesGrowth, EBIT, AssetTurn, R&D, CAPEX, PP&E, HHI*) and the second set examines changes in these industry ratios ($\Delta_{t-2/0}$*MtoB*, $\Delta_{t-2/0}$*SalesGrowth*, $\Delta_{t-2/0}$*EBIT*, $\Delta_{t-2/0}$*AssetTurn*, $\Delta_{t-2/0}$*R&D*, $\Delta_{t-2/0}$*CAPEX*).

To test industry effects on long- and short-term value creation, a linear regression model is used. The model pairs transaction BHAR and CAR with annual industry metrics. The linear regression model is outlined in Equation (7.6):

$$
\begin{aligned}
AbnormalReturn\ (CAR/BHAR) = {} & a_0 + a_1 MtoB + a_2\, SalesGrowth + \\
& a_3\, EBIT + a_4\, AssetTurn + a_5\, R\&D + a_6\, CAPEX + a_7\, PP\&E + \\
& a_8\, HHI + a_9 \Delta_{t-2/0}\, MtoB + a_{10}\, \Delta_{t-2/0}\, Growth + a_{11}\, \Delta_{t-2/0}\, EBIT + \\
& a_{12} \Delta_{t-2/0} AssetTurn + a_{13} \Delta_{t-2/0} R\&D + a_{14} \Delta_{t-2/0} CAPEX
\end{aligned}
\tag{7.6}
$$

AbnormalReturn is the dependent variable for value creation of major transactions. It is measured as 3-day CAR and 24-month BHAR to sellers' shareholders. The dependent variables pair with annual industry level and industry dynamic variables for the respective industry year.

7.4 Results

In a first step, industry determinants of divestment activity are tested with linear and logistic regressions. Based on the findings this paper then examines the power of the applied industry determinants to predict short- and long-term abnormal returns.

7.4.1 Divestment activity

The industry overview in Table 7.1 provides the aggregated 10-year activity index for the 20 ICB sectors in the sample. The results show large variations in aggregated activity level across industries. The mean industry transaction activity for the 10-year sample period is 33%. The activity level ranges from 9% (Health Care Equipment and Services) to 53% (General Industrials). Differences in activity between industries are tested with Pearson Chi-squared-tests as in Mitchell and Mulherin (1996). Resulting p-values are reported. The outcome shows significant differences in divestiture activity across industries. The null hypothesis of equality in industry activity is rejected with a confidence level of above 99%.

The effect of industry characteristics on annual divestment activity is tested in order to identify drivers of variations. Table 7.2 shows the logistic regression outcome for individual firms' decision to divest in a given industry year. Dependent variables are industry level (Panel A.) and industry dynamic indicators (Panel B.) for 200 industry years. Table 7.7 in the Appendix shows multinomial regression results for divestments in core-industries and refocusing sell-offs of non-core businesses.

The results show that industries with high valuation levels and high growth rates are less likely to divest. This indicates that managers are less willing to divest parts of their business when growth prospects in their industry are favorable. The reverse view suggests that divestments are more frequent when growth is flat or negative within an industry. This finding appears intuitive, as managers are less eager to sell when demand is growing and financial pressure to sell is low (Lang et al. 1995). Companies in low growth industries are, thus, more likely to reduce capacity and focus operations. This finding differs to some extent from results by Maksimovic and Phillips (2001) for a data sample of US plant sales during the 1980s. Maksimovic and Phillips (2001) set forth that asset sale activity is higher in growing industries. This effect is attributed to growing opportunity costs of poorly managed plants. Hence, in expanding industries, pressure to sell to more productive owners rises. The deviation in results is attributed to their focus on individual manufacturing plans limiting the industry scope opposed to the applied broader understanding of divestitures across all industries as well as to a difference in time period and geography.

The industry dynamic variables in Panel B. show differing results from the industry level view. Positive changes in M/B ratios (valuation shocks) lead to increased divestment activity. The results for inter- and intra-industry transactions in Table 7.7 show that increased activity mainly stems from divestments in core industries rather than in unrelated businesses. This notion underlines the market-timing hypothesis. Demand shocks (change in industry growth), in contrast, also have a positive sign but increased activity is mainly driven by non-related asset sales when managers reallocate resources to their expanding core industries.

The regression outcome shows that asset productivity and asset structure influence divestment activity. The result suggests that industries with relatively large productive asset stocks are more actively trading assets than industries that operate lower asset stocks. Companies with high asset turnover are typically more human capital intensive (e.g., service industries). The highly positive effect of PP&E share in industry assets supports this view and indicates that particularly industries relying on tangible productive assets are more actively trading assets (Maksimovic and Phillips 2001). Hence, asset reallocation within an industry is more likely when transferring physical assets instead of human capital. Wang and Chung (2009) provide a possible explanation for this observation by pointing out that human capital is hard to retain in M&A transactions and is therefore less liquid.

Industries with high profitability levels are more active compared to high growth industries. EBIT is highly correlated to industry CAPEX levels that also have highly significant positive effects on divestment activity. In an industry dynamic view the EBIT change variable has an insignificant negative sign while changes in industry CAPEX requirements increase the likelihood of asset sales significantly. The related and non-related asset view in Table 7.7 confirms the intuitive notion that managers react to investment shocks by selling assets in unrelated industries, reallocating resources to their core industry.

R&D intensive industries show lower divestment activity. A potential explanation for this effect is lower liquidity of specific technology assets due to uncertainty with regard to the valuation of technology as pointed out by Benou et al. (2008). Another potential reason is the often smaller value of technology assets which may lead to exclusion from the transaction sample. The inter-industry view in Table 7.7 provides an indication that managers react to increasing R&D investment requirements by selling assets in industries that experience technology shocks.

Table 7.2: Industry determinants of divestment activity

	(1)	(2)	(3)	(4)	(5)	(6)	(7)	(8)	(9)	(10)
					A. Industry Levels					
Intercept	-2.917	-3.219	-3.514	-2.915	-3.120	-3.171	-3.563	-3.320	-4.046	-4.017
	[0.000]	**[0.000]**	**[0.000]**	**[0.000]**	**[0.000]**	**[0.000]**	**[0.000]**	**[0.000]**	**[0.000]**	**[0.000]**
MtoB	-0.140								-0.063	-0.154
	[0.002]								[0.484]	[0.175]
SalesGrowth		-0.340							0.840	-0.521
		[0.348]							[0.200]	[0.647]
EBIT			4.813						1.489	3.556
			[0.000]						[0.498]	[0.202]
AssetTurn				-0.284					0.112	0.221
				[0.006]					[0.475]	[0.193]
R&D					-2.501				-0.624	-0.931
					[0.000]				[0.512]	[0.360]
CAPEX						9.080			5.207	10.147
						[0.000]			[0.125]	**[0.027]**
PP&E							0.906		0.879	0.253
							[0.000]		**[0.016]**	[0.568]
HHI								2.554	1.363	1.110
								[0.002]	[0.137]	[0.232]
Company yrs					N=45'810					
Pseudo R^2	0.010	0.001	0.017	0.011	0.021	0.027	0.027	0.014	0.017	**cont.**
					B. Industry Dynamic					
Intercept	-3.192	-3.197	-3.193	-3.199	-3.195	-3.160	-3.158			**cont.**
	[0.000]	**[0.000]**	**[0.000]**	**[0.000]**	**[0.000]**	**[0.000]**	**[0.000]**			
$\Delta_{t-2/0}$ MtoB	0.073						0.068			0.109
	[0.021]						[0.306]			[0.248]
$\Delta_{t-2/0}$ Growth		0.462					0.550			0.913
		[0.031]					[0.290]			[0.250]
$\Delta_{t-2/0}$ EBIT			-0.582				-4.211			-3.374
			[0.548]				[0.479]			[0.174]
$\Delta_{t-2/0}$ AssetTurn				-0.112			0.005			-0.381
				[0.590]			[0.987]			[0.253]
$\Delta_{t-2/0}$ R&D					0.916		0.895			1.315
					[0.572]		[0.687]			[0.626]
$\Delta_{t-2/0}$ CAPEX						6.645	7.674			5.704
						[0.018]	**[0.029]**			[0.168]
Company years					N=31'104					
Pseudo R^2	0.005	0.005	0.000	0.000	0.000	0.011	0.015	0.014	0.017	0.028

This table presents logistic regressions of divestment activity. The logistic regressions indicate the likelihood of an individual company to divest in a specific year in dependence of tested industry characteristics. The tested dataset consists of 31'104 company years. The dependent variable (logit) takes the value 1 for companies that performed at least one divestment in the specific year. It takes the value 0 if no activity occurred. P-values from t-statistics are provided in brackets below coefficients. Significant values are marked in bold. Nagelkerkes Pseudo R-squared is provided.

Industry concentration has a positive effect on divestment likelihood. Komlenovic et al. (2011) argue that mature, concentrated industry buy less within their industry due to lack of investment opportunities. The divestment results propose, however, that managers in mature industry are more active in optimizing their capital allocation than managers in less mature industries with higher growth.

Overall, the results show that industry level variables have higher predictive power (R^2) than industry dynamic variables. When included in an overall regression model, no industry dynamic coefficient remains significant (however, this needs to be interpreted with caution due to significant multicollinearity in an integrated model). The second part of hypothesis 7.H2 is, therefore, rejected for activity predictors. This finding stands in contrast to M&A specific results from Mitchell and Mulherin (1996) who show that increased M&A activity is driven by industry shocks rather than industry levels indicators.

7.4.2 Value creation of corporate divestitures

In addition to industry factors influencing divestment activity, focus of this analysis is on industry implications on sellers' shareholder wealth. This study tests short- and long-term abnormal stock market performance to examine value creation from a shareholders' perspective. Short-term effects are measured as 3-day CAR. Long-term effects are measured with 24-month BHAR. Results for the overall sample (Table 7.1) show, in line with previous studies, that divestitures increase shareholder wealth regardless of examined time horizon. It is not surprising to find abnormal returns both at announcement and over 24 months following the announcement. Bates (2005) points out that the value creation of corporate divestiture depends on the use of proceeds. At announcement, the use of proceeds is not fully transparent to investors leading to re-assessment of divestment decisions over time when further information about investment choices becomes available.

The mean CAR for the 579 sample transactions is 2.03%. The mean BHAR is also positive at 8.05%. Both means are statistically significant within the 99% confidence interval. This finding is largely in line with previous research on corporate divestitures. Positive abnormal returns are frequently explained by a more efficient allocation of assets following divestments and the lack of agency conflicts that often negatively affect M&A success (e.g., Boone and Mulherin 2000, Schlingemann et al. 2002, Veld and Veld-Merkoulova 2004). However, in a cross-industry comparison, large variations in mean industry divestment performance can be found in the data sample. CAR range from 5.17% for Health Care Equipment & Services (ICB 453) to -1.94% for Beverages (ICB 353). The long-term BHAR results range from a highly positive abnormal return of 41.88% in the Oil Equipment & Services (ICB 57) sector to significantly negative BHAR of -14.98% in Industrial Transportation (ICB 277).

Table 7.3: Regression of 3-day CAR -Divestments

	(1)	(2)	(3)	(4)	(5)	(6)	(7)	(8)	(9)	(10)	(11)
Intercept	-0.004	0.009	0.009	0.001	-0.006	0.020	0.020	0.020	0.016	0.014	-0.044
	[0.742]	[0.181]	[0.329]	[0.939]	**[0.012]**	**[0.000]**	**[0.000]**	**[0.000]**	**[0.000]**	**[0.000]**	[0.131]
Industry Levels											
MtoB	0.012				0.063						-0.003
	[0.024]				[0.255]						[0.831]
SalesGrowth		0.061			-0.068						-0.112
		[0.181]			[0.333]						[0.220]
EBIT			0.167		0.461						0.609
			[0.210]		**[0.043]**						**[0.021]**
AssetTurn				0.024	0.042						0.044
				[0.022]	**[0.003]**						**[0.004]**
R&D				-0.036	-0.004						0.067
				[0.950]	[0.966]						[0.511]
CAPEX				-0.158	-0.086						0.254
				[0.519]	[0.456]						[0.528]
PP&E				-0.030	0.099						-0.049
				[0.332]	**[0.078]**						[0.238]
HHI				-0.022	-0.050						-0.048
				[0.781]	[0.568]						[0.599]
Industry Dynamic											
$\Delta_{t-2/0}$ MtoB						0.023				0.027	0.024
						[0.003]				**[0.006]**	**[0.038]**
$\Delta_{t-2/0}$ Growth							0.104			-0.058	0.024
							[0.032]			[0.388]	[0.751]
$\Delta_{t-2/0}$ EBIT								0.125		0.214	0.043
								[0.256]		[0.479]	[0.903]
$\Delta_{t-2/0}$ AssetTurn									-0.147	-0.168	-0.098
									[0.003]	**[0.002]**	[0.125]
$\Delta_{t-2/0}$ R&D									-0.216	-0.074	0.025
									[0.259]	[0.725]	[0.909]
$\Delta_{t-2/0}$ CAPEX									-0.390	-0.582	-0.876
									[0.156]	[0.135]	[0.098]
Transactions						N=579					
Industry years						N=200					
F-Statistic	5.14^{b}	1.79	1.57	1.35	2.23^{b}	8.61^{a}	4.62^{a}	3.55^{a}	3.29^{a}	3.44^{a}	2.20^{a}
R^2 adjusted	0.009	0.001	0.001	0.011	0.029	0.015	0.008	0.006	0.017	0.035	0.052

The table presents OLS regressions of short-term announcement returns (CAR) for a 3-day event window around the announcement of major corporate divestitures. Major divestitures are defined as transactions with a deal value that equals or exceed 10% of the seller's market capitalization in the month before the announcement. Independent variables are industry characteristics which are aggregated for 20 ICB sectors (3-digit ICB codes) from individual firm financial data of industry constituents. Industry characteristics are divided in industry medians of the announcement years (Industry Levels) and average median changes (Industry Dynamics) over three years (t=-2 to t=0). In addition, industry concentration is included applying the Herfindahl-Index (HHI). All industry characteristics are calculated for the 200 industry years of the 10-year sample period between 1998 and 2007. The table returns p-values from t-statistics of the coefficients in brackets. P-values are marked in bold if below 10%. The F-statistic of the OLS regression are marked with "a" in the 1% confidence interval, "b" in the 5% confidence interval, and "c" in the 10% confidence interval.

An ANOVA test of mean differences for industry CAR and BHAR is performed to test whether these industry variations are statistically significant. Table 7.1 reports the resulting p-values. Mean differences for both industry CAR and BHAR are highly significant within the 1% confidence interval. The results underline the intuition that average value creation of corporate divestitures varies in different industry settings.

To further evaluate the effects of industry characteristics on value creation, linear regressions of CAR and BHAR are estimated. Table 7.3 shows results for 3-day CAR as independent variable. Table 7.4 shows regressions of 24-month BHAR. Finally, Table 7.8 in the Appendix provides results from regressions of inter- and intra-industry divestment subsample CAR and BHAR. For the analysis of inter- and intra-industry transaction the test focuses on industry dynamic variables. Previous research points out that change in industry structure promote refocusing or diversification decisions (Colak 2009).

The short-term results in Table 7.3 show that investors react positively to divestments when industry valuations are high and increasing. The positive effects on firm value are only significant when companies are selling assets within their highly valued core industry (Table 7.8). The results suggest that higher proceeds from sales when valuations are high are favored by investors. Divestments under depressed valuations yield lower shareholder returns in the short-term when applying the reverse view. CAR are also higher when positive demand shocks appear within a seller's core industry. This effect is driven by positive investor reactions to refocusing transactions when core industries expand (Table 7.8). The finding is intuitive as managers reallocate their assets to a more promising investment environment. The predictions advanced by Yang (2008) with regard to positive implication of asset sales in expanding industries support this result.

Industry productivity measures show a reversed picture compared to the activity view. While industries with lower asset turnover see more corporate control transactions, CAR are higher for less asset intensive industries with high asset turnover. The PP&E coefficient remains insignificant indicating no significant influence of tangible asset share on CAR.

Change in asset turnover has a negative sign suggesting that investors perceive announcement returns from divestments in industries with growing asset productivity negatively. The reverse view proposes positive announcement effects in industries that experience a decline in asset productivity. The notion that asset reallocation in industries that see productivity shocks is in line with predictions from Yang (2008) and Warusawitharana (2008). Both authors predict positive valuation effects when managers adjust the productive asset stock to a (lower) optimal level. The long-term results in Table 7.4 show comparable but less significant results for changes in asset turnover.

The long-term BHAR results in Table 7.4 are in line with short-term CAR findings. Shareholder value creation from divestments is larger in industries with high valuation levels. The finding indicates that higher proceeds from highly valued assets benefit shareholders also beyond transaction announcement. High CAPEX levels within an industry appear to positively affect the value creation of corporate divestitures when managers finance CAPEX investments by reallocating internal assets. The coefficient remains, however, insignificant at the 10% confidence interval. The results also show that shareholder benefit in the long-run when managers restructure and sell assets in their core industry amid declining industry profitability levels ($\Delta_{t-2/0}$ EBIT). This finding is consistent with value implications from Yang (2008) and Warusawitharana (2008).

Increases in R&D spending have a positive effect on divestment success. Companies appear to benefit from freeing up capital to invest in R&D internally or through M&A.

Overall, short-term announcement returns appear mainly driven by industry changes in valuation levels and growth indicators. Long-term value creation depends more strongly on productivity measures and investment requirements. This finding proposes that investors make their initial investment decision based on short- to mid-term growth prospects in an industry and potential temporary misevaluation. In the longer term, abnormal returns are driven by structural changes in productivity and investment requirements.

With regard to value creation, the results also show that changes in industry structure have generally higher predictive power (R^2) than industry level variables. Hypothesis 7.H2 is, thus, supported for value creation.

Table 7.4: Regression of 24-month BHAR - Divestments

	(1)	(2)	(3)	(4)	(5)	(6)	(7)	(8)	(9)	(10)	(11)
Intercept	-0.004	0.031	0.061	-0.062	-0.054	0.081	0.085	0.081	0.053	0.055	-0.044
	[0.742]	[0.491]	[0.527]	[0.669]	[0.822]	**[0.004]**	**[0.003]**	**[0.004]**	[0.117]	[0.118]	[0.131]
Industry Levels											
MtoB	0.120				0.167						0.138
	[0.019]				[0.103]						[0.224]
SalesGrowth		0.642			-0.460						-0.319
		[0.155]			[0.511]						[0.224]
EBIT			0.294		-2.254						0.624
			[0.827]		[0.155]						[0.820]
AssetTurn				-0.066	-0.065						0.064
				[0.502]	[0.619]						[0.640]
R&D				0.399	-0.663						-1.154
				[0.588]	[0.484]						[0.266]
CAPEX				2.742	2.632						7.734
				[0.122]	[0.134]						**[0.070]**
PPE				-0.774	-0.628						-0.604
				[0.005]	**[0.067]**						[0.135]
HHI				0.155	0.180						-0.410
				[0.854]	[0.831]						[0.182]
Industry Dynamic											
$\Delta_{t-2/0}$ MtoB						-0.056				0.034	0.087
						[0.135]				[0.710]	[0.436]
$\Delta_{t-2/0}$ Growth							-0.303			-0.321	0.024
							[0.283]			[0.621]	[0.592]
$\Delta_{t-2/0}$ EBIT								-2.470		-1.500	-0.142
								[0.027]		[0.343]	[0.269]
$\Delta_{t-2/0}$ AssetTurn									-0.329	-0.907	-0.255
									[0.206]	**[0.077]**	[0.668]
$\Delta_{t-2/0}$ R&D									0.648	0.584	0.494
									[0.001]	**[0.008]**	**[0.043]**
$\Delta_{t-2/0}$ CAPEX									0.292	0.497	-1.438
									[0.124]	[0.861]	[0.458]
Transactions						N=452					
Industry years						N=200					
F-Statistic	5.52^a	1.79	1.57	2.63^b	2.06^b	2.25	1.16	4.90^a	3.29^a	3.19^a	2.47^a
R^2 adjusted	0.012	0.004	0.001	0.029	0.036	0.005	0.003	0.010	0.037	0.041	0.073

The table presents OLS regressions of 24-month buy-and-hold returns (BHAR) to shareholders of firms that undertake a major divestment. Major divestitures are defined as transactions with a deal value that equals or exceed 10% of the seller's market capitalization in the month before the announcement. Independent variables are industry characteristics, which are aggregated for 20 ICB sectors (3-digit ICB codes) from individual firm financial data of industry constituents. Industry characteristics are divided in industry medians of the announcement years (Industry Levels) and average median changes (Industry Dynamics) over three years (t=-2 to t=0). In addition, industry concentration is included applying the Herfindahl-Index (HHI). All industry characteristics are calculated for the 200 industry years of the 10-year sample period between 1998 and 2007. The table returns p-values from t-statistics of coefficients in brackets. P-values are marked in bold if below 10%. The F-statistics of the OLS regressions are marked with "a" in the 1% confidence interval, "b" in the 5% confidence interval, and "c" in the 10% confidence interval.

7.5 Conclusions

The presented study examines effects of industry characteristics on the activity level and on value creation of corporate divestments. Value creation and activity are analyzed based on 20 ICB sectors (3-digit ICB codes). The results support the starting intuition that activity levels and value creation of corporate divestiture differ significantly across industries. The findings suggest that industry characteristics determine activity and success of corporate restructuring.

First, industry drivers of activity are analyzed. The results show that firms are more likely to divest assets in industries with low valuation levels and weak growth rates. (Temporary) increases in valuation levels drive activity, suggesting that managers time their divestments to enhance proceeds. Increasing CAPEX investment requirements foster refocusing divestments when managers attempt to reallocate non-core assets to meet capital needs in their core industry. A further result of the activity examination indicates that industries with low asset turnover rates and large tangible asset stocks are more actively trading assets.

The second part of the analysis examines the effects of industry characteristics on shareholder wealth creation from divestments. Although announcement returns as well as long-term investor returns are positive on average, large differences between industries exist. Factors driving these variations differ for immediate announcement returns and long-term performance of divestitures. These differences across time horizons can be explained by uncertainty of investors with regard to the future use of the proceeds from asset sales. This leads to positive investor reactions when divestments are made during high and increasing valuations when asset prices are high. Investors also favor refocusing on core industries when these expand. Surprisingly, announcement returns are lower in asset heavy industries despite higher activity levels.

Long-term returns, in contrast to short-term results, are less driven by valuation levels and growth prospects then by industry wide productivity changes. Shareholders profit in the long-term when firms sell assets in industries that see declining profitability levels, adjusting their productive assets stocks to a new optimal levels. These findings are largely in line with predictions from recent studies by Yang (2008) and Warusawitharana (2008) that relate asset reallocation to changes in an optimal firm size that is determined by industry dynamics.

Increases in R&D investment needs also see significant value creation potential from divestments when managers reassess their asset allocation to non-core industries and potentially shift resources to core industries that experience technology shocks.

7.6 Appendix

7.6.1 Overview of data sample

Table 7.5 shows the derivation of the applied transaction and industry data sample. The table provides the scope of the company data sample used to calculate industry financials, the transaction sample applied to derive CAR and BHAR as well as the activity index and, finally, the resulting number of industries that are included in the examination. Table 7.6 provides an overview of the aggregated 10-year industry medians and standard deviations of the calculated industry financials.

Table 7.5: Derivation of data sample

A. Transaction data sample	**Sample size**
Acquisitions of European companies with transaction value > EUR 10mn between 1998-2007	16'295
thereof partial firm acquisitions/divestments	9'307
thereof transactions from private companies/no matching CUSIP or SEDOL code	4'268
Total number of allocated public company divestitures	5'039
Divestitures > 10% of seller's market cap	945
Number of transactions with all available data to calculate CAR	872
Number of transactions with all available data to calculate BHAR	662
Average transactions value in EUR mn	639
B. Industry data sample	
Total number of 3-digit ICB sectors	41
thereof financial industries with investment focus	5
Number of industry with strategic divestment focus	36
Number of industries with more than 10 major transactions of listed firms	31
Number of industries with sufficient data availability to calculate 10 3-day CAR	27
Number of industries with sufficient data availability to calculate 10 24-month BHAR	20
C. Company data sample	
Total European (based on region code) company identifiers in database	14'557
thereof ADR identifiers	535
Non-ADR European Company identifiers	14'022
thereof in-active between 1998 and 2007	1'487
Total active European Company identifiers	12'535
thereof no primary industry classification available (ICB codes)	3'076
Total industry classified companies	9'459
thereof public companies	6'383
thereof private companies	3'076
D. Applied data sample	
Number of industries (based on BHAR data availability)	20
Number of transactions with reported deal value > EUR 10mn in considered industries	2'758
Number of public companies in considered 20 ICB industries	4'581
Number of CAR in considered industries	579
Number of BHAR in considered industries	454

The table gives an overview of the transaction, industry, and company sample derivation. Excluded from the analysis are real estate firms, investment firms and investment vehicles. The data sample focuses on companies headquartered in Europe based on the regional code provided in Thomson Financials. Transaction data was downloaded from SDC; Company and stock market information was obtained from Thomson Financials and Datastream.

Table 7.6: Overview of aggregated industry characteristics 1998 to 2007

ICB sector (codes)	MtoB		Sales Growth		EB IT Margin		AssetTurn		R&D		CAPEX		PP&E		HHI	
	MD	**StDev**	**MD**	**StDev**	**MD**	**StDev**	**MD**	**StDev**	**MD**	**StDev**	**MD**	**StDev**	**MD**	**StDev**	**MD**	**StDev**
Oil Equipment, & Services (57)	1.80	0.89	12.3%	12.0%	8.8%	3.2%	0.72	0.07	0.5%	0.2%	6.0%	3.0%	49.6%	14.8%	0.06	0.00
Chemicals (135)	1.50	0.22	4.9%	3.0%	7.4%	1.0%	0.95	0.04	2.4%	0.2%	5.2%	0.8%	63.6%	3.6%	0.04	0.01
Forestry & Paper (173)	1.09	0.13	2.0%	2.9%	6.3%	1.3%	0.90	0.07	0.5%	0.1%	4.8%	0.7%	70.6%	5.0%	0.09	0.01
Construction & Materials (235)	1.48	0.36	8.4%	3.5%	7.5%	1.1%	1.01	0.04	0.8%	0.1%	4.4%	0.6%	48.3%	3.2%	0.02	0.00
General Industrials (272)	1.43	0.15	6.2%	4.2%	7.4%	1.4%	0.99	0.05	0.9%	0.2%	5.3%	0.7%	60.8%	4.0%	0.09	0.02
Electronic & Equipment (273)	2.14	0.51	8.5%	7.4%	6.3%	2.0%	1.17	0.04	4.6%	0.5%	3.0%	1.1%	39.3%	6.9%	0.16	0.01
Industrial Engineering (275)	1.75	0.43	6.0%	5.0%	6.6%	1.4%	1.17	0.02	2.3%	0.3%	3.6%	0.6%	46.6%	3.2%	0.03	0.00
Industrial Transportation (277)	1.48	0.41	7.3%	4.3%	9.7%	3.1%	0.59	0.06	0.7%	0.5%	6.3%	1.3%	58.8%	5.6%	0.06	0.02
Support Services (279)	2.38	0.41	13.1%	7.2%	5.5%	1.4%	1.32	0.12	1.8%	0.6%	2.9%	1.0%	25.3%	5.0%	0.03	0.00
Automobiles & Parts (335)	1.43	0.26	7.1%	4.1%	5.4%	0.9%	1.16	0.04	3.6%	0.4%	6.3%	0.8%	61.9%	3.8%	0.07	0.01
Beverages (353)	2.13	0.30	3.6%	1.5%	8.8%	1.4%	0.74	0.06	0.2%	0.1%	5.2%	0.8%	52.3%	8.4%	0.06	0.01
Food Producers (357)	1.72	0.27	6.3%	3.1%	6.0%	0.7%	1.15	0.12	0.6%	0.1%	4.4%	0.7%	59.3%	3.0%	0.06	0.00
Household Goods (372)	1.34	0.23	6.0%	3.3%	6.3%	1.1%	1.16	0.06	1.1%	0.1%	3.5%	0.8%	52.9%	6.3%	0.05	0.01
Health Care Eqpmt. & Serv. (453)	2.43	0.48	9.1%	4.9%	8.3%	2.1%	0.84	0.05	6.1%	1.0%	4.0%	0.8%	29.5%	5.0%	0.06	0.01
Pharmaceuticals & Biotech. (457)	3.38	0.60	7.7%	4.6%	9.1%	1.8%	0.50	0.09	21.3%	4.1%	2.9%	1.1%	23.9%	6.7%	0.06	0.00
General Retailers (537)	1.94	0.28	8.2%	3.0%	5.2%	0.5%	1.55	0.05	1.7%	1.0%	4.8%	0.7%	42.6%	5.0%	0.04	0.01
Media (555)	2.25	0.67	8.0%	9.6%	8.5%	2.2%	0.82	0.09	1.7%	0.8%	2.2%	0.9%	17.8%	5.3%	0.03	0.01
Travel & Leisure (575)	1.72	0.26	6.1%	3.5%	7.4%	2.0%	0.60	0.03	1.1%	0.9%	5.2%	1.5%	62.4%	10.9%	0.03	0.00
Nonlife Insurance (853)	1.56	0.18	8.0%	2.9%	7.3%	3.1%	0.31	0.02	0.0%	0.0%	0.3%	0.1%	5.6%	1.0%	0.06	0.01
Software & Computer Serv. (953)	2.39	1.52	13.5%	20.3%	4.8%	3.3%	1.08	0.16	12.3%	1.6%	2.1%	1.2%	16.2%	3.8%	0.03	0.00
Average	**1.87**	**0.43**	**7.62%**	**5.52%**	**7.13%**	**1.74%**	**0.94**	**0.06**	**3.21%**	**0.65%**	**4.12%**	**0.97%**	**44.4%**	**5.5%**	**0.06**	**0.01**
Standard Deviation	**0.92**	**0.26**	**4.30%**	**3.70%**	**8.50%**	**1.31%**	**0.46**	**0.04**	**2.71%**	**0.52%**	**2.31%**	**0.59%**	**23.9%**	**3.8%**	**0.06**	**0.02**

The table provides an overview of the industry factors applied in the previous analyses. In contrast to the data used for the analyses the table returns aggregated values over the ten-year sample period. The ten-year median (MD) and standard deviation (StDev) are shown. The annual industry factors are calculated for every year between 1998 and 2007 from all active listed firms with the respective 3-digit ICB code (4'581) that show valid entries for the examined financial data in the Worldscope data base.

7.6.2 Results for inter- and intra-industry divestments

An important aspect when analyzing industry determinants of divestment activity and value creation is the management decision to refocus operations or to dispose parts of the core business. Core business transactions are defined as sell-offs of assets that share the same SIC code with the selling parent. Refocusing transactions, on the other hand, show different SIC codes of seller and divested entity. The presented results pertain to differences in 2-digit SIC codes. The results are mostly robust to changes in this regime towards 4- and 3-digit SIC codes (available on request). Although the ICB classification scheme is applied for the general industry classification underlying the analyses, SIC, despite a number of short-comings (Weiner 2005), are more suitable to identifying differences in industry between sold asset and seller. Main reason is a consistent SIC classification in the SDC database for divested assets.

Table 7.7 provides multinominal logistic regression results for an individual firm's choice to divest assets within its core industry (Panel B) or to refocus by selling a non-core asset (Panel A). The results indicate that managers are more likely to sell assets in their core industry when its valuation levels are rising. This finding underlines the market timing view. Managers appear to conduct asset sales when proceeds are highest. The significantly positive coefficient for sales growth in this inter-industry sample suggests that companies in industries experiencing a demand shock tend to refocus their resources towards their expanding core industry. The regression outcome also indicates that managers react to falling industry asset productivity by diversifiying. However, the coefficients remain insignificant close to the 10% confidence interval. The results also provide only an indication that technology shocks (strong increases in R&D investments) lead managers to sell assets in their core industry. The most significant finding, however, shows that increases in CAPEX requirement in an industry is frequently addressed by selling non-core business units.

Panel B. indicates that long-term returns are positively affected when firms sell assets in industries that see a negative profitabilty shock. The reversed view suggests that selling assets in industries that show increasing profitability levels leads to lower relative shareholder return in the long run. The coefficient for technology shocks (change in R&D investment levels) is significant for both inter- and intra-industry transactions with different signs. Selling assets in core industries when industry R&D expenditure increases leads to lower long-term returns for shareholders. Refocussing, on the other hand, increases long-term returns. This result suggests companies fare better when reallocating assets and investing in new technolgies rather than pulling away from industries that experience technology shocks. This result stands in contrast to the observed tendencies of firms to allocate resources in non-core areas when R&D requirements go up (Table 7.7).

Table 7.7: Multinomial regression of inter- and intra-industry divestments

	(1)	(2)	(3)	(4)	(5)	(6)	(7)
A. Refocusing transactions (inter-industry) - Ln(inter/non)							
Intercept	-3.192 **[0.000]**	-3.926 **[0.000]**	-3.852 **[0.000]**	-3.840 **[0.000]**	-3.850 **[0.000]**	-3.807 **[0.000]**	-3.767 **[0.000]**
$\Delta_{t-2/0}$ MtoB	0.071 [0.114]						0.053 [0.569]
$\Delta_{t-2/0}$ Growth		0.539 **[0.081]**					1.033 [0.159]
$\Delta_{t-2/0}$ EBIT			-0.063 [0.662]				-8.909 **[0.001]**
$\Delta_{t-2/0}$ AssetTurn				0.234 [0.423]			0.340 [0.393]
$\Delta_{t-2/0}$ R&D					-1.290 [0.573]		-3.206 [0.317]
$\Delta_{t-2/0}$ CAPEX						9.194 **[0.016]**	14.059 **[0.003]**
B. Divestments in core industry (intra-industry) - Ln(intra/non)							
Intercept	-3.192 **[0.000]**	-3.854 **[0.000]**	-3.923 **[0.000]**	-3.949 **[0.000]**	-3.928 **[0.000]**	-3.902 **[0.000]**	-3.948 **[0.000]**
$\Delta_{t-2/0}$ MtoB	0.075 **[0.088]**						0.088 [0.348]
$\Delta_{t-2/0}$ Growth		0.392 [0.182]					0.010 [0.986]
$\Delta_{t-2/0}$ EBIT			1.277 [0.356]				0.825 [0.772]
$\Delta_{t-2/0}$ AssetTurn				-0.464 [0.109]			-0.346 [0.376]
$\Delta_{t-2/0}$ R&D					3.158 [0.160]		4.848 [0.104]
$\Delta_{t-2/0}$ CAPEX						3.855 [0.338]	0.729 [0.885]
Company years				N=31'104			
Pseudo R^2	0.009	0.004	0.001	0.003	0.000	0.014	0.015

This table presents results from multinomial logistic regressions of divestment activity in dependence of the seller's industry characteristics. In Panel A., the multinomial regression model tests the likelihood of a firm to make a refocusing (inter-industry) divestment relative to making no divestment. Inter-industry divestments show a difference in 2-digit SIC code between seller and divested asset. Panel B. tests the likelihood of an investment within the core industry of the seller (intra-industry). Intra-industry transaction have equal 2-digit SIC codes between asset and seller. The regression is based on 31'104 active company years for the 4'581 companies within the 20 ICB sectors in the industry sample between 1998 and 2007. P-values from t-statistics are provided in brackets below coefficients. Significant values are marked in bold.

Table 7.8: Regression of CAR and BHAR for inter- and intra-industry sub-samples

	(1) Inter	(2) Intra	(3) Inter	(4) Intra	(5) Inter	(6) Intra	(7) Inter	(8) Intra	(9) Inter	(10) Intra
					A. CAR					
Intercept	0.021	0.018	0.126	-0.009	0.128	-0.004	0.013	0.023	0.013	0.017
	[0.000]	[0.345]	**[0.001]**	[0.190]	**[0.001]**	[0.342]	**[0.007]**	**[0.000]**	**[0.009]**	**[0.023]**
$\Delta_{t-2/0}$ MtoB	0.015	0.033							0.007	0.048
	[0.188]	**[0.002]**							[0.646]	**[0.001]**
$\Delta_{t-2/0}$ Growth			0.164	-0.007					0.188	-0.150
			[0.009]	[0.929]					**[0.028]**	[0.102]
$\Delta_{t-2/0}$ EBIT					1.141	0.103			0.184	0.249
					[0.703]	[0.500]			[0.467]	[0.589]
$\Delta_{t-2/0}$ AssetTurn							-0.263	0.014	-0.091	-0.058
							[0.000]	[0.686]	**[0.048]**	[0.157]
$\Delta_{t-2/0}$ R&D							-0.246	-0.130	-0.070	-0.096
							[0.404]	[0.604]	[0.833]	[0.729]
$\Delta_{t-2/0}$ CAPEX							-0.851	0.489	-0.599	0.175
							[0.012]	[0.333]	**[0.076]**	[0.730]
Transactions									N=351	N=228
Industry years									N=200	N=200
F-Statistic	1.74	9.53^{a}	6.88^{a}	0.01	0.15	0.455	5.50^{a}	0.611	2.15^{b}	2.49^{b}
R^2 adjusted	0.005	0.039	0.020	0.000	0.001	0.001	0.047	0.008	0.037	0.061
					B. BHAR					
	0.127	0.018	0.130	0.005	0.125	0.011	0.084	-0.020	0.085	-0.012
	[0.001]	[0.236]	**[0.001]**	[0.904]	**[0.001]**	[0.785]	**[0.060]**	[0.698]	**[0.065]**	[0.831]
$\Delta_{t-2/0}$ MtoB	-0.050	-0.058							0.047	0.003
	[0.304]	[0.322]							[0.732]	[0.977]
$\Delta_{t-2/0}$ Growth			-0.250	-0.287					-0.481	0.060
			[0.496]	[0.507]					[0.587]	[0.952]
$\Delta_{t-2/0}$ EBIT					-1.840	-2.175			-1.202	-1.495
					[0.204]	**[0.069]**			[0.560]	[0.544]
$\Delta_{t-2/0}$ AssetTurn							-1.041	-0.398	-1.299	-0.517
							[0.102]	[0.539]	**[0.069]**	[0.483]
$\Delta_{t-2/0}$ R&D							0.747	-0.606	0.622	-0.513
							[0.009]	**[0.014]**	**[0.059]**	**[0.078]**
$\Delta_{t-2/0}$ CAPEX							-1.013	-1.253	-0.448	0.108
							[0.740]	[0.787]	[0.901]	[0.983]
Transactions									N=284	N=168
Industry years									N=200	N=200
F-Statistic	1.06	0.90	0.46	0.44	1.62	3.36^{a}	3.52^{a}	2.67^{a}	1.87^{c}	1.35^{a}
R^2 adjusted	0.004	0.005	0.002	0.003	0.006	0.020	0.036	0.046	0.039	0.028

This table presents OLS regressions of 3-day CAR and 24-month BHAR to shareholders of firms that complete a major divestiture between 1998 and 2007. The dependent variables are CAR (Panel A.) and BHAR (Panel B.) of refocusing transactions (inter) and divestments within the core industry of the seller (intra). Difference or equality of industry between sold asset and seller is determined based on 2-digit SIC codes as provided in the SDC M&A database. Independent variables are the sum of median changes of industry characteristics (Industry Dynamics) over 3 years (t=-2 to t=0). Indicators of industry dynamics are aggregated for 20 ICB sectors (3-digit ICB codes) from individual firm financial data of industry constituents for every year in the sample period. The table returns p-values from the t-statistics of the coefficients in brackets. P-values are marked in bold if below 10%. The F-statistic of the OLS regression are marked with "a" in the 1% confidence interval, "b" in the 5% confidence interval, and "c" in the 10% confidence interval.

Table 7.8 provide linear regression results of transaction sub-sample for refocusing transactions (inter) and divestments of core-industry assets (intra). Independent variables are short-term abnormal return to seller's shareholder measured as 3-day CAR (Panel A.) and long-term abnormal returns measured as 24-month BHAR (Panel B.). The short-term results in Panel A. suggest that investors favor divestments of core-industry assets when core industries see an increase in asset valuations (increase in MtoB). With regard to demand shocks (change in sales growth), CAR are positively affected when firms refocus on their growing core industry by selling non-core businesses. However, investor react negatively when firms refocus amid growing core industry asset productivity and CAPEX requirement.

7.6.3 Univariate results

This section provides descriptive results for divestment value creation in different industry groups based on their aggregated characteristics. Tabel 7.9 shows effects of industry fundamental levels and changes in these fundamentals on mean short-term value creation (3-day CAR) for different industry groups. Table 7.10 provides the corresponding results for long-term effects (24-month BHAR). The total sample of transactions is split in three equally sized groups to analyze the value effects. Groups are constructed based on the annual ranking of industries with regard to the respective industry factor. The top 33% group returns all transactions in industries that showed a characteristic with the highest 33% of values in the announcement year of the transaction. The bottom 33% group contains the lowest 33% of values, respectively. The tables then report a mean difference test of the top and bottom group. This analysis shows whether significant differences between high and low industry determinants exist.

The findings provide support for the multiple regression results. In addition, they give an indication for the actual level of abnormal returns realized in different industry groups. They also show the outcome of potential investment strategies. Table 7.9 suggests that valuation levels have a positive effect on announcement return to sellers' shareholders. The mean difference between top and bottom MtoB industry level groups is significant at 1.48% in line with the multivariate finding. Industries with high relative asset turnover rates also outperform the lowest third of industries by 1.05% at announcement. However, the univariate result remain insignificant.

Table 7.9: 3-day CAR results for industry groups - Divestments

Groups	MtoB	Sales Growth	EBIT	Asset Turnover	R&D	CAPEX	PP&E	HHI
				A. Industry Level				
Bottom 33%	1.50% (2.51**)	1.64% (2.55**)	2.00% (3.45***)	1.37% (2.36**)	1.58% (3.46***)	2.33% (4.18***)	2.37% (4.56***)	2.16% (5.07***)
Top 33%	3.84% (5.35***)	2.07% (4.48***)	2.24% (4.29***)	2.42% (4.26***)	2.12% (3.85***)	1.27% (2.73***)	1.32% (2.14**)	1.56% (3.04**)
Top - Bottom	1.48% (1.81*)	0.43% (0.55)	0.24% (0.31)	1.05% (1.29)	0.54% (0.45)	-1.06% (-1.45)	-1.05% (-1.52)	-0.60% (-0.90)
				B. Industry Dynamics				
Bottom 33%	1.46% (2.32**)	1.35% (2.01**)	1.03% (1.50*)	3.15% (6.24***)	2.32% (4.94***)	2.23% (3.74***)		
Top 33%	2.50% (6.12***)	2.34% (4.90***)	1.68% (4.10***)	1.64% (2.57**)	1.98% (3.25***)	1.45% (3.47***)		
Top - Bottom	1.04% (1.39)	1.00% (1.20)	0.65% (0.84)	-1.51% (1.86*)	-0.33% (-0.43)	-0.77% (-1.06)		

The table shows results from an analysis of short-term abnormal returns (3-day CAR) to acquirers' shareholders from an industry perspective. Each industry transaction year (200 over the ten-year period) is ranked based on the absolute level of the tested variable in the transaction year. The ranked industry years are then divided into three groups (top 33%, bottom 33%, and a middle group) to test the effect of the relative size of variables on the transaction success. The table reports the top and bottom group results and the mean differences between the two. Industry level parameters (Panel A.) are calculated as median values of industry characteristics in the transaction year. Industry dynamic measures (Panel B.) are calculated as the sum of annual change in the three years from two years before transaction year to the transaction year. Statistical significance is tested using the standardized cross-sectional test by Boehmer et al for the group means. Significance of mean differences is tested with a t-test for mean differences. Statistical significance is indicated with *** in the 1% confidence interval, with ** in the 5% confidence interval, and with * in the 10% confidence interval.

Table 7.10 provides the corresponding results for 24-month BHAR. The results also underline the multivariate conclusions. Divestments of firm assets in highly valued industries return higher abnormal returns than asset sales in low MtoB industries. The mean difference is highly significant at 20.38%. The multivariate results for CAPEX and PP&E show the same signs as for the multivariate regression coefficients with a mean difference between top and bottom groups of 3.64% and -5.40% respectively. The grouped view, however, shows lower significance levels. With regard to the effect of changes in industry characteristics the outcome of the mean difference analysis shows that long-term value creation, in contrast to the short-term view, is influenced by changes in industry wide productivity. The bottom group of industry with negative EBIT level changes outperforms the top group with large positive changes by 16.54%. The mean differences between top and bottom groups for changes in Asset Turnover are significant at -11.15%. In line with the multivariate findings large increases in industry wide technology investments have a positive effect on long term value creation of divestments. The outperformance of the top group amounts to 22.45%.

Table 7.10: 24-month BHAR results for industry groups - Divestments

Groups	MtoB	Sales Growth	EBIT	Asset Turnover	R&D	CAPEX	PP&E	HHI
				A. Industry Level				
Bottom 33%	-1.41%	6.46%	10.52%	3.54%	1.58%	10.17%	10.02%	7.78%
	(-0.27)	(1.30)	(2.22**)	(0.66)	(3.46***)	(1.94*)	(2.23**)	(2.02**)
Top 33%	18.98%	10.25%	12.43%	13.11%	2.12%	13.84%	4.62%	10.52%
	(3.81***)	(2.17**)	(2.31**)	(2.57**)	(3.85***)	(2.92***)	(0.85)	(1.85*)
Top - Bottom	20.38%	3.79%	1.91%	9.57%	0.54%	3.64%	-5.40%	2.74%
	(2.82***)	(0.54)	(0.25)	(1.26)	(0.45)	(0.53)	(-0.80)	(0.41)
				B. Industry Dynamics				
Bottom 33%	11.62%	8.98%	14.92%	14.73%	-0.57%	15.02%		
	(2.41**)	(1.80*)	(2.82***)	(3.06***)	(-0.12)	(3.20***)		
Top 33%	3.79%	6.54%	-1.63%	3.58%	21.88%	8.04%		
	(0.77)	(1.44)	(-0.32)	(0.73)	(4.32***)	(1.50)		
Top - Bottom	-7.83%	-2.43%	-16.54%	-11.15%	22.45%	-6.98%		
	(-1.17)	(-0.34)	(-2.27**)	(-1.59*)	(3.14***)	(-0.98)		

The table shows results from an analysis of long-term abnormal returns (24-month BHAR) to acquirers' shareholders from an industry perspective. Each industry transaction year (200 over the ten-year period) is ranked based on the absolute level of the tested variable in the transaction year. The ranked industry years are then divided into three groups (top 33%, bottom 33%, and a middle group) to test the effect of the relative size of the variable on the transaction success. The table reports the top and bottom group results and the mean differences between the two. Industry level parameters (Panel A.) are calculated as median values of industry characteristics in the transaction year. Industry dynamic measures (Panel B.) are calculated as the sum of annual change in the three years from two years before transaction year to the transaction year. Statistical significance is tested using a t-test for the group means. Significance of mean differences is tested with a t-test for mean differences. Statistical significance is indicated with *** in the 1% confidence interval, with ** in the 5% confidence interval, and with * in the 10% confidence interval.

7.6.4 Robustness to calendar time long-term returns

In addition to the event-time analysis of abnormal long-term returns, a calendar-time approach is applied to test for robustness of the results. The Fama-French-4-Factor model (FF4F) addresses some of the shortcomings of the BHAR methodology, e.g., the cross-sectional correlation of firms in event-time (Mitchell and Stafford 2000). However, it is potentially exposed to other pitfalls, e.g., heteroscedasticity. The 4-factor model determines excess returns of a portfolio of sample firms by regressing the time series of (i) the markets excess return, (ii) the differences in return between small and big firms, (iii) the excess returns of high vs. low book-to-market (B/M) companies, and (iv) the Carhart (1997) momentum factor. The model takes the form of Equation (7.7).

(7.7) $$R_{pt} - R_{ft} = a_p + b_p\left(R_{mt} - R_{ft}\right) + s_p SMB + h_p HML + m_p PR1YR + e_{pt}$$

Rpt is the return of a continuously changing portfolio of companies or subgroups of these companies that conducted divestments within the preceding 24 months. The acquirer portfolio is reconstructed on a monthly basis when new bidders are included and inactive companies leave after the 24-months period. Rmt - Rft represents the market factor, calculated by subtracting the risk free rate (three months Libor until 1999, Euribor after 1999) from the value weighted market portfolio (Europe DS-Total Market index). SMB is the size factor which is determined by the return of a portfolio of big company stocks minus the return of a portfolio of small company stocks. All European companies included in the data sample are ranked based on their market value on the last trading day of June each year. The median is used to split the companies into big (B) and small (S) portfolios. HML is the book-to-market factor which is formed by subtracting high B/M value stocks and low B/M growth stocks. The portfolios are formed by ranking the companies according to their B/M level and distributing the top and bottom 30% to the respective portfolios (H and L) and the remaining 40% in a medium portfolio (M). Six portfolios are created each year (S/L, S/M, S/H, B/L, B/M, and B/H). The SMB portfolio is supposed to replicate the risk factor in returns related to size. It is calculated using the average of the monthly returns on the three small (S) portfolios minus the three big (B) portfolios. The HML portfolio mimics the risk factor related to book-to-market valuation and is calculated in the same way using the two high (H) and the two low (L) portfolios. Due to simple averaging of the portfolios the factors should be largely free of the other factor's effect. In addition, a momentum factor is included to account for portfolio momentum effects as proposed by Carhart (1997). PR1YR is the return differential of two equally weighted portfolios constructed out of firms with the highest and lowest 30% of eleven months returns prior to the announcement month. The coefficients bp, sp, hp, and mp determine the loading of the respective factor indicating the composition of the sample portfolio and the factor's effect on returns. The ap coefficient is the intercept of the model and represents the monthly return of the sample portfolio over a 24 months period that cannot be explained by the four factors. The sum of the error terms ept is assumed to be zero.

In order to test the effect of industry fundamentals on abnormal returns, monthly returns of acquirer portfolios formed with companies from the top third and the bottom third of the tested industry variable are regressed with the Fama-French factors. These groups are constructed based on the yearly ranking of industries based on their characteristics. The first quintile, for example, returns all transactions of the ten or eleven industries that had the lowest 33% of values in the announcement year of the transaction. The fifth quintile contains the highest

33% of values, respectively. Abnormal returns are then indicated by the intercept of the model. In addition, returns of a long-short portfolio of top and bottom group companies are regressed to determine performance differences between the two groups.

The calendar-time analysis emphasizes the negative effect of increasing industry profitability levels. In the reverse view this means that companies that divest assets when productivity is going down in an industry generate long-term abnormal returns for their shareholders. A second significant finding with regard to industry dynamics is the positive effect of technology shocks on the value creation potential of divestments.

Table 7.11: FF4F results for different industry groupings

Groups	MtoB	Sales Growth	EBIT	Asset Turnover	R&D	CAPEX	PP&E	HHI
				A. Industry Level				
Bottom 33%	-0.001 [0.975]	0.004 [0.537]	0.010 [0.175]	0.019 [0.163]	-0.004 [0.580]	-0.009 [0.132]	0.008 [0.212]	0.005 [0.147]
Top 33%	0.005 [0.288]	0.000 [0.968]	0.021 [0.433]	0.004 [0.406]	0.008 **[0.086]**	0.004 [0.342]	-0.002 [0.435]	0.016 **[0.051]**
Top - Bottom	0.007 [0.599]	0.008 [0.498]	0.016 [0.664]	-0.014 [0.294]	0.013 [0.141]	0.011 [0.158]	-0.009 [0.154]	0.013 [0.175]
				B. Industry Dynamics				
Bottom 33%	0.001 [0.913]	0.016 [0.721]	0.009 [0.274]	0.001 [0.921]	-0.021 **[0.031]**	0.002 [0.818]		
Top 33%	0.011 [0.454]	-0.008 [0.529]	-0.050 **[0.075]**	0.010 [0.105]	0.002 [0.686]	0.008 [0.113]		
Top - Bottom	-0.006 [0.851]	-0.023 [0.105]	-0.060 **[0.033]**	0.009 [0.243]	0.022 **[0.035]**	0.010 [0.376]		

This table presents alphas from 4-factor (FF4F) portfolio regressions. The reported intercept (a_p) represents the monthly abnormal return of a continuously adapted portfolio of divesting companies selling within the 24 months preceding the respective month. The analysis is conducted for portfolios constructed from companies in an industry that belongs to the bottom third and top third of industries ranked by the respective tested variable. In addition, a long-short portfolio of the two groups is regressed. The coefficients "b", "s", "h", and "m" representing the loadings of the regressed market factors are not reported (available on request). The classic t-statistic is conducted to test significance. The statistical fit of the model is indicated by the adjusted determination coefficient R^2 adjusted (not reported). P-values of the coefficients are provided in brackets.

Table 7.11 shows the results of the calendar-time analysis. In general, it is found that the calendar-time returns underline the BHAR findings with comparable results for the industry group comparisons (the reported coefficients represent monthly alphas and need to be multiplied by 24 months to come to comparable results for 24-month BHAR). Another general finding is that industry level outcomes are less significant in the long-short view. Industry dynamic long-short portfolios show more significant outperformance. This is in line with the hypothesis (7.H3) that in particular changes in industry structure (industry shocks) determine abnormal capital market performance following divestments.

7.6.5 Panel regression results

In addition to the cross-sectional view applied so far, the robustness of these industry findings to time series effects is tested. This study uses linear panel regressions to analyze the 20 industry groups over 10 years between 1998 and 2007 in the divestment sample. Equation (7.8) illustrates the applied model.

$$\begin{aligned} ActivityIndex\,/\,AbnormalReturn = {} & a_0 + \beta_1 MtoB + \beta_2\, SalesGrowth + \\ & \beta_3\, EBIT + \beta_4\, AssetTurn + \beta_5\, R\&D + \beta_6\, CAPEX + \beta_7\, PP\&E + \\ & \beta_8\, HHI + \beta_9 \Delta_{t-2/0}\, MtoB + \beta_{10}\, \Delta_{t-2/0}\, Growth + \beta_{11}\, \Delta_{t-2/0}\, EBIT + \\ & \beta_{12} \Delta_{t-2/0} AssetTurn + \beta_{13} \Delta_{t-2/0} R\&D + \beta_{14} \Delta_{t-2/0} CAPEX\; + \varepsilon \end{aligned} \tag{7.8}$$

First, panel regressions of industry specific divestment activity is estimated for the ten sample years. The annual *ActivityIndex* is measured as share of companies within one of 20 industry (panel) groups that engage in at least one divestiture in a sample period year. *AbnormalReturn* is the dependent variable for value creation of major transactions. It is measured as 3-day CAR and 24-month BHAR to sellers' shareholders. Average abnormal returns are calculated for each of the 20 ICB industries in every sample year to form panel groups. Industry years without transaction activity are excluded. The dependent variables pair with annual industry level and industry dynamic variables for the respective industry year.

The specification test introduced by Hausman (1978) choses between fixed and random effect panel models. The results show that there is no statistically significant difference between the covariance matrices of the two models (activity: p-value = 0.376; CAR: p-value = 0.547; BHAR: p-value = 0.432). Hence the random effects estimation can be applied for this analysis.

The results, in general, reflect the outcome of the cross-sectional analyses. However, the significance of coefficients decreases in the panel perspective. Table 7.12 reports results for divestment activity. Panel A. includes regressions of industry activity levels with industry level determinants. Panel B. entails respective regression results for industry dynamic variables. Table 7.13 presents CAR results and table 7.14 shows BHAR panel results.

Table 7.12: Panel results for divestment activity

	(1)	(2)	(3)	(4)	(5)	(6)	(7)	(8)	(9)	(10)
A. Industry Levels										
Intercept	0.048	0.043	0.041	0.050	0.047	0.031	0.032	0.041	0.050	-0.072
	[0.000]	**[0.000]**	**[0.000]**	**[0.000]**	**[0.000]**	**[0.000]**	**[0.000]**	**[0.000]**	**[0.000]**	**[0.082]**
MtoB	-0.002								-0.007	0.027
	[0.366]								**[0.045]**	[0.153]
SalesGrowth		0.034							0.047	-0.227
		[0.317]							**[0.074]**	**[0.023]**
EBIT			0.046						0.048	0.053
			[0.378]						[0.518]	[0.165]
AssetTurn				-0.006					-0.010	0.034
				[0.447]					[0.274]	[0.107]
R&D					-0.067				-0.025	-0.063
					[0.193]				[0.668]	[0.674]
CAPEX						0.294			0.315	0.366
						[0.000]			**[0.007]**	[0.526]
PP&E							0.028		-0.001	-0.024
							[0.016]		[0.959]	[0.704]
HHI								0.067	0.077	-0.193
								[0.360]	[0.292]	[0.568]
B. Industry Dynamic										
Intercept	0.044	0.044	0.044	0.043	0.047	0.045	0.043			**cont.**
	[0.000]	**[0.000]**	**[0.000]**	**[0.000]**	**[0.000]**	**[0.000]**	**[0.000]**			
$\Delta_{t-2/0}$ MtoB	-0.001						-0.005			-0.004
	[0.258]						**[0.030]**			[0.769]
$\Delta_{t-2/0}$ Growth		0.005					0.042			0.179
		[0.620]					**[0.025]**			[0.122]
$\Delta_{t-2/0}$ EBIT			-0.025				-0.063			-0.193
			[0.514]				[0.297]			[0.563]
$\Delta_{t-2/0}$ AssetTurn				-0.018			-0.021			0.036
				[0.043]			[0.210]			[0.466]
$\Delta_{t-2/0}$ R&D					0.006		-0.047			-0.167
					[0.925]		[0.635]			[0.635]
$\Delta_{t-2/0}$ CAPEX						0.094	0.152			-0.754
						[0.420]	[0.209]			[0.114]
Industry years	N=200									

This table presents linear panel regression results for divestment activity in industry groups. The dependent variable is annual transaction activity in 20 ICB industries. The tested annual ratio is calculated as share of listed companies executing at least one divestment in the specific year. Panel regressions are estimated with a random effects model. Independent variables are industry characteristics which are aggregated for 20 ICB sectors (3-digit ICB codes) from individual firm financial data of industry constituents. Industry characteristics are divided in industry medians of the announcement years (Industry Levels) and average median changes (Industry Dynamics) over three years (t=-2 to t=0). In addition, industry concentration is included applying the Herfindahl-Index (HHI). All industry characteristics are calculated for the 200 industry years of the 10-year sample period between 1998 and 2007. P-values for from t-statistics for the panel coefficients are provided in brackets below the respective coefficient. Significant values are marked bold.

Table 7.13: Panel results for short-term (3-day CAR) value creation

	(1)	(2)	(3)	(4)	(5)	(6)	(7)	(8)	(9)	(10)	(11)
Intercept	0.001	0.019	0.002	-0.002	-0.076	0.017	0.017	0.020	0.015	0.014	-0.083
	[0.928]	**[0.005]**	[0.891]	[0.939]	**[0.018]**	**[0.001]**	**[0.003]**	**[0.001]**	**[0.005]**	**[0.000]**	[0.131]
Industry Levels											
MtoB	0.008				0.024						0.024
	[0.269]				[0.255]						[0.255]
SalesGrowth		-0.044			-0.219						-0.219
		[0.513]			**[0.022]**						**[0.022]**
EBIT			0.211		0.533						0.533
			[0.273]		**[0.043]**						**[0.043]**
AssetTurn				0.019	0.036						0.036
				[0.316]	**[0.059]**						**[0.059]**
R&D				0.064	-0.061						-0.061
				[0.588]	[0.648]						[0.648]
CAPEX				-0.181	-0.227						-0.227
				[0.653]	[0.586]						[0.586]
PP&E				-0.032	0.029						0.029
				[0.449]	[0.543]						[0.543]
HHI				-0.139	-0.154						-0.154
				[0.408]	[0.249]						[0.249]
Industry Dynamic											
$\Delta_{t-2/0}$ MtoB						0.038				0.041	0.041
						[0.000]				**[0.006]**	**[0.006]**
$\Delta_{t-2/0}$ Growth							0.124			-0.073	-0.073
							[0.074]			[0.418]	[0.418]
$\Delta_{t-2/0}$ EBIT								0.479		0.391	0.391
								[0.096]		[0.275]	[0.275]
$\Delta_{t-2/0}$ AssetTurn									-0.012	-0.062	-0.098
									[0.858]	[0.388]	[0.125]
$\Delta_{t-2/0}$ R&D									-0.021	0.260	0.260
									[0.957]	[0.507]	[0.507]
$\Delta_{t-2/0}$ CAPEX									-0.791	-0.971	-0.876
									[0.112]	**[0.055]**	[0.098]
Industry yrs						N=200					

This table presents linear panel regression results for average annual short-term announcement returns (3-day CAR) in 20 ICB industry groups. The tested annual value is calculated as average from transactions executed in an industry year. Industry years without major divestment transactions are left empty. Panel regressions are estimated with a random effects model. Independent variables are industry characteristics which are aggregated for 20 ICB sectors (3-digit ICB codes) from individual firm financial data of industry constituents. Industry characteristics are divided in industry medians of the announcement years (Industry Levels) and average median changes (Industry Dynamics) over three years (t=-2 to t=0). In addition, industry concentration is included applying the Herfindahl-Index (HHI). All industry characteristics are calculated for the 200 industry years of the 10-year sample period between 1998 and 2007. P-values for from t-statistics for the panel coefficients are provided in brackets below the respective coefficient. Significant values are marked bold.

Table 7.14: Panel results for long-term (24-month BHAR) value creation

	(1)	(2)	(3)	(4)	(5)	(6)	(7)	(8)	(9)	(10)	(11)
Intercept	-0.137	0.051	0.065	-0.038	-0.006	0.097	0.101	0.095	0.016	0.014	-0.044
	[0.229]	[0.348]	[0.582]	[0.826]	**[0.012]**	**[0.013]**	**[0.005]**	**[0.025]**	**[0.000]**	**[0.000]**	[0.131]
Industry Levels											
MtoB	0.126				0.184						0.254
	[0.029]				[0.139]						**[0.069]**
SalesGrowth		0.644			-0.410						-0.357
		[0.248]			[0.607]						[0.736]
EBIT			0.466		-2.958						-6.091
			[0.771]		[0.250]						**[0.037]**
AssetTurn				0.024	-0.092						0.044
				[0.022]	[0.567]						**[0.004]**
R&D				0.953	-0.237						-0.634
				[0.228]	[0.832]						[0.599]
CAPEX				0.732	0.731						1.00
				[0.016]	**[0.039]**						**[0.031]**
PP&E				-0.550	-0.324						-0.918
				[0.104]	[0.422]						**[0.079]**
HHI				-0.034	0.014						0.275
				[0.974]	[0.990]						[0.803]
Industry Dynamic											
$\Delta_{t-2/0}$ MtoB						-0.026				0.162	0.276
						[0.956]				**[0.052]**	**[0.011]**
$\Delta_{t-2/0}$ Growth							-0.256			-0.858	-2.045
							[0.471]			[0.222]	**[0.048]**
$\Delta_{t-2/0}$ EBIT								-2.524		-1.088	-0.943
								[0.061]		[0.632]	[0.728]
$\Delta_{t-2/0}$ AssetTurn									-0.056	-0.408	-0.253
									[0.868]	[0.281]	[0.545]
$\Delta_{t-2/0}$ R&D									0.774	-0.714	0.685
									[0.000]	**[0.004]**	**[0.013]**
$\Delta_{t-2/0}$ CAPEX									2.454	0.702	-5.063
									[0.212]	[0.823]	[0.176]
Industry yrs						N=200					

This table presents linear panel regression results for average long-term returns to sellers' shareholders (24-month BHAR) in 20 ICB industry groups. The tested annual value is calculated as average from transactions executed in an industry year. Industry years without major divestment transactions are left empty. Panel regressions are estimated with a random effects model. Independent variables are industry characteristics which are aggregated for 20 ICB sectors (3-digit ICB codes) from individual firm financial data of industry constituents. Industry characteristics are divided in industry medians of the announcement years (Industry Levels) and average median changes (Industry Dynamics) over three years (t=-2 to t=0). In addition, industry concentration is included applying the Herfindahl-Index (HHI). All industry characteristics are calculated for the 200 industry years of the 10-year sample period between 1998 and 2007. P-values for from t-statistics for the panel coefficients are provided in brackets below the respective coefficient. Significant values are marked bold.

8. Summary and Conclusion

The presented study examines short- and long-term value creation of corporate restructuring from a market cycle and industry perspective. An initial analysis of corporate restructuring in Europe in Chapter 2 shows that large variations exist with regard to shareholder wealth effects of corporate restructuring over time and between industries. This finding forms the research interest of this thesis. The question arose whether market cycles and industry determinants are able to explain or eventually even predict these variations in corporate restructuring success. In contrast to the majority of previous studies, this analysis entails both forms of corporate restructuring: mergers and acquisitions (M&A) as well as corporate divestitures. The analysis is based on a large sample of European corporate restructuring transactions allowing for a comprehensive analysis of the determinants of shareholder wealth creation. The study focuses on value effects from an acquirer's (for the analysis of M&A) and seller's (for the analysis of divestments) shareholder perspective. Subject of analysis are corporate restructuring transactions that result in the transfer of majority stakes and subsequently control rights between unrelated buyers and sellers. In order to identify value effects, various empirical methods are applied. Focus of the analysis are stock market effects that result from corporate restructuring events. Event studies in a short- and long-term perspective are applied. In addition to the widely used announcement return analysis, both commonly used long-term approaches, buy-and-hold abnormal returns in event-time, and calendar-time abnormal returns based on a 4-factor model are used. To complement the return analysis, an accounting analysis of improvements in profitability after corporate restructuring is conducted.

This final summary provides an overview of the results from the analysis of market valuation effects on M&A and divestment success discussed in Section A. of this thesis as well as results from the examination of industry determinants of corporate restructuring success outlined in Section B.. In addition, potential topics for further research are proposed.

The results based on the overall transaction sample show that, on the one hand, announcement effects of M&A transactions and corporate divestments have been significantly positive for the analyzed sample of European corporate restructuring transactions between 1989 and 2007. Long-term stock market returns, on the other hand, vary significantly depending on examined time period, industry selection, and applied long-term methodology.

With regard to M&A, the overall results differ remarkably from the majority of US-focused studies that report insignificant or negative announcement returns and frequently negative long-term returns following takeovers. The findings from studies of US transactions in earlier time periods lead to two possible conclusions. The first is that transactions from European acquirers have been more successful on average. This explanation proposes that European transactions are less exposed to agency costs that lead to value decreasing takeover decisions. Since previous studies from the US rely on older samples, another explanation for the variation in results could be a general improvement in M&A performance over time.

With regard to corporate divestment success, the positive results for short-term announcement returns are mostly consistent with previous findings. With regard to long-term value creation the results from previous studies remain inconclusive and depend on chosen methodology, regional focus, and time period.

The focus of this thesis is, however, not on overall value effects of corporate restructuring, but on detecting determinants that explain variations in results over time and across industries.

In Section A., value implications of different market cycles are studied. In order to analyze variations in corporate restructuring over time, the European stock market is categorized in high, neutral, and low market valuation phases based on industry price-to-earnings ratios (P/E). This classification provides an approximation of the market prospects in the month of the transaction announcement. The overall sample of corporate restructuring transactions between 1989 and 2007 is then split into transactions that have been announced in time-periods that fall in one of the three valuation phases (high, neutral, and low). In addition to this general split, further sub-samples are formed based on specific transaction characteristics that potentially affect the success of corporate restructuring in the different market phases.

The results show that market valuation levels have had a significant influence on M&A and divestment success in the examined time period. The results for M&A transactions in Chapter 4 suggest that short-term announcement effects of transactions in high valuation market are significantly higher than in low valuation markets. Investors appear to favor acquisitions when the market outlook is positive. The results from a long-term perspective, however, challenge this market assessment. The BHAR and calendar-time results show that acquisitions in booming, high valuation markets created less value for shareholders than takeovers in depressed markets over 24 months after the announcement. This long-term underperformance of takeovers in high valuation markets can be explained by behavioral arguments. Strong markets and subsequent high valuation levels create agency costs that lead to reduced value creation potential of M&A when managers follow their own interests in times when their companies are highly valued and growing. In the absence of market-induced overvaluation, low market acquirers appear to apply superior target selection and make sounder investment decisions when financing resources are scarce and when integration risks are high in declining markets.

In a next step, specific transaction characteristics of M&A in low valuation markets are examined to determine the success factors of acquisitions in weak market environments. The results show that the long-term success of down-market M&A depends on a number of transactions characteristics. Takeovers paid for with undervalued shares destroy value for shareholders of the purchasing company in weak markets. Distressed targets also have a clearly negative effect on value creation. In down-markets, turnarounds seem to be more difficult to achieve than in stronger market environments. Small acquisition targets relative to the buyer's size show the largest positive long-term value creation in weak markets. Cautiously selected smaller sized transactions with limited capital requirements for buyers appear especially value creating in lean times. Surprisingly, higher transaction complexity assumed for cross-border transactions and diversifying M&A investments, does not appear to negatively influence acquisition performance in weak markets.

The results also indicate that the purchase of divested business units can create more value for shareholders in weak markets compared to boom-markets (see Chapter 5). This finding indicates that corporate sellers are more likely to sell attractive subsidiaries in difficult market environments when they are under pressure to generate additional liquidity to weather bad market conditions. Based on this indication, it appears relevant to also take the seller's perspective into account when analyzing corporate restructuring in different market phases. Chapter 5 of this thesis, therefore, conducts an analysis of shareholder wealth creation from corporate divestitures in high, neutral, and low market valuation phases.

The overall results in Chapter 5 show that European divestments in the analyzed period had positive announcement returns while the long-term capital market returns over 12 and 24 months were insignificantly different from zero or negative. The difference in shareholder wealth creation across time horizons illustrates that investors have difficulties to assess the effects of divestments on firm value at announcement due to intransparency with regard to the future use of proceeds. Negative effects on wealth creation following divestments indicate agency costs of management discretion when proceeds are re-invested in value decreasing projects which are not anticipated by investors at announcement.

Market cycle results provide evidence that the overall market condition significantly affects shareholder returns of divestments. The main finding is that divestments in weak markets, when companies are under pressure to restructure and growth projects to reinvest proceeds are rare, significantly underperform compared to divestitures in stronger markets. Possible explanations for this effect are a tendency of managers to focus on short-term liquidity and internal improvements rather than on long-term strategic objectives in down markets. In strong markets, on the other hand, managers appear to better align their decisions with long-term strategic goals and are able to time their divestment decisions to obtain higher proceeds that can be reinvested to grow the remaining business.

In addition, differences between refocusing and core-industry divestments are examined. Evidence is found that refocusing drives outperformance of divestments in high valuation markets. A likely explanation is superior shareholder wealth creation of divestments that target efficiency gains through refocusing compared to divestments meant to provide additional liquidity. Refocusing decisions during strong markets, in the absence of market wide liquidity and financing constraints, are more likely to be targeted at efficiency improvements and increase shareholder wealth.

Additional findings from the multivariate analysis show that larger divestments create more shareholder wealth while large sellers perform relatively weaker than small firms after divestments. Results also show that companies that perform weakly compared to their industry peers profit most from divestments.

The results suggest that it is a value increasing strategy from a shareholder's perspective for managers to reassess the current asset allocation for potential efficiency gains during booming markets in the absence of immediate need to restructure. Especially firms that underperform compared to their peers can increase shareholders wealth significantly when valuation levels are high.

Section B. of this thesis further examines the second finding of the initial analysis of European corporate restructuring in Chapter 2. The observations suggest that M&A and divestment success differ significantly between industries. This initial finding proposes that characteristics of the industry in which acquirers and sellers are active play an important role to predict the value creation potential of corporate restructuring. In order to identify relevant industry characteristics, an examination of corporate restructuring on an industry level is conducted. First, all European companies that were active during the ten years from 1998 to 2007 are allocated to ICB industry sub-sectors. Based on this comprehensive data sample, industry characteristics are aggregate from individual company data to measure industry characteristics and to identify significant changes in the structure of individual industries over the sample period that potentially affect corporate restructuring activity and value creation. In a next step, major corporate restructuring transactions that have been conducted by the industry sample firms are identified and analyzed with regard to their short- and long-term value creation from an acquirers' and a sellers' shareholder perspective. Finally, the industry determinant of seller and buyer industry are tested with regard to their effect on value creation from corporate restructuring.

Chapter 6 discusses the role of industry characteristics on M&A activity and value creation. First, industry drivers of activity are analyzed. The results show that companies in industries which experience increases in demand and in industries that show high levels of profitability are more actively engaging in M&A. This effect is largest for intra-industry transactions when companies seek to increase market share in strong industries. A positive effect on activity is also found for industries that show high levels of intangible assets, while industries with large stocks of physical assets are less active.

The second part of the analysis examines the effects of industry characteristics on M&A value creation. The results show that transactions in industries with strong growth prospects create more value for shareholders than takeovers in stagnant or declining industries. Positive value effects from M&A are also observed in industries that see increases in capital investment needs. Another significant effect is based on the nature of company assets in the buyer's industry. Physical productive assets like manufacturing plants are difficult to combine and, therefore, show lower value creation potential. Industries with large intangible asset bases, on the other hand, realize more value on the market for corporate control. Further results show that takeovers in already highly concentrated are likely to reduce shareholder value.

The results provide evidence that M&A in growing industries with increasing capital requirements bears the largest potential to increase shareholder wealth.

Chapter 7 analyzes the role of industry characteristics on the value creation potential of corporate divestitures. The results show that also for divestitures, activity levels and value creation differ significantly across industries.

Applying the same approach as in Chapter 6 for the M&A discussion, first, industry drivers of activity are analyzed. The results show that disposals are more frequent in industry with low valuation levels and weak growth rates. (Temporary) increases in valuation levels drive activity, suggesting that managers may time divestments to increase potential proceeds. Increasing CAPEX investment requirements foster refocusing divestments when managers attempt to reallocate unrelated assets to meet capital needs in their core industry. A further result of the activity examination indicates that industries with low asset turnover rates and large tangible asset stocks are more actively trading assets than labor intensive industries.

The second part of the analysis then examines the effects of industry characteristics on shareholder wealth creation from divestments. In general, announcement returns and long-term returns are positive on average. The results show, however, large differences between industries. Factors driving these variations differ for immediate announcement returns and long-term performance of divestitures. The results show positive investor reactions when divestments are made during high and increasing valuations when asset prices are high. Investors also favor refocusing when core industries expand. Surprisingly, announcement returns are lower in asset heavy industries despite higher activity levels.

Long-term returns are less affected by valuation levels and growth prospects. Instead, productivity variables play an important role in explaining variations in long-time shareholder wealth creation following major divestments. Shareholders profit in the long-term, when firms sell assets in industries that see declining profitability levels. The finding illustrates that companies can increase value for their shareholders when they actively reallocate assets to reach an optimal size that best matches industry productivity.

Increases in R&D investment needs see significant value creation potential from divestments when managers reassess their asset allocation to non-core industries and potentially shift resources to core industries that experience technology shocks. Increasing investment needs can also be effectively addressed by either substituting internal investment with M&A or by reallocating capital through divestments.

The analysis of corporate restructuring in a market and industry context raise a number of additional research questions that have not been addressed in this study. Potentially fruitful areas for further research on market cycle and industry effects are outlined in the following list.

Market cycle effects

- The market cycle analysis presented takes a separated look at both forms of corporate restructuring. The finding that shareholders of acquirers in weak markets profit from M&A transactions while selling firms underperform provides room for further examination. In particular a combined view by matching the value implications for buyers and sellers in dependence of market environments could yield further insights with regard to the determinants of value creation from corporate restructuring.

Industry effects

- The examination of industry effects on value creation from corporate restructuring proposes a relation between the nature of productive assets of an industry and the value creation potential of corporate restructuring. Further research interest exists with regard to the specific sources of value creation and synergies in different industry contexts.
- The industry analysis in this thesis focuses on characteristics of the buyer/seller industry. It does not consider the specific characteristics of industries in which assets are acquired or sold. A combined analysis of acquirer/seller industry and target industry could, therefore, yield further insight with regard to the sources of value creation.

- The industry analysis focuses on differences in industry characteristics between industries. It does not account for variations in performance within an industry that could be an additional source of value creation. Further research could include the inter-industry perspective in the analysis of industry factors that affect value creation of corporate restructuring.

References

Ali, A./Klasa, S./Yeung, E. (2009): The Limitations of Industry Concentration Measures Constructed with Compustat Data: Implications for Financial Research. In: Review of Financial Studies, Vol. 22, 2009, pp. 3839-3871.

Almazan, A./De Motta A./Titman S./Vahap, U. (2010): Financial Structure, Acquisition Opportunities, and Firm Locations. In: Journal of Finance, Vol. 65, 2010, 529-563.

Andrade, G./Mitchell, M. L./Stafford, E. (2001): New Evidence and Perspective on Mergers. In: Journal of Economic Perspective, Vol. 15, 2001, pp. 103-120.

Andrade, G./Stafford, E. (2004): Investigating the economic role of mergers. In: Journal of Corporate Finance, Vol. 10, 2004, pp. 1-36.

Ang, J. S./Cheng, Y. (2006): Direct Evidence on the Market-driven Acquisition Theory. In: Journal of Financial Research, Vol. 29, 2006, pp. 199-216.

Aw, M. S. B./Chatterjee, R. A. (2004): The performance of UK firms acquiring large cross-border and domestic takeover targets. In: Applied Financial Economics, Vol. 14, 2006, pp. 337-349.

Baker, M./Foley, C. F./Wurgler, J. (2009): Multinationals as Arbitrageurs: The Effect of Stock Market Valuations on Foreign Direct Investments. In: Review of Financial Studies, Vol. 22, 2009, pp. 337-369.

Balasubramanian, N./Sivadasan J. (2009): Capital Resalability, Productivity Dispersion, and Market Structure. In: Review of Economics & Statistics, Vol. 91, 2009, pp. 547-557.

Barber, B. M./Lyon, J. D. (1997): Detecting long-run abnormal stock returns: The empirical power and specification of test statistics. In: Journal of Financial Economics, Vol. 43, 1997, pp. 341-372.

Bartsch D./Börner J. (2007): Werteffekte strategischer Desinvestitionen - Eine empirische Untersuchung am deutschen Kapitalmarkt. In: Zeitschrift für Betriebswirtschaftliche Forschung (zfbf), Vol. 59, 2007, pp. 2-34.

Bartholdy, J./Olson D./Peare/P. (2007): Conducting Event Studies on a Small Stock Exchange. In: European Journal of Finance, Vol. 13, 2007, pp. 227-252.

Bates, T. W. (2005): Asset sales, investment opportunities, and the use of proceeds. In: Journal of Finance, Vol. 60, 2005, pp. 105–135.

Beitel, P./Schiereck, D./Wahrenburg, M. (2004): Explaining M&A Success in European Banks. In: European Financial Management, Vol. 10, pp. 109-139.

Berger, P. G./Ofek E. (1995): Diversification's effect on firm value. In: Journal of Financial Economics, Vol. 37, 1995, pp. 39-65.

Benou, G./Madura, J/Ngo, T. (2008): Wealth creation from high-tech divestitures. In: The Quarterly Review of Economics and Finance, Vol. 48, 2008, pp. 505-519.

Black, F. (1972): Capital market equilibrium with restricted borrowing. In: Journal of Busyness, Vol. 45, 1972, pp. 444-454.

Boehmer, E./Musumeci, J./Poulsen, A. (1991): Event-Study Methodology under Conditions of Event-induced Variance. In: Journal of Financial Economics, Vol. 30, 1991, pp. 253-272.

Boone, A. L./Mulherin, J. H. (2000): Comparing Acquisitions and Divestments. In: Journal of Corporate Finance, Vol. 6, 2000, pp. 117-139.

Bougette, P (2010): Preventing merger unilateral effects: A Nash-Cournot approach to assets divestitures. In: Research in Economics, Vol. 62, 2010, pp.162-174.

Bouwman, C. H. S./Fuller, K./Nain, A. S. (2009): Market Valuation and Acquisition Quality: Empirical Evidence. In: The Review of Financial Studies, Vol. 22, 2009, pp. 633-678.

Brealey, R./Myers, S. (2003): Principles of Corporate Finance. McGraw-Hill, New York, 2003.

Brown C./Fung, C. (2009): Keiretsu Affiliation and Stock-Market-Diven Acquisitions. In: Journal of Financial Research, Vol. 32, 2009, pp. 479-503.

Brown, S. J./Warner, J. B. (1980): Measuring Security Price Performance. In Journal of Financial Economics, Vol. 8, 1980, pp. 205-258.

Brown, S. J./Warner, J. B. (1985): Using Daily Stock Returns: The Case of Event Studies. In Journal of Financial Economics, Vol. 14, 1985, pp. 3-31.

Bruner, R. F. (2002): Does M&A Pay? A Survey of Evidence for the Decision Maker. In: Journal of Applied Finance, Vol. 12, 2002.

Capaldo, A./Cogman, D./Suonio, H. (2009): What's different about M&A in this downturn? In: McKinsey on Finance, Winter 2009, pp. 31-36.

Carapeto, M./Moeller, S./Faelten, A. (2010): The good, the bad, and the ugly: A survival guide to M&A in distressed times. Cass Business School, Working Paper, 2010, available at http://69.175.2.130./ ~finman/Reno/Papers/DistressedAcquisitions.pdf.

Cahart, M. M. (1997): On Persistence in Mutual Fund Performance. In: Journal of Finance, Vol. 52, 1997, pp. 57-82.

Chari, A./Ouimet, P. P./Tesar, L. L. (2010): The Value of Control in Emerging Markets. In: Review of Financial Studies, Vol. 4, 2010, pp. 1741-1770.

Celikyurt, U./Sevilir, M./Shivdasani, A. (2010): Going public to acquire? The acquisition motive in IPOs. In: Journal of Financial Economics, Vol. 96, 2010, pp. 345-363.

Chidambaran, N. K./Kose, J./Zhaoyun, S./Gopala, V. (2010): Hot and cold merger markets. In: Review of Quantitative Financial Accounting, Vol. 34, 2010, pp. 327-349.

Clark, K./Ofek E. (1994): Mergers as a Means of Restructuring Distressed Firms: An Empirical Investigation. In: Journal of Financial & Quantitative Analysis, Vol. 29, 1994, pp. 541-565.

Cremers, M./Nair, V. B./Kose, J. K. J. (2009). Takeovers and the Cross-Section of Returns. Review of Financial Studies. In: Review of Financial Studies. Vol. 22, 2009, pp. 1409-1443.

Colak, G. (2009): Refocusing and Firm Value. In: European Financial Management, Vol. 16, 2009, pp. 422-448.

Cooney, J.W./Moeller, T./Stegemoller, M. (2009): The Underpricing of Private Targets. In: Journal of Financial Economics. Vol. 93, 2009, pp. 51-66.

Copeland, T. E./Weston, J. F. (1988). Financial Theory and Corporate Policy. Reading, MA: Addison-Wesley.

Cowan, A./Nandkumar, N./Singh, A. (1990): Stock Returns Before and After Calls of Convertible Bonds. In: Journal of Financial and Quantitative Analysis, Vol. 25, 1990, pp. 549-555.

Custodio, C./Metzger, D. (2010): The Value of CEOs Industry Expertise - Evidence from Mergers & Acquisitions. London School of Economics, Working Paper, 2010, available at SSRN: http://ssrn.com/abstract=1647073.

Damodaran, A. (2004). Valuing Acquisitions and Takeovers. In A. Damodaran (Ed.), Corporate Finance: Theory and Practice (2nd ed., pp. 834-878). New York,NY: John Wiley & Sons Inc.

Danbolt,, J. (2004): Target company cross-border effects in acquisitions into the UK. In: European Financial Management, Vol. 10, pp. 83-108.

Devos, E./Kadapakkam, P.-R./Krishnamurthy, S. (2009): How do Mergers Create Value? A Comparison of Taxes, Market Power, and Efficiency Improvements as Explanations for Synergies. In: Review of Financial Studies, Vol. 22, pp. 1179-1211.

Denis, D.J./Denis, D.K., Yost, K. (2002): Global Diversification, industrial diversification, and firm value. In: The Journal of Finance, Vol. 52, 2002, pp. 1951-1980.

Desai, H./ Jain P.C. (1999): Firm Performance and Focus: Long-run Stock Market Performance Following Spin-Offs. In: Journal of Financial Economics, Vol. 54, 1999, pp. 75-101.

Desai, C. A./Savickas, R. (2010): On the causes of volatility effects of conglomerate breakups. In: Journal of Corporate Finance, Vol. 16, 2010, pp. 554-571.

Dutz, M. A. (1989): Horizontal Mergers in Declining Industries. Theory and Evidence. In: International Journal of Industrial Organization, Vol. 7, 1989, pp. 11-33.

Eckbo, E.B. (1992). Mergers and the value of antitrust deterrence. In: Journal of Finance, Vol. 47, 1992, pp. 1005–1029.

Eisfeldt, A. L./ Rampini, A. A. (2006): Capital reallocation and liquidity. In: Journal of Monetary Economics, Vol. 53, 2006, pp. 369-399.

Espenlaub S./Iqbal, A./Strong, N. (2009): Datastream returns and UK open offers. In: European Journal of Finance, Vol. 15, 2009, pp. 61-69.

European Central Bank (ECB) (2008): Business investment in the euro area and the role of firms' financial position. In: ECB Monthly Bulletin April 2008, pp. 57-68.

Fama, E. F./French, K. R. (1993): Common risk factors in the returns on stocks and bonds. Journal of Financial Economics, Vol. 33, 1993, pp. 3-56.

Fama, E. F./French, K. R. (1997): Industry cost of equity. In: Journal of Financial Economics. Vol. 43, 1997, pp. 153-193.

Ferreira, M. A./Massa, M./Matos, P. (2010): Shareholders at the Gate? Institutional Investors and Cross-Border Mergers and Acquisitions. In: Review of Financial Studies, Vol. 23, 2010, pp. 601-644.

Fuller, K./Netter, J./Stegemoller, M. (2002): What Do Returns to Acquiring Firms Tell Us? Evidence from Firms That Make Many Acquisitions. In: Journal of Finance, Vol. 57, 2002, pp. 1763-1793.

Gell, J./Kengelbach, J./Roos, A. (2008): The Return of the Strategist: Creating value with M&A in a Downturn. The Boston Consulting Group, 2008.

Gell, J./Kengelbach, J./Ross, A. (2009): Be daring when others are fearful. Seizing M&A Opportunity While They Last. The Boston Consulting Group, 2009.

Gleason, K. C./Gregory, D. W./Wiggins, R. A. (2002): Wealth Effects of US Acquisitions in the Pacific Rim. In: Journal of Business & Economic Studies, Vol. 8, 2002, pp. 28-48.

Goel, A. M./Thakor, A. V. (2010): Do Envious CEOs Cause Merger Waves? In: Review of Financial Studies, Vol. 23, 2010, pp. 487-517.

Gort, M. (1969): An Economic Disturbance Theory of Mergers. In: Quarterly Journal of Economics, Vol. 83, 1969, pp. 624-642.

Gorton, G./Kahl, M./Rosen, R. (2009): Eat or be Eaten: A Theory of Mergers and Firm Size. In: Journal of Finance, Vol. 64, 2009, pp. 1291-1344.

Gregory, A./McCorriston, S. (2005): Foreign acquisitions by UK limited companies: short- and long-run performance. In: Journal of Empirical Finance, Vol. 12, 2005, pp. 99-125.

Harford, J. (2005): What drives merger waves. In: Journal of Financial Economics, Vol. 77, 2005, pp. 529-560.

Harford, J./Klasa, S./Walcott, N. (2009): Do firms have leverage targets? Evidence from acquisitions. In: Journal of Financial Economics, Vol. 93, 2009, pp. 1-14.

Hausman, J. A. (1978): Specification tests in econometrics. In: Econometrica, Vol. 46, 1978. pp. 1251-1271.

Healy, P. M./Palepu, K. G./Ruback, R. S. (1992): Does corporate performance improve after mergers? In: Journal of Financial Economics, Vol. 32, 1992, pp. 135-175.

Heron, R./Lie E. (2002): Operating Performance and the Method of Payment in Takeovers. In: Journal of Financial & Quantitative Analysis, Vol. 37, 2002, pp. 137-155.

Hillier, D./McColgan, P./Werema, S. (2009): Asset sales and firm strategy: an analysis of divestitures by UK companies. In: The European Journal of Finance, Vol. 15, 2009, pp. 71-87.

Hite, G. L./ Owers, J. E./ Rogers, R. C. (1987). The market for inter-firm asset sales: Partial sell-offs and total liquidation. Journal of Financial Economics, Vol. 18, 229-252.

Hoberg, G. and Philiips, G. (2010): Product Market Synergies and Competition in Mergers and Acquisitions. In: Review of Financial Studies, Vol. 23, 2010, pp. 3773-3811.

Hou, K./Robinson D. T. (2006): Industry Concentration and Average Stock Returns. In: Journal of Finance, Vol. 61, 2006, pp. 1927-1955.

Hirshleifer, D./Lim S. S./Teoh, S. H. (2009): Driven to Distraction: Extraneous Events and Underreaction to Earnings News. In: Journal of Finance, Vol. 54, 2009, pp. 2289-2325.

Hyland, D. C./Nail L. (2006): Intersecurity Wealth Redistribution in Conglomerate Mergers: Re-Examination over three Decades. In: Corporate Ownership & Control, Vol. 3, 2006, pp. 178-189.

Ince, O. S./Porter, R.B. (2006): Individual Return Data from Thomson Datastream: Handle with Care! In: Journal of Financial Research, Vol. 29, 2006, pp. 463-479.

Jensen, M. C. (1986): Agency Cost Of Free Cash Flow, Corporate Finance, and Takeovers. In: American Economic Review, Vol. 76, 1986, pp. 323-329.

Jensen, M. C. (1993): The Modern Industrial Revolution, Exit, and the Failure of Internal Control Systems. In: Journal of Finance, Vol. 48, 1993, pp. 831-880.

Jensen, M. C. (2005): Agency Costs of Overvalued Equity. In: Financial Management, Vol. 34, 2005, pp. 5-19.

Jensen, M. C./Ruback, R. S. (1983): The Market for Corporate Control: The Scientific Evidence. In: Journal of Financial Economics, Vol. 11, 1983, pp. 5-50.

John, K./Ofek, E. (1995): Asset sales and increase in focus. In: Journal of Financial Economics, No. 37, 1995, pp. 105–126.

Jovanovic, B./Rousseau, P. L. (2008): Mergers as Reallocation. In: Review of Economics and Statistics, Vol. 90, 2008, pp. 765-776.

Komlenovic, S./Mamun, A./Mishra, D. (2011): Business cycle and aggregated industry mergers. In: Journal of Economics and Finance, Vol. 35, 2011, pp. 239-259.

Jope, F./Schiereck D./Zeidler, F. (2009): Value generation of mergers and acquisitions in the technology, media, telecommunication industry. In Journal of Telecommunication Management, Vol. 2, 2009, 369-386.

Kothari, S.P./Warner, J.B. (2007): Econometrics of Event Studies. In B. E. Eckbo (Ed.), Handbook of Corporate Finance, 1st edition, 2007, North Holland: Amsterdam, The Netherlands, pp. 34-56.

Laabs, J.-P./Schiereck, D. (2010): The long-term success of M&A in the automotive supply industry: determinants of capital market performance. In: Journal of Economics & Finance, Vol. 34, 2010, pp. 61-8.

Lambrecht, B. M. (2004): The timing and terms of mergers motivated by economies of scale. In: Journal of Financial Economics, Vol. 72, 2004, pp. 41-62.

Lang, L./Poulsen, A./Stulz, R. (1995). Asset sales, firm performance, and the agency costs of managerial discretion. In: Journal of Financial Economics, No. 37, 1995, pp. 3–37.

Lee, E./Lin, S. (2008): Corporate Sell-offs in the UK: Use of Proceeds, Financial Distress and Long-run Impact on Shareholder Wealth. In: European Financial Management, 2008, Vol. 14, pp. 222-244.

Lin, L./Fu, F. (2008): Mergers Driven by Stock Overvaluation: Are They Good Deals? Singapore Management University, Working Paper, 2008, available at SSRN: http://ssrn.com/abstract=1099842.

Loughran, T./Ritter J. R. (2000): Uniformly least powerful tests of market efficiency. In: Journal of Financial Economics, Vol. 55, 2000, pp. 361-389.

Loughran, T./Vijh, A. M. (1997): Do Long-Term Shareholders Benefit From Corporate Acquisitions? In: Journal of Finance, Vol. 52, 1997, pp. 1765-1790.

Lubatkin, M./Chatterjee, S. (1991): The Strategy-Shareholder Relationship: Testing Temporal Stability Across Market Cycles. In: Strategic Management Journal, Vol. 12, 1991, pp. 251-270.

Lyon, J. D./Barber, B. M./Tsai, C.-L. (1999): Improved Methods for Tests of Long-Run Abnormal Returns. In: Journal of Financial Economics, Vol. 54, 1999, S. 165-201.

Maksimovic, V./Phillips G. (2001): The Market for Corporate Assets: Who Engages in Mergers and Asset Sales and Are There Efficiency Gains? In: Journal of Finance, Vol. 56, 2001, S. 2019-2065.

Maksimovic, V./Phillips G. (2002): Do Conglomerate Firms Allocate Resources Inefficiently across Industries? Theory and Evidence. In: Journal of Finance, Vol. 57, 2002, S. 721-767.

Martynova, M./Oosting, s./ Renneboog, L. (2006). "The Long-Term Operating Performance of European Mergers and Acquisitions, Working Paper, 2006, available at SSRN: http://ssrn.com/ abstract=944407.

Maquieira, C. P./ Megginson, W. L./Nail, L. (1998): Wealth creation versus wealth redistributions in pure stock-for-stock mergers. In: Journal of Financial Economics, Vol. 48, 1998, pp. 3-33.

McConnell, J. J./Ozbilgin, M./Wahal, S. (2001): Spin-Offs, Ex-Ante. In: Journal of Business, Vol. 74, 2001, pp. 245-280.

Ming, D./Hirshleifer, D./Richardson, S./Siew Hong, T. (2006): Does Investor Misvaluation Drive the Takeover Market? In: Journal of Finance, Vol. 61, 2006, pp. 725-762.

Mitchell, M. L./Mulherin, J. H. (1996): The impact of industry shocks on takeover and restructuring activity. In: Journal of Financial Economics, Vol. 41, 1996, pp. 193-229.

Mitchell, M. L./Stafford, E. (2000): Managerial Decisions and Long-Term Stock Price Performance. Journal of Business, Vol. 73, 2000, pp. 287-331.

Miyazaki, H. (2009): An analysis of the relation between R&D and M&A in high-tech industries. In: Applied Economic Letters, Vol. 16, 2009, pp. 199-201.

Moeller, S. B./Schlingemann, F. P./Stulz, R. M. (2004): Firm size and the gains from acquisitions. In: Journal of Financial Economics, Vol. 73, 2004, pp. 201-228.

Morck, R./Shleifer, A./Vishny, R. W. (1990): Do Managerial Objectives Drive Bad Acquisitions. In: Journal of Finance, Vol. 35., 1990, pp. 31-48.

Mußhoff, J. (2007): Erfolgreiche M&A-Transaktionen in der europäischen Bankenindustrie. Wiesbaden: Deutscher Universitätsverlag.

Rhodes-Kropf, M./Viswanthan, S. (2004): Market Valuations and Merger Wave. In: Journal of Finance, Vol. 59, 2004, pp. 2685-2718.

Rhodes-Kropf, M./ Robinson, D. T./ Viswanthan, S. (2005): Valuation waves and merger activity: The empirical evidence. In: Journal of Financial Economics, Vol. 77, pp. 561-603.

Ravenscraft, D. J./Scherer, F. M. (1987): Life after Takeover. In: Journal of Industrial Economics, 1987, Vol. 36, pp. 147-156.

Roll, R. (1986): The Hubris Hypothesis of Corporate Takeovers. In: Journal of Business, Vol. 59, 1986, pp. 197-216.

Rustige, M./Grote M. H. (2009): Der Einfluss von Diversifikationsstrategien auf den Aktienkurs deutscher Unternehmen. In: Zeitschrift für Betriebswirtschaftliche Forschung (zfbf), Vol. 61, 2009, pp. 470-498.

Shahrur, H./Venkateswaran, A. (2009): Industry Prospects and Acquirer Returns in Diversifying Takeovers. In: Journal of Financial Research, Vol. 32, 2009, pp. 23-51.

Savor, P. G./Lu, Q. (2008): Do Stock Mergers Create Value for Acquirers? Working Paper, 2008, available at SSRN: http://ssrn.com/ abstract=881513.

Schlingemann, F. P./Stulz, R. M./Burns, N. (2002): Divestiture and the liquidity of the market for corporate control. In: Journal of Financial Economics. Vol. 64, 2002, pp. 117-144.

Schwert, G. W. (2006): Markup pricing in mergers and acquisitions. In: Journal of Financial Economics, Vol. 41, 2006, pp. 153-192.

Shahrur, H. (2005): Industry structure and horizontal takeovers: Analysis of wealth effects on rivals, suppliers, and corporate customers. In: Journal of Financial Economics, Vol. 76, 2005, pp. 61-98.

Shleifer, A./Vishny, R. W. (2003): Stock Market Driven Acquisitions. In: Journal of Financial Economics, Vol. 70, 2003, pp. 295-311.

Shleifer, A./Vishny, R. W. (1992): Liquidation Values and Debt Capacity: A Market Equilibrium Approach. In: Journal of Finance, Vol. 47, 1992, pp. 1343-1366.

Veld C./Veld-Merkoulova, Y. V. (2004): Do spin-off really create value? The European case. In: Journal of Banking and Finance, Vol. 28, 2004, 1111-1135.

Wang, C./Chung, K. S. (2009): Corporate Governance Transfer and Synergistic Gains from Mergers and Acquisitions. In: Review of Financial Studies, Vol. 22, 2009, pp. 829-858.

Warusawitharana, M. (2008): Corporate asset purchases and sales: Theory and evidence. In: Journal of Financial Economics. Vol. 87, pp. 471-497.

Weston, J. F./Chung, K. S. (1990): Takeovers and Corporate Restructuring: An Overview. In: Business Economics, Vol. 25, 1990, pp. 6-11.

Yang, L. I. U. (2008): The Real Determinants of Asset Sales. In: Journal of Finance, Vol. 63, pp. 2231-2262.

Corporate Finance and Governance

Herausgegeben von Dirk Schiereck

Band 1 Sebastian Michael Gläsner: Return Patterns of German Open-End Real Estate Funds. An Empirical Explanation of Smooth Fund Returns. 2010.

Band 2 Patrick Ams: Directors' Dealings and Insider Trading in Germany. An Empirical Analysis. 2010.

Band 3 Joachim Vogt: Value Creation within the Construction Industry. A Study of Strategic Takeovers. 2011.

Band 4 Fabian Braemisch: Underpricing, Long-Run Performance, and Valuation of Initial Public Offerings. 2011.

Band 5 Matthäus Markus Sielecki: Creating and Governing an Integrated Market for Retail Banking Services in Europe. A Conceptual-Empirical Study of the Role of Regulation in Promoting a Single Euro Payments Area. 2011.

Band 6 Arne Wilkes: Determinants of Credit Spreads. An Empirical Analysis for the European Corporate Bond Market. 2011.

Band 7 Dirk Schiereck / Martin Setzer (Hrsg.): Bankerfolg und Akquisitionen. Aktuelle Erkenntnisse zur Konsolidierung und Restrukturierung der Finanzindustrie. 2011.

Band 8 Steffen Meinshausen: M&A Activity, Divestitures and Initial Public Offerings in the Fashion Industry. 2012.

Band 9 Malte Helmut Raudszus: Financial Return Risk and the Effect on Shareholder Wealth. 2012.

Band 10 Ramit Mehta: Mergers and Acquisitions in the Global Brewing Industry. A Capital Market Perspective. 2012.

Band 11 Marcel Normann: The Influence of German Top Executives on Corporate Policy and Firm Performance. 2012.

Band 12 Christoph Böhm: Risk-Adjusted Performance and Bank Governance Structures. 2013.

Band 13 Christian Thamm: Minority Shareholder Monitoring and German Corporate Governance. Empirical Evidence and Value Effects. 2013.

Band 14 Robert M. Fraunhoffer: Mergers and Acquisitions in the Energy Sector. The Impact of Synergy Disclosures on Shareholder Wealth and Operating Performance. 2013.

Band 15 Heiko Schön: Pharma M&A versus alliances and its underlying value drivers. Are M&A or alliances the right therapy for an ailing pharmaceutical industry? A capital market perspective. 2015.

Band 16 Sascha Kolaric: Bank mergers and acquisitions in the Asia-Pacific region. An investigation of the shareholder wealth effects of the financial sector consolidation and its impact on the acquirer's cost of debt. 2015.

Band 17 Ulrich Erxleben: Value Creation of Corporate Restructuring. A Market Cycle and Industry View. 2015.

www.peterlang.de